THE ROOTS OF
OBAMA'S
RAGE

THE ROOTS OF
OBAMA'S
RAGE

DINESH D'SOUZA

Since 1947
REGNERY
PUBLISHING, INC.
An Eagle Publishing Company • Washington, DC

First paperback edition © 2011
ISBN: 978-1-59698-276-5

The Library of Congress has cataloged the hardcover edition as follows:

    D'Souza, Dinesh, 1961-
      The Roots of Obama's Rage / by Dinesh D'Souza.
        p. cm.
      Includes bibliographical references and index.
      ISBN 978-1-59698-625-1
      1. Obama, Barack. 2. Presidents—United States—Biography. I.
Title.
      E908.D76 2011
      973.932092--dc22
      [B]
                             2010035703

Published in the United States by
Regnery Publishing, Inc.
One Massachusetts Avenue, NW
Washington, DC 20001
www.regnery.com

Manufactured in the United States of America
10 9 8 7 6 5 4 3 2 1

Books are available in quantity for promotional or premium use. Write to Director of Special Sales, Regnery Publishing, Inc., One Massachusetts Avenue NW, Washington, DC 20001, for information on discounts and terms or call (202) 216-0600.

Distributed to the trade by:
Perseus Distribution
387 Park Avenue South
New York, NY 10016

For Ed McVaney
Friend and Co-Conspirator

CONTENTS

INTRODUCTION

BY DINESH D'SOUZA

This is a book unlike any other on Barack Obama. It is not the typical effusive book of apostolic praise, but neither is it a crude bashing of Obama. Rather, it is an effort to understand Obama, to discover what motivates him, and to formulate a theory that explains his actions in the White House. It offers a completely original theory for what drives Obama, and yet remarkably the theory is derived from Obama's own autobiography and Obama's own self-description. If you read this book, it will not only help you to understand Obama, it will also help you to predict what he is going to do next. I make three specific predictions in the last chapter, and in the twelve months following the book's original hardcover publication, all three have already come to pass.

I wrote this book in two months in the summer of 2010. I have written ten books, and this is the first one that I have written in sixty days. But the central thesis came to me as a kind of epiphany, shortly after reading Obama's *Dreams from My Father* and after discussing its ideas with my friend Bruce Schooley. I was struggling to reconcile Obama's self-presentation as an African American with his father's experience as an anti-colonialist from Kenya. How, I wondered, could the son's experience and the father's dream fit together? Then it hit me. The son's account of his own experience was largely bogus. Obama never sat at a segregated lunch counter, and neither did any of his ancestors. He is not descended, as most African Americans are, from slaves. In fact, his accounts of prejudice in his autobiography are very slight and, it turns out, largely made up. In fact, the son's formative experiences in Hawaii, Indonesia, Pakistan, and Kenya very closely track the anti-colonial journey of his father, and thus there is no conflict to be resolved. The son consciously chose to make himself in the image of his father, just as he tells us in his book.

So finally I had a theory to work with, and once I put on the anti-colonial spectacles, literally everything about Obama fell into place. Suddenly weird things that he was saying and doing started to make perfect sense. I saw that the broad sweep of Obama's actions in the first two years of his presidency, from expanding the role of the government at home to shrinking the imprint of America's role in the world, could now be fully explained. No, Obama wasn't anti-American and he wasn't a secret Muslim; within the framework of his ideology, he was doing things that he believed were good for America. But now I also could see why many people suspected him of being anti-American and a closet Muslim. From Obama's ideological perspective, it was and is a good thing to shrink America's global footprint, to cut America down to size, if you will. Obama views Muslims who are fighting against America in Iraq and Afghanistan as freedom-fighters, somewhat akin to Indians or Kenyans fighting to push out their British colonial occupier. So the beauty of my (or rather Obama's) anti-colonial theory is that it makes sense of the facts in the world, facts that have eluded other comprehensive attempts to explain Obama.

When I finished the manuscript, I gave it to Steve Forbes, the editor of *Forbes*, and asked him to read it and see what he thought. Right away he called me in to meet the senior editors, and together we agreed that I would write the cover story for the next issue. My article, "How He Thinks," proved to be a sensation. The reason was that many business guys voted for Obama, hoping that he would govern like Bill Clinton. Now they were having buyer's remorse. The prevailing idea was that Obama is clueless; Obama has never run a business and he doesn't understand business. My argument was that Obama *hates* business. He is captive to an ideology that sees capitalism as a form of neocolonialism. Bringing down the rich and the big, bad corporations is the central focus of Obama's agenda. I backed up the article with telling facts and telling quotations from Obama himself. The article landed like a bombshell. It was virally circulated on the web, and resulted in a flurry of inquires to the White House. Then White House press secretary Robert Gibbs went on the attack. He denounced my article as a revival of the so-called birther controversy, the issue of whether Obama was born in Hawaii or in Kenya. But the birther claim was nowhere discussed in the article, and it is specifically repudiated in this book. My book was confirmed, not refuted, when Obama finally produced his birth certificate. So the birther allegation was pure distortion. Then Gibbs suggested that the article was somehow racist, because it raised the issue of Obama's African background. But again, the article specifically noted that Obama's ideology has nothing to do with race. The whole point is that Obama is not a race guy, he is an anti-colonial guy, and anti-colonialism is only peripherally about race. (The British didn't conquer India because the natives were brown; they conquered it in order to benefit themselves and rule the place.)

Not content to attack me before the media and in his blog, Gibbs then called in representatives of *Forbes* and berated them for publishing the article. Under White House pressure, the magazine agreed to internally fact-check the article. Turns out that it contained two very minor errors. In one case I suggested that Obama went to Pakistan before he was seventeen years old, while in fact he went a couple of years later. In the second case I cited Obama saying America has 2 percent of the world's energy but uses 25 percent. In fact, Obama said America has 2 percent of the world's oil but uses 25 percent. None of this detracted from the central thesis of the article. *Forbes* ran a correction on its website, but stood by the article.

The effect of Gibbs's mania, probably directed by the man who was the subject of my book, activated the Obama Choir. This group interrupted its unceasing songs of praise for Obama to savagely attack my article and book. Out of the gate came Media Matters, the left-wing watchdog group, with a flurry of accusations. Most of it was rhetorical humbug, but the multiple press releases from the group did contain a couple of specific allegations of falsehood. First, I had quoted Obama faulting "British Petroleum" for the BP oil spill; Media Matters noted that Obama didn't use the company's former name "British Petroleum" in his original speech. True, but he used it more than once in his subsequent comments on the issue. If Media Matters had bothered to Google-search "Obama and British Petroleum," the group would see multiple references, from the *New York Times* to the BBC to the British press, of Obama using the term "British Petroleum." In fact, Obama's own ambassador to Great Britain, Louis Susman, is quoted by the BBC saying that Obama used the term but intends to stop doing so in the future.

Media Matters also faulted me for saying that the Obama administration had approved, through the Export-Import Bank, a $2 billion loan guarantee to the Brazilian company Petrobras for oil-drilling in Brazil.

The group protested that there were Bush appointees on the board who approved the transaction. Yes, but left-over appointees at government agencies are often eager to go along with the policies of a new administration. Moreover, the Export-Import Bank decision had to be cleared by the Obama White House. So obviously Obama bears the responsibility for policies proposed by a federal executive agency and signed off on by the White House. In its customary obfuscating way, Media Matters was trying to clear Obama of accountability for the decisions of his own administration. In March 2011, six months after this book came out, Obama went to Brazil and openly praised the Brazilians for their U.S.-subsidized oil drilling program.

Also taking up the cue from the White House was Maureen Dowd, who wrote a column in the *New York Times* calling me an "Ann Coulter in pants." The general theme of Dowd's article was a communication of Dowd's own sputtering rage and incredulity. Keith Olbermann on MSNBC promptly declared me the second most dangerous man in America, which I found a bit offensive; I had been working hard to be, in Olbermann's fevered world, the most dangerous man. I was attacked on Chris Matthews's show *Hardball*, and one TV network even trotted out Colin Powell, who had endorsed Obama, to warn that we should focus on Obama's ideas and not trace them back to his African roots. Powell's disagreement is less with me than with Obama: between his 2004 Democratic National Convention Speech and his election to the presidency in 2008, Obama was the one who was handing out his autobiography tracing his ideas to his African roots.

My favorite skirmish was on the C-SPAN program *After Words*, in which I was interviewed for an hour by journalist Jonathan Alter. Alter is a former editor of *Newsweek* and an incorrigible Obama sycophant. His book *The Promise* is a kind of hymn to Obama. On the show Alter went into major attack mode, but so eager was he to vindicate his man that he went over the line, contesting every single point, refusing to consider counter-evidence, and ultimately making himself look ridiculous. A sample exchange was when Alter lectured me that in America we don't judge people by the character of their fathers. Reagan's father was an alcoholic, Alter said, but we don't assume that Reagan's personality or values were shaped by his father. Yes, I responded, but then Reagan didn't write a book titled *Dreams from My Father*. Again, I am only following Obama's lead in making his father the central figure in the formation of his identity and ideals.

Despite Alter's bluster, he was raising a point that many other critics have raised, namely that Obama hardly knew his father so how could he be so heavily influenced by him? To anyone familiar with Freud or modern psychology, the question seems naïve. Indeed, there is a whole body of psychological literature on the powerful and traumatic impact that absentee fathers have on their sons. More significant, I cannot see how any careful reader of Obama's book or this book could still be mystified by such a question. Both books provide a clear answer: the larger-than-life image of the absentee father was cultivated in young Obama's mind by his mother. Repeatedly, unceasingly, she convinced her son that he should develop his values and identity in imitation of the senior Obama. Strangely enough the father's absence helped this myth to grow in young Obama's mind; if the real father had been around, his son would have discovered promptly enough that Barack Obama Sr. was a deeply flawed man. In fact, Obama discovered these harsh truths about his father much later, mainly through his sister. The discovery provoked a massive crisis of identity which young Obama resolved only by making a month-long pilgrimage to Africa, culminating in a life-changing visit to his father's grave.

As with my previous books, I have never objected to genuine and thoughtful concerns and objections, and have always been willing to engage them. My only objection is to uncritical analysis and uninformed attacks. Still, these attacks turned out to be a blessing in this case. The benefit of all the agitation by the Obama Choir was that it activated an equally intense response from the right. Newt Gingrich called *The Roots of Obama's Rage* "stunning . . . the most profound insight I have read in six years about Barack Obama." In other words, Gingrich considered mine the best analysis of Obama since he emerged into the national spotlight with his 2004 speech at the Democratic National Convention in 2004. Rush Limbaugh also praised the book, calling it "indispensable" and "irrefutable." Limbaugh interviewed me for a profile in his *Limbaugh Letter*, which probably didn't hurt sales. I did Glenn Beck's radio show and got a wildly enthusiastic response, after which I was on Glenn Beck's show two nights in a row. We did the blackboards, the charts, everything. Beck came dressed as a student and he designated me the professor. I was able not only to present my thesis but offer explanatory background and telling examples. It is very rare to get this kind of time on national TV. Naturally all the exposure drove my book onto the bestseller lists: Number 1 on Amazon, number 4 on the *New York Times* bestseller list.

Still, my objective in writing this book was not merely to sell a lot of copies but also to help shape the national debate. This I was able to do in the months leading up to the mid-term election, one in which Obama took a heavy and much-deserved shellacking. Since then, however, the Obama Choir has gone into a sullen silence about this book and its thesis. That's why I'm delighted to have the book coming out in paperback.

Notice that in the book's last chapter, I use my central thesis about Obama to make some specific predictions about him. I say that Obama will do nothing in the rest of his term to seriously prevent Iran from getting a nuclear bomb. I say that Obama will make no genuine attempt to reduce the deficit or the national debt, and if he is pressured to do so, he will seek to raise taxes on the rich and to cut funding for the military. Since the book's publication, Obama has in a sense acted out the script that I laid out for him. One TV producer even emailed me, "From now on, Dinesh, I am going to start calling you Elijah."

This is the real measure of an argument's validity: not only can it explain the things that have happened; it can also predict with reasonable accuracy what is going to happen. Moreover, a good theory should even be able to contend with facts that seem, at first glance, to contradict it. For instance, Obama's decision to order the killing of Osama bin Laden has flummoxed right-wing claims that Obama is anti-American, or a dithering incompetent, or a man allergic to the use of military force. But Obama's action is in no way inconsistent with my theory and his defense of the killing—as an act of justice, not an act of war—fits perfectly with my account of his ideology. So the anti-colonial theory has so far held up extremely well, and I promise you that if you put on the anti-colonial spectacles, in the manner suggested by this book, you will understand Obama in a new way and you will see him as you have never seen him before.

Either way, I'd like to hear from you, so read the book and then send me your comments to dineshjdsouza@gmail.com.

CHAPTER 1

A TALE OF THREE DREAMS

reams are powerful things. Sometimes they have motivational power, as with Martin Luther King's dream. King aspired to a color-blind society, and this guided his difficult striving. Dreams can also provide artistic inspiration, as when the Muse of the mind supplies ideas and images to the creative imagination. Here I think of Blake's sketches, Shakespeare's comedies, Milton's *Paradise Lost*. For Freud, dreams were clues to repressed desires, wishes that could not be expressed, not only to society but even to the self. There are sweet dreams and whimsical dreams, but there are also dark dreams. Think of the war veteran who has nightmares of being tied up in a hut, or being starved and beaten by his captors. That's a man who can wake up screaming. And there have been cases of men who are so preoccupied with their dark dreams that they have difficulty adjusting to contemporary reality. The dream, as it were, becomes a time machine. They live in the time machine, continuing to quixotically charge imaginary

1

windmills and slay fictitious evil knights. The windmills and knights were real enough, but they belonged to another world, a world that is long gone, but a world etched into the fabric of human memory. Men who have dreams like that can be great visionaries, or leaders with a dangerous obsession. This book is about one such man, who happens to be the president of the United States.

Barack Obama is an enigmatic figure, a puzzle both to his adversaries and to his supporters. Somehow the Obama of the 2008 election campaign seems to have metamorphosed into a very different President Obama. The two men are not merely politically different—different in their policy agenda—but also psychologically different. The centrist, reassuring Obama is gone and has been replaced by a more detached, unreadable and, to some, even menacing Obama. It's hard for Americans to respond to Obama because we aren't sure where he is coming from, what motivates him.

"Who is Barack Obama?" Richard Cohen titled a recent article in the *Washington Post*. Cohen's answer: no one really knows. "He led no movement, was spokesman for no ideology . . . he casts no shadow." Cohen contrasts Obama with Reagan. He notes that unlike Reagan, who connected so intimately with his supporters and so effectively with the country, Obama has left his own backers and indeed the nation at large guessing. "Americans know Obama's smart, but we still don't know him."[1]

Come to think of it, what did we ever really know about Obama? He is certainly the least-known figure ever to reach the presidency. The political mystery of his agenda is compounded by the psychological mystery of the man. Since he is our president, however, we had better try to figure out who he is and what he intends to do to America and the world. This book supplies the key.

This is not the book I set out to write. In fact, it represents my third take on Obama. If it took me, who shares so much in common with the man, three times to get this guy, I can see why he has eluded so many others. Despite our differences, I'm a lot like Obama. I'm a native of Mumbai, India, so I grew up in a different part of the world, as Obama did. I'm nonwhite, as he is. He had a white mom and grew up in an interracial family; I have a white wife, and we have a mixed-race daughter. Like Obama, I see America both from the inside and from the outside. We were born in the same year, 1961, so we're the same age. Obama and I attended Ivy League colleges, graduating in the same year, 1983; we also got married in the same year, 1992. He went into elective politics, while I have spent my life writing about politics and once served in the White House as a policy adviser. In sum, both of us have cosmopolitan backgrounds, grew up in the same era, and have made our careers in American politics.

I'm a conservative, and I didn't vote for Obama. During the 2008 presidential campaign, I read an interesting article in the London *Telegraph* titled "Barack Obama's 'Lost' Brother Found in Kenya." The article featured a picture of a 26-year-old man standing inside a ramshackle hut on the outskirts of Nairobi. CNN confirmed the story, reporting, "We found Barack Obama's half-brother living in a Nairobi slum." He was George Hussein Obama, the product of a liaison between Barack Obama Sr. and an African woman. "I live here on less than a dollar a month," George said. Humiliated by his poverty, he confessed he never mentioned his famous half-brother. "I say we are not related. I am ashamed." In 2006, George briefly met Barack Obama, who was then a United States senator from Illinois, but felt as though he was talking to a "total stranger." I found it remarkable that Barack Obama, who had a net worth of several million dollars and who was within striking distance of the world's highest office, hadn't lifted a finger to help a destitute close relative.

Seeing from the article that George Obama aspired to be a mechanic, I started the "George Obama Compassion Fund." On a daily blog I wrote for AOL at the time, I invited people to make small contributions to help George move out of his hut and get some training to realize his dreams. We raised a couple thousand dollars, and a Christian missionary promised he would deliver the money in person to George. Then I was contacted by a reporter for a large newspaper in Kenya who told me that the Obama family had refused the money. Evidently they had consulted with the Obama campaign and been told to go into hiding. My attempts to locate George proved unavailing. So I tore up the checks, figuring that perhaps I had jostled Obama into doing something for George, if only to save himself from political embarrassment.[2]

While I was puzzled by Obama's indifference to George, I did not join the conservative chorus bashing Obama. On the contrary, when Obama was elected I wrote a column for Townhall.com on "Obama and Post-Racist America." In it I confessed I was moved by the sight of him taking the oath of office. To me, Obama wasn't just America's first African American president; he also represented the promise of "the end of racism." *The End of Racism* was the title of a controversial book I published in 1995. In it I contended that racism was no longer systemic; it was now episodic. It existed, but it no longer controlled the lives of blacks and other minorities. Racism could no longer explain why some people in America succeeded and others didn't.

That book might have been ahead of its time, but Obama's election seemed to show that I was basically right. Consider the oceans of ink that have been spilled in the past several decades about how America is a racist society, how bigotry runs in the veins of white America, how little real progress has been made, how far we still have to go, and so on.

Would anyone who had been drinking this intellectual Kool-Aid for the past several years have been prepared for Obama's election? True, Obama was no Jesse Jackson. But precisely the difference between the two showed that individual conduct and demeanor, not skin color, was decisive. Obama didn't come across as a race hustler. He didn't seek to turn victimization into profit. Rather, he made his claims on their merits and appealed to shared American ideals. To borrow a line from Martin Luther King, Jr. he sought to be judged not by the color of his skin but by the content of his character. So Obama's election, I wrote, means that we are living in post-racist America. And that's something we could all celebrate.[3]

Since Obama's inauguration, I have written virtually nothing about him, because I didn't want to judge him too early. Personally, I liked Obama—a nice man with a nice family. What a refreshing contrast from the previous Democratic occupants of the White House, the Clintons! I felt confident Obama would not entertain interns under his desk or leave with the White House china. The man had class, not to mention an undeniable gravitas. Besides, he had inherited a huge financial mess. He deserved a chance to clean it up. I recall saying in one of my campus speeches, "We have to give this guy a year to see what he is going to do."

As Obama launched his spending spree—a bailout plan followed by a stimulus plan followed by an automobile industry rescue plan followed by a national health care plan and then new environmental and financial regulations—I became alarmed. Obama insisted that his policies were aimed at rescuing America's economy from the precipice, but many of them, notably in energy, the environment, education, and health care, had nothing to do with the financial crisis. The proposed solutions were unconnected to the original problems. Moreover, by piling on public debt and driving up costs to business, they threatened to worsen the economic crisis.

I didn't fear only the economic repercussions, but also the degree of government control over the economy and over the lives of free citizens. I talked to my publishers and proposed a book called "Obama's Leviathan." I planned to contrast two types of liberalism, one with its roots in Locke and the other in Hobbes. Both were liberals, yet Lockean liberalism implies limited government, while Hobbes argued that in order to enjoy security we should concede all our rights to an all-powerful state. Hobbes called this state "Leviathan," a reference to the massive sea beast in the Bible. I set out to document how Obama and his team were moving America further away from the Lockean liberalism of the founders toward a more menacing Leviathan.

But even as I worked on the book I felt I was missing something, and that something was Obama himself. Somehow the Hobbesian explanation was too philosophical; it didn't capture what motivated Obama. That's when I got my second idea. I intended to contrast Martin Luther King's dream with Obama's ongoing scheme of taking advantage of the civil rights movement. My basic premise was that Obama had to be understood as a product of that movement. That was the milieu in which he grew up; those were the ideals that shaped him. In one sense, Obama had embraced King's color-blind aspiration. He was a nonracial candidate, and as president he did not appeal to race. At the same time, my thesis held that Obama got his Big Government philosophy from the civil rights era.

Here, a bit of explanation is necessary. For the American founders, rights were seen as a limitation on government. That's why the Bill of Rights typically begins its specifications of rights with the phrase, "Congress shall make no law. . . ." Congress can pass no laws regulating freedom of speech, or the press, or assembly, and so on. In the founders' view, the rights of citizens are protected by restricting the power of the federal government. For American blacks, however, the federal government was the indispensable securer and guarantor of rights. The federal government ended slavery and Jim Crow. It took federal troops to enable black kids to attend public schools in the segregated South. Through its Great Society programs, the federal government was the biggest employer of African Americans and is largely responsible for the creation of a black middle class. Surveys have consistently shown that blacks are much more sympathetic toward Big Government than any other group; many blacks believe that because of their history America owes them, and therefore they are entitled to jobs, benefits, health insurance, and retirement income at society's expense.[4] I sought to show that Obama had adopted the viewpoint of black America but removed the black label. Essentially he was applying black remedies to all of America, and the danger—I intended to argue—was that if he succeeded, all of us as citizens would become more dependent on the state and consequently less free as individuals.

But I found that this theory is also wrong—or at least seriously inadequate. A couple of things tipped me off. The first is the chorus of complaint by black activists and scholars that Obama doesn't care about their agenda. Obama's indifference to black issues was the central theme of a 2010 summit organized by the African American TV host Tavis Smiley. Smiley echoed the sentiments of many of the speakers when he said, "The time has come for . . . the president to be more aggressive about an African American agenda." The black literary scholar Michael Eric Dyson put the point even more bluntly in an MSNBC television interview: "This president runs from race like a black man runs from a cop."[5]

At first I thought that this approach represented a tactical decision by Obama to eschew race-specific issues. After all, the man does have to convince the country that he represents the national interest, not just the black interest. But as the political philosopher Cornel West—an adviser to Obama's presidential campaign—recently pointed out, this does not require Obama to avoid black issues altogether. West noted that Obama certainly pays attention to environmentalists' concerns about oil spills, and union concerns about contracts. "But when it comes to black people ... we don't have an agenda? He must be losing his mind. ... We've got a black president who needs to be saved from himself." Saved from himself! I pondered the arresting phrase as well as why, in West's view, Obama steadfastly refuses to attend to the African American agenda, focused as it is on affirmative action and inner-city poverty programs. Then a startling thought hit me. Maybe Obama pays no attention to race because he doesn't care about race. Maybe race is not what drives this guy after all.[6]

This got me to my second reason for doubting my race theory: it does not jibe with Obama's actual life story. I realized I had been placing Obama the whole time in the civil rights movement, thinking of him as African American, when in reality he has a very different history. Obama is not the descendant of slaves as African Americans typically are. Obama never sat at a segregated lunch counter, and neither did any of his ancestors. Obama's father was an immigrant from Africa who studied at Harvard and returned to Africa. His mother was white. Moreover, Obama grew up in Hawaii and Indonesia and lived a life of relative privilege, attending private school before enrolling at Columbia and then Harvard. So what did Obama have in common with black America? Virtually nothing.

Of course, Obama went through a phase growing up in which he thought of himself as an American black. And it is a political necessity for him to identify as an African American. This is not only because such identification brings near-universal black support and white support from many quarters, but also because it guarantees Obama's place in history. Obama isn't going down in history as the first child of an immigrant to become president, but rather as the first black president. So Obama has carefully cultivated a racial identity for himself, one that seeks to bind him to black America. But a little scrutiny shows that Obama's effort is contrived. This isn't so hard to figure out: all you need to do is read Obama's writings and speeches with some good knowledge of black history and the civil rights tradition. The reason we haven't figured out Obama's tenuous relationship to black America is because so many people—especially in the press—are so eager to see an African American president who looks and sounds like Obama that they have suspended their critical faculties.

My critical antennae were alerted when I came across a passage in Obama's self-revealing autobiography *Dreams from My Father*. While waiting for his mother in the lobby of the American embassy in Indonesia, Obama recalls picking up a copy of *Life* magazine. Thumbing through the articles, he came across a story about a black man who underwent chemical treatments to lighten his skin. Obama notes that the man looked sickly, like "a radiation victim or an albino." His reaction was one of horror. "I felt my face and neck get hot. My stomach knotted; the type began to blur on the page ... I had the desperate urge to jump out of my seat ... to demand some explanation or assurance." Then his white mother entered the room and, with heroic effort, Obama suppressed his anger. The incident is a dramatic revelation to Obama that blackness stands condemned in America to such a degree that black people have to attempt to make themselves white.[7]

Obama's story was reported in *Newsweek* and many other places before journalists at the *Chicago Tribune* decided to locate the original story and, well, it turns out there wasn't one. *Life* never published such an article. When Obama was asked about this, he suggested that maybe *Ebony* or some other magazine carried this particular article. Actually, no. The search for the article has been sufficiently thorough that we can say with confidence that it does not exist. Now a book published in the early 1960s, *Black Like Me*, does describe a fellow who took skin treatments to change his color. But the author, John Howard Griffin, was a white guy from Dallas who was trying to make himself look black. Griffin's purpose was to masquerade as a black man so he could personally experience and then expose racism in the South. It seems doubtful that Griffin was Obama's source, but if he was, then Obama not only distorted but completely inverted the facts. In any event Obama's intense emotional response now seems bogus and contrived. Obama's defenders have suggested that "Obama was after an emotional truth here."[8] Quite obviously he was searching for a morality tale to dramatize the impact that American racism had on him in his formative years. Still, he could easily have found some other true incident to make the same point. Instead, he seems to have engaged in some very creative writing. Yet if the whole episode was fantasy, why this particular fantasy?

I was about to despair in my attempt to figure out Obama when I heard Obama make his now-famous remark about whether America is an exceptional country. The notion that in many respects America is unique in the world is called American "exceptionalism." Now in one sense I knew that obviously Obama believed in American exceptionalism. In his 2004 speech at the Democratic National Convention Obama said, "I stand here knowing that . . . in no other country on earth is my story even possible," a refrain he repeated many times during the campaign.[9] Obama was acknowledging that no other country allows outsiders like him (or me, for that matter) full entry and full acceptance in society. But here in America, foreigners of all races can "become American" and rise to the very top of the political and social ladder.

Yet when Obama was asked at a 2009 press conference in Europe whether he believed in American exceptionalism, he replied, "I believe in American exceptionalism just as I suspect the Brits believe in British exceptionalism and the Greeks in Greek exceptionalism."[10] What did Obama mean by this? In a banal sense, every country is unique, with its own distinctive history, mores, and cuisine. We all know that Americans eat hot dogs, Greeks eat souvlaki, and the British eat horrible British food. But this is not what exceptionalism means. It refers to the claim that the rest of the world does things in one way and we do things in a different way. Our ideals distinguish us from those of other cultures or, as I put it in one of my earlier books, America offers a new and original way to be human. If this is true, then it's wrong to say that American exceptionalism is no different from British or Greek exceptionalism. Obama seems to be insisting, in effect, that there is nothing especially unique about America. Why would Obama, of all people, make such a remarkable statement? Something seemed terribly wrong here, not with Obama, but with my understanding of Obama.

So I went back and re-read Obama's two books, *Dreams from My Father* and *The Audacity of Hope*. Both are autobiographical, but the first tells us far more about Obama because it is not couched in political language. It was written in 1995, shortly before Obama was a state senator and a decade before he was a U.S. senator. Earlier I had read these books to discover Obama's positions on various issues. This time I read them to find Obama. In the process, I found myself plunged into Obama's world, a world not of segregated lunch counters or separate water fountains, but rather a world much like the one that I grew up in: the Third World. As I read about Obama in Hawaii, Indonesia, Pakistan, and Africa, I remembered growing up as a boy in the suburbs of Mumbai, surrounded by the helter-skelter of poverty and chaos, naked children running around, rickshaws and beggars, cows crossing the road. Sometimes I wondered how I made the long journey from the world of my childhood, growing up without television or telephone or even hot showers in the bathroom, to the world I live in now. How, I ask myself, did I go from the periphery of the modern world to its epicenter? Others, like the novelist V. S. Naipaul, who grew up in Trinidad and moved to London, have written about this.

This is Obama's story, a story of a little boy who emerged from the hinterlands and somehow was elected to the highest office in the land. Obama's formative history, I realized, was crucial to understanding who Obama is now. And suddenly it hit me that all along I had been looking for Obama in the wrong place. I had been trying to fit Obama into some version of American history, and in the process I had ignored Obama's own history. How absurd of me, since Obama's history in important respects resembled my own. What made this discovery especially fascinating is that Obama interpreted this history in a way radically different from how I see it.

Obama's story is both enthralling and incredibly revealing of his current motivation and outlook, but I don't want to get too far ahead of myself. Let me just say here that Obama's books are about three dreams. The first one is the American dream, and this refers to what the American founders termed the "novus ordo seclorum," the new order for the ages. The founders sought to build a society never before seen in Europe or anywhere else in the world. They were, in this sense, the original champions of American exceptionalism. The American dream has been very good for Obama, making his success possible. But it is not what he cares most about; as we have seen, he explicitly rejects the idea that America is somehow unique. Perhaps for him the American dream is not very different from the British dream or the Greek dream.

Second, there is Martin Luther King's dream. Less obviously, this is also not Obama's dream. Again, he depends on it. He campaigned as a non-racial candidate, and he counted on whites to vote for him or against him, not on the basis of his skin color, but on who he was as a politician and as a man. Without a realization of King's dream within the soul of the body politic, Obama would not be president today. Even so, Obama is not fundamentally guided by Martin Luther King's dream. The best evidence of this is that he rarely talks about that dream, and he does not seem to be moved or motivated by it. When is the last time you heard Obama speak with conviction about the importance of a color-blind society? If you go back and read Obama's speeches, including his famous Philadelphia address on race, King's dream gets short shrift. In this area, Obama's actions are equally important. As president, Obama has done nothing to alter race-conscious policies or even urge that Americans get beyond race. Even as he benefits from King's dream, he treats it with benign neglect.

Finally, there is Obama's dream, and if you want to know what that is, all you have to do is look at the title of Obama's book: *Dreams from My Father.* So there it is: according to Obama himself, his dream comes from his father. And who was his father and what were the ideals and values that moved him? I withhold the answer to these questions until the next chapter, but let's just say that Obama's dream, as derived from Barack Obama Sr., is very different from the one espoused by George Washington, Benjamin Franklin, and Abraham Lincoln. It is just as distant from the dream of Frederick Douglass and Martin Luther King. In fact, to discover Obama's dream we have to leave the American mainland and join Obama on his lifelong quest to discover his father and, through that experience, himself.

When we go abroad, leaving behind familiar shores and signposts, we encounter a rich mélange of political and intellectual figures from all over the globe. We discover names like Jomo Kenyatta, Tom Mboya, Oginga Odinga, Kwame Nkrumah, Chinua Achebe, Frantz Fanon, Roberto Mangabeira Unger, Edward Said, Amilcar Cabral, Wole Soyinka, and Aimé Césaire. Many of these names appear in Obama's books, although—for reasons that will become clear—some of them are deliberately omitted. Fortunately for me, this is intellectual terrain that I know well. Steeped as I am in the politics and history of the Third World, these are figures whom I have studied. This is also the world of Barack Obama Sr., and it is in this mental and moral universe that his son found his ideals and his place. Obama's policies are incomprehensible without this intellectual landscape.

This book will clearly establish the relevance of this body of ideas to Obama's worldview—and a little detail here will set us on the right track. In *Dreams from My Father*, Obama writes about being influenced by Frantz Fanon. Born in Martinique, Fanon became a psychiatrist who joined the Algerian liberation movement, the Front de Liberation Nationale, or FLN. I'd like to quote an interesting passage from Fanon's book *Black Skin, White Masks*, a book first published in 1952 in French, and then widely reprinted in translation in America. "For some years now, certain laboratories have been researching for a 'denegrification' serum. In all seriousness they have been rinsing out their test tubes and adjusting their scales and have begun research on how the wretched black man could whiten himself and thus rid himself of the burden of his bodily curse."[11] Fanon is writing about the North African Negro who is desperately eager to alter his skin color and become white like the French rulers of his country. Here, I believe, is where Obama got his skin treatment story. He found it in Fanon and altered the setting and the facts to invent a personal experience instructive about American racism.

Clearly in Barack Obama we are dealing with a strange, complex man. Ironically we have ironed out that strangeness by making Obama the embodiment of American multiculturalism. Somehow we have taken this lonely, driven figure and turned him into an image of diversity. He is our Kumbayah man, our post-ideological president, an ultra-modern leader with a twenty-first century agenda. Obama recognizes this; he has himself commented that "I serve as a blank screen on which people of vastly different political stripes project their own views."[12] As we will see, Obama is happy to accommodate these projections, which are vital to his transcendent image and political success. But whatever Obama is, he is not diverse or multicultural, at least not in his thinking or his fundamental values. Moreover, as we will soon discover, Obama is not even a twenty-first century man. He is fighting a private war that started far away and goes back to the middle of the last century, with roots that are even earlier. If we want to understand his actions in America and in the world, we have to understand Obama as he really is, not as we want him to be.

CHAPTER 2

THE BLACK MAN'S BURDEN

Barack Obama is a radiant figure on the world stage. He looks the way an American president should look, and he talks the way many in the world want the American president to talk. As a personality, he conveys dignity and calm; he seems to be what Aristotle called the great-souled man. As an orator, Obama is cerebral and yet confident, a man who is not afraid to occupy large shoes or undertake large ventures. Commenting after one of Obama's orations, *Newsweek* writer Evan Thomas commented, "In a way Obama's standing above the country, above the world, he's sort of God."[1]

Obama is also a consequential president. Less than two years into his first term, he has revamped the Bush administration's foreign policy: no more invasions, no more preemptive wars, plans for withdrawals both from Iraq and Afghanistan, a new approach for punishing terrorists, and in general a very different understanding of America's role in the world. At the same time, Obama has transformed the relationship between

American citizens and their government. He has passed the most significant raft of laws since the Great Society: the bank rescue plan, the auto industry bailout, the stimulus package, sweeping regulation of Wall Street, a complete remaking of the health care system. In a way, Obama has altered the political trajectory of the past quarter century: no longer is the American economy steered by the invisible hand of the market; now it is increasingly controlled by the visible hand of the federal government.

Obama stands astride American politics like a colossus. All political movements in the country are responses to Obama in one form or another; the midterm election in November 2010 is almost entirely a referendum on him and his policies. Whatever one might think of his policies and priorities, no one since Reagan has been able to accomplish changes of such magnitude. If Obama serves two terms, he will likely leave America a very different country than it is now. This is certainly his objective; he has set himself the task, as he put it in his inauguration address, of "remaking America."[2]

Obama is also a complex man, a fact often lost both on his supporters and detractors, who like to portray him in simple colors. As a personality, Obama is much more fascinating than George W. Bush, Bill Clinton, George H. W. Bush, or Jimmy Carter. Even Reagan, for all his accomplishments, was a much easier guy to figure out: what you saw was mostly what you got. Obama is more like Richard Nixon, a man of ambition and intellect, but at the same time an elusive man, an inward man, a surprise to see in the world of politics. He is a figure of psychological depth that carries about him an aura of mystery. Obama, like Nixon, would have interested Thucydides or Dostoyevsky.

These writers would have been struck by the dramatic contrast between the two faces of Obama. What then are these two faces? The first is the face of the healer and unifier. This is the Obama who wrote in his book *The Audacity of Hope*, "We will need to remind ourselves, despite all our differences, just how much we share: common hopes, common dreams, a bond that will not break." Obama promised "a new kind of politics, one that can excavate and build upon those shared understandings that pull us together as Americans." The same Obama spoke at the Democratic convention in 2004, in which he said, "There is not a liberal America and a conservative America; there is a United States of America. There is not a black America and a white America, a Latino America and an Asian America. . . . We are one people, all of us pledging allegiance to the Stars and Stripes, all of us defending the United States of America." That speech resounded with conservative themes, as when Obama described "the people I meet in small towns and big cities and diners and office parks—they don't expect government to solve all of their problems. Go into the collar counties around Chicago, and they'll tell you that they don't want their tax money wasted by a welfare agency or by the Pentagon. Go into any inner-city neighborhood and folks will tell you that government alone can't teach kids to learn." This is the kind of talk you normally hear at the Republican convention. And when Obama was elected he pledged, "And to those Americans whose support I have yet to earn—I may not have won your vote, but I hear your voices, I need your help, and I will be your president too." Let's call the Obama who uttered these inspirational words Obama I.[3]

We haven't seen very much of Obama I in the White House. Instead, we regularly encounter Obama II, a very different character. This is the Obama who lambasts the banks and investment houses and forces them to succumb to federal control; the Obama who gives it to the pharmaceutical and the health insurance companies, bending them to his will; the Obama who demonizes his predecessor and his opponents, portraying them as the source of all the problems that only he can solve.

This Obama pushed through health care reform, essentially establishing government control over one-sixth of the U.S. economy, and he did it without a single Republican vote in either the House or the Senate. Nor did it matter to Obama that a majority of the American people, in poll after poll, rejected the proposed changes. Despite Scott Brown's stunning victory in Massachusetts, turning Ted Kennedy's Senate seat over to the Republicans, Obama found a way to make his health care reform the law of the land. This same Obama seeks to impose expensive environmental regulations on companies in the form of cap and trade legislation; he is going to sharply hike taxes on business and the affluent; he is scaling back the military budget and has announced a withdrawal of American troops both from Iraq and Afghanistan. Here, as before, Obama can be expected to trample over his opposition to achieve his goals. This Obama has dismayed Republicans and conservatives, and an activist Tea Party movement has mobilized against him.

So which is the real Obama? For conservatives, it is Obama II and Obama I is just a mask and a camouflage. So far, conservative opposition to Obama has been shrill, focusing on several familiar themes: Obama is not an American citizen; Obama is a pawn of radical extremists; Obama is an unscrupulous power-seeker; Obama is a Muslim; and Obama is a socialist. These javelins, however, have at best grazed Obama; they have not fully found their target. Was Obama born in America? The best evidence is that he was. He was born in Honolulu on August 4, 1961. His birth was mentioned in two local papers, the Honolulu *Sunday Advertiser* and the *Star Bulletin*. This makes him a "natural born" American, as the Constitution requires of a president. No evidence has been produced that Obama is anyone's pawn. Sure, there are radical elements associated with him, but quite possibly they are his pawns. Obama is certainly ambitious, and like most presidents he seeks power, but power to do what? Power for what end?

I certainly don't think that Obama is a closet Muslim extremist who seeks to destroy America from within. I realize that his first name, Barack, refers to a Muslim blessing; his middle name, Hussein, is Islamic; and his last name, Obama, is eerily similar to Osama. Even so, the charge that Obama has an allegiance to Islam is unsubstantiated. His biological father Barack Sr. was born a Muslim, and so was Obama's Indonesian stepfather Lolo Soetoro, but neither practiced his faith. Of his dad, Obama writes, "By the time he met my mother he was a confirmed atheist, thinking religion to be so much superstition, like the mumbo-jumbo of witch doctors that he had witnessed in the Kenyan villages of his youth." When Obama lived in Indonesia, he attended schools with Muslim teachers and Muslim students. Undoubtedly he was also exposed to Islam as part of the curriculum. But he also learned about Catholicism. Neither made much of an impact. In fact, Obama writes, "When it came time to pray, I would pretend to close my eyes, then peek around the room. Nothing happened. No angels descended. Just a parched old nun and thirty brown children, muttering words."[4] This is a more believable account of Obama's religious—or non-religious—views than conjectures that he was raised as a Muslim.

The charge of socialism, now furiously leveled against Obama, seems to bring us closer to the mark. Here is a president who has no business background and very few people with business experience around him; as he goes about slicing the economic pie, it is not clear that he has any idea how to make a pie. As Jonathan Alter remarks in *The Promise*, "entrepreneurship" is a word Obama rarely uses and a concept with which he seems uncomfortable.[5] More troubling, Obama is a president who spends the taxpayer's money with shameless promiscuity. He runs up debt not in the billions, but in the trillions. Just when it seems that he has broken the bank, he proposes new spending. He has also increased federal control over major industries: the home mortgage industry, the investment banking industry, the pharmaceutical industry, the health industry, the energy industry, and so on. Never before have the tentacles of government reached so deeply into the private sector. Obama even woke up one day and decided to fire the CEO of General Motors. To his conservative critics, Obama is a kind of amnesiac. Somehow he lived through the second half of the twentieth century without witnessing the collapse of socialism, without learning the obvious lesson that socialism doesn't work.

Yes, Obama was around during those years, but as we will discover, his mind was elsewhere. Still, the charge of socialism isn't quite right. Even if it could account for Obama's economic policy, it certainly could not explain his foreign policy. Moreover, socialism as a description of Obama's domestic priorities doesn't really work. Strictly speaking socialism means that private property is forfeited to the government, and Obama hasn't even proposed that. He isn't trying to take away your car or your computer. Now there are other forms of socialism—such as the kind espoused by socialist parties in Europe—but these are nothing more than welfare state capitalism: the market produces wealth, and the government takes an active role in redistributing it.

Obama is certainly closer to this European model of socialism. But even as I say this, I am struck by the fact that while Obama has massively increased government spending and regulation, he typically seeks to achieve this goal by working through the private market. During the height of the financial crisis, Obama could have nationalized the banks, but he chose not to. Instead he bailed them out with infusions of capital, in return for which the government took preferred stock. Obama's health law didn't nationalize the hospitals and the insurance companies; rather, it established new government rules that will require everyone to own health insurance provided for the most part by private companies. So too, Obama's proposed cap and trade legislation involves government-imposed limitations on carbon use, but these limitations take the form of emissions permits that can be bought and sold on the free market, thus enabling the normal rules of price and scarcity to operate.

Psychologically, too, the socialist label doesn't fit Obama. If you heard the old socialists, they became passionate when they spoke about equality and the poor. I think of the socialist stalwarts like Marx, Eugene Debs, or Norman Thomas. Even liberal Democrats like Howard Dean and John Edwards, whose views were progressive rather than strictly socialist, addressed poverty and social injustice with animated conviction. Listen to Obama talk about the poor, and he sounds like he is reading from his tax return. Even equality is not a big theme with him; on the rare occasions when he mentions the subject, he does so without passion. None of this is to suggest that the socialist allegation is flat-out wrong; rather, it is inadequate, incomplete, and needs to be integrated into a larger, fuller theory.

If the conservative reading of Obama is not entirely convincing, the liberal assessment of him is also implausible. For many of his ardent defenders, there is no Obama II. Obama I is the real Obama, and the only appropriate response to him is adulation and genuflection. I call these people the Obama Choir. A leading member of this group is Chris Matthews, host of the television show *Hardball*, who is known to respond to Obama's speeches with exceptional gusto. On February 12, 2008, Matthews found one of Obama's orations so titillating that, in his words, "I felt this thrill going up my leg." Another Choir member is columnist Mark Morford of the *San Francisco Chronicle*, who is persuaded that Obama is "that rare kind of attuned being who . . . can actually help usher in a new way of being on the planet. . . . These kinds of people actually help us evolve."[6] The issue raised by the Obama Choir is not whether Obama is worthy of unceasing hosannas, but what it is about Obama that causes normal people to lose their reason. Since the phenomenon is widespread in the mainstream media, this in itself is a condition that demands explanation.

I do not mean to suggest that all Obama's supporters are borderline delusional. There are many thoughtful and rational people who support Obama. Even many of them, however, are baffled by the man they voted for. He seems to be coming from an entirely different place than they are. Some of them are even unnerved by him. Perhaps, these Obama backers say, it comes down to the man's peculiar temperament. Maureen Dowd speculates in the *New York Times* that "Obama has a bit of Mr. Spock in him.... He has a Vulcan-like logic and detachment." Writing in the online magazine *Slate*, Jacob Weisberg worries that this man is too withdrawn for a politician. "Obama's relationship with the world is primarily rational and analytical rather than intuitive or emotional."[7]

One explanation for this is that Obama is playing against type. He doesn't want to be the stereotypical "angry black man," so he holds back. But as we will see, Obama does not always hold back, and the instances when he explodes or lashes out are crucial to understanding what really matters to him. Moreover, Obama watchers have noticed something artificial and even contrived in the president's public image. Appearing on the *Charlie Rose* show, Evan Thomas said he found himself curiously repelled by a man whose ideas he generally agreed with. Thomas called Obama "slightly creepy" and "deeply manipulative." Thomas suggested that there was something fake and unreal about Obama's public persona. "This creature he's designed isn't necessarily a real person."[8]

Perhaps the most consistent liberal view of Obama is that he is the fulfillment of a civil rights tradition. This argument is presented in David Remnick's book *The Bridge*. Remnick's theme can be summarized in this way: Frederick Douglass, Martin Luther King, and now Obama. Reading Remnick's book you get the distinct impression that he wrote it while wearing his "Yes We Can" button. The book is devoid of intellectual skepticism: somehow Remnick never pauses to wonder why Jesse Jackson, who ran twice for president, was never taken seriously as a candidate, while Obama, who was merely a state senator a few years ago, made it on his first try. Nor does Remnick ask why a privileged fellow like Obama, who by his own account never experienced any serious racism, can claim a genuine kinship with a former slave like Douglass or a man like King who faced down the dogs and hoses of segregation in the South. Remnick details Obama's family history in Hawaii and Indonesia and Kenya without making a serious attempt to relate that history to the American civil rights movement. Like so many others who write about this president, Remnick is so eager to insert Obama into the American story that he entirely misses the significance of Obama's story.[9]

To grasp Obama's story, we have to put aside the multicultural mantras and the conservative boilerplate and enter Obama's world. In a sense, we are in search of Obama III, an account that transcends and reconciles Obama I and Obama II. We need to discover Obama's own narrative, one that makes psychological sense of the man, and that helps to explain his policies and his deepest beliefs. Where can we find this interpretive key that unlocks the mystery and helps us understand Obama? Remarkably, it is Obama himself who supplies it, and we can comprehend Obama if we are willing to take off our blinders and listen to his story as told in his own words.

Imagine a little boy growing up in the sunbathed beauty of Hawaii, soaking in the culture, hearing about how the innocent natives were crushed and overrun by horrible invaders and profiteers. Imagine a slightly older child on a bicycle on the crowded streets of Indonesia, learning from his stepfather the harsh code of a developing country, shaped out of the history of European colonialism. Now imagine a young man undertaking a journey to Kenya, for many people a journey to nowhere, but for him a journey to his own past, where through inner soul-searching and conversations with relatives he discovers who his father really was, and what he must do to make good on the dead man's unfulfilled dreams. This is Barack Obama. But for him these aren't imaginings; they are memories. These memories are formed out of the indelible ink of experience, and they have by his own account marked the man. By attentively examining his experience as he tells it himself, and as elaborated by others who have researched his background, we can understand Obama in a way that he has not been understood before.

I will outline Obama's personal and political development over the next few chapters, but here I distill the essence of the man: he is his father's son, and his dreams are derived from his father's aspirations and failures. Everyone who knows Obama well says this about him. His "granny" Sarah Obama—not his actual grandmother but one of his grandfather's other wives—told *Newsweek*, "I look at him and I see all the same things—he has taken everything from his father. The son is realizing everything the father wanted. The dreams of the father are still alive in the son." Obama of course makes the same point in his title—*Dreams from My Father*—and his whole book is an elaboration of how he internalized his father's dreams and goals. Obama calls his memoir "the record of a personal, interior journey—a boy's search for his father and through that search a workable meaning for his life as a black American." And again, "It was into my father's image, the black man, son of Africa, that I'd packed all the attributes I sought in myself."[10]

Obama even took his father's name in order to cement his explicit identification with him, and the way he did so is even more revealing. Young Obama's parents named him Barack, after his father. But from birth until his young adult years, he was known as Barry. Actually, Obama's dad was also called Barry; Barry was the name he adopted when he came as a student from Kenya to America. While the father went from Barack to Barry, however, the son went in the opposite direction. As a young man, Obama asked people to stop calling him Barry and instead to call him Barack. For Obama's father, the switch from Barack to Barry was no big deal; he was just doing what many immigrants do in order to fit in. For the son, by contrast, the move from Barry to Barack was a very big deal. He didn't just take his father's identity; he self-consciously rejected his father's American name in favor of the senior Obama's African identity.[11]

There is something deeply Freudian about this, and even Shakespearean. Obama never knew his father, who abandoned his mother and him shortly after he was born, and whom he met only once when he was a young boy. Even so, Obama identified more with his father than anyone else, and he undertook an intense psychological and ultimately actual journey to Africa in order to discover his dad and, in the process, to find himself. Unable to find his father, he did the next best thing: he embraced his father's ideals and decided to live out the script of his father's unfulfilled life. Obama ultimately recognized that his father was not the great romantic figure he had long envisioned him to be. But Obama concluded that, despite his flaws, his father had great vision, great ideals, a great plan of reform. Since Obama Sr. was unable to achieve those ideals, Obama Jr. figured he would undertake this heroic mission. In changing the world into the image of his father, he would complete the task that his father couldn't, and thus he would become worthy of his father, a real African and a real man.

As we trace this remarkable story, we will see how Obama's mother and maternal grandparents figure into his voyage of self-discovery. We will also discover how Obama found along the way a number of surrogate dads; these men helped to form his personality and outlook. Drawing on this ensemble of characters, Obama crafted an identity that is at once the product of his family history and yet distinctively his own. By an act of intellectual and willful striving, Obama defined himself in relation

to his absent father and a host of paternal surrogates. Therefore, to discover Obama, we have to begin with his father because it is from his
father, more than from anyone else, that Obama got the worldview that
defines his presidency.

Who was Barack Obama Sr.? First and foremost, he was an anti-
colonialist. He grew up under British rule in Kenya, and he came of age
during the struggle for independence. He was considered one of his
country's bright young stars, one of an elite group of African scholars
who came to study in the United States, and then returned to their
home countries with a goal of helping them form their independent
identities. This Obama was an economist, and as an economist he was
influenced by socialism, but he was never a doctrinaire socialist; rather,
his quasi-socialism sprang from and was integrated into an anti-colonial
outlook that was shared by many of his generation, not only in Africa
but also in Asia and South America. Here I want to outline the main
themes of that anti-colonial ideology, which formed the core of the
philosophy of Barack Obama Sr., and which is closely tied to what his
son Barack Obama Jr. is doing in the White House today.

Empire is nothing new in world history. The Athenians, the Romans,
the Mongols, and the Ottomans all established empires and ruled over
subject peoples. We are concerned here with European empire, with the
white man's discovery, conquest, and settlement of Asia, Africa, and the
Americas—a process that began with Columbus and Vasco da Gama in
the fifteenth century and was largely completed by the end of the nineteenth century. Our specific focus here is the conquest of Africa. This
conquest was preceded by the Scramble for Africa. In the mid-1880s,
representatives of the leading European powers showed up at a Berlin
conference to carve up Africa. The Europeans were bumping into each
other all over Africa in their colonizing frenzy, and the Berlin conference
was an attempt to amicably share the land and the loot. The usual

suspects were all present—the English, the French, the Dutch, the Portuguese, the Germans—but there were also some surprise guests, including the conniving and avaricious King Leopold of Belgium.[12]

Well, it was quite a picnic while it lasted. Once the bargains were struck in Berlin, the rest of Africa was taken by force and parceled out to various European occupiers. Except for a few outposts of freedom—such as Ethiopia and Liberia—virtually the entire continent came under European rule. The French controlled North Africa, notably Algeria, Tunisia, and Morocco. The Portuguese had Angola and Mozambique, and a few small holdings on the west coast. The Belgians secured the Congo. The Germans grabbed Southwest Africa, Tanganyika, Cameroon, Rwanda, Burundi, and Togo. And the British had pretty much everything else. In fact, by the end of the nineteenth century, Queen Victoria reigned over an empire that encompassed approximately half the real estate on the planet. No wonder it was said that the sun never sets on the British empire.

This situation lasted around half a century. Then, over the next few decades, Europe itself was convulsed by two disastrous world wars that virtually bankrupted the continent and almost ruined the greatest of the colonial powers, Britain. Around this time, fierce cries of resistance emanated from the ranks of the colonized. Sometimes these were peaceful, as in the case with Gandhi in India. But often they were not, and movements of guerilla resistance emerged to challenge and overthrow European rule. Despite the toll of the two world wars—which were actually European civil wars—Europe was not ready to relinquish its colonial possessions. The guerillas directly assaulted the European settlers in their countries, and the European powers brought all their remaining might against this armed opposition. These were the anti-colonial wars of the twentieth century. As we will see, they left deep scars on Obama's father and grandfather.

Anti-colonialism is the movement of ideas that rallied opposition to European rule. It is also the outlook that guided many of the newly independent nations in the aftermath of the European retreat. This is the ideology that was espoused by Barack Obama Sr. and many of his generation. As a movement, anti-colonialism had its passionate advocates: among them were the Algerian physician Frantz Fanon, the Tunisian writer Albert Memmi, the Martiniquan poet Aimé Césaire, the African writer Chinweizu, the Ghanaian political leader Kwame Nkrumah, and the Palestinian scholar Edward Said. The anti-colonialists were anti-Western and oriented toward national self-determination, but their ideology also contained noticeable strains of Marxism and socialism. Let us identify the main tenets of anti-colonialism and also trace the connections between anti-colonialism, Marxism, and socialism.

The first tenet of anti-colonialism is that empires are produced by murderous conquest and sustained by unceasing terror and violence. As the African writer Chinweizu puts it, "White hordes have sallied forth from their western homelands to assault, loot, occupy, rule and exploit the world." Fanon insists that torture and massacres are the modus operandi of all the imperial regimes in Africa. Césaire asserts that during World War II the British and the French hated Hitler not because he was a mass murderer, but because he was a mass murderer of Europeans. According to Césaire, Hitler's real crime in the European view was "the inflicting on Europeans of European colonialist procedures which until now were reserved for the Arabs of Algeria, the coolies of India and the Negroes of Africa."[13]

A second tenet of anti-colonialism is that colonial regimes are racist—they systematically cause the dehumanization of the colonized. Said blames Western racism for the sufferings of "ravaged colonial peoples who for centuries endured summary injustice, unending economic oppression, distortion of their social and intimate lives, and a recourseless submission that was a function of unchanging European superiority." In *The Colonizer and the Colonized*, Albert Memmi argues that racism dehumanizes the ruler no less than the native. Césaire writes that this is because the colonizer "gets into the habit of seeing the other man as an animal, accustoms himself to treating him like an animal, and tends objectively to transform himself into an animal."[14]

A third anti-colonialist tenet is that colonialism is a system of piracy in which the wealth of the colonized countries is systematically stolen by the colonizers. In *The Wretched of the Earth*, Fanon writes, "The well being and progress of Europe have been built up with the sweat and the dead bodies of Negroes, Arabs, Indians and the yellow races." The Marxist scholar Walter Rodney makes the same point in *How Europe Underdeveloped Africa*. Anti-colonialist writers insist that the former colonized countries are poor because the West is rich; the West, they say, became rich by looting the wealth and resources of other countries.[15]

A fourth tenet of anti-colonialism is that the colonial powers have a new leader: the United States. As Said puts it, "The United States has replaced the great earlier empires and is the dominant outside force." Lest you naïvely think that America was not a colonial power and does not have a history of oppression like Britain or France, historians Michael Omi and Howard Winant draw our attention to what has happened within America. "The broad sweep of U.S. history is characterized not by racial democracy but by racial despotism, not by trajectories of reform but by implacable denial of political rights, dehumanization, extreme exploitation and policies of minority extirpation." Omi and Winant are referring to the displacement of the native Indians, the seizure and occupation of their territory, the ideology of Manifest Destiny, the war with Mexico and the capture of large tracts of Mexican land, and the annexation of Hawaii, all aimed at expanding the settlement we now call the United States.[16]

Anti-colonial critics also point to the 1823 promulgation of the Monroe Doctrine, in which America basically declared that Central and South America were "our" sphere of influence, telling the European powers to stay out of "our" neighborhood. In the twentieth century, the United States routinely intervened in Central and South America to protect U.S. political interests and also the interests of U.S. corporations such as the United Fruit Company. Anti-colonialists also highlight America's 50-year imperial adventure in the Philippines, which was short-lived by European standards but by itself discredits any attempt to declare America innocent of participation in colonial escapades.

And today? Well, anti-colonial critics say that the problem is worse than ever. While America's global dominance has been evident since World War II, it has only increased with the end of the Cold War and the disappearance of the Soviet Union as a serious rival. So now America has the power and uses it to subjugate other countries and bring them under the American jackboot. Sometimes this is outright colonial occupation, as when American troops invade and occupy another country, such as Afghanistan or Iraq, but mostly America exercises its domination through political and economic strong-arm tactics. The effect is the same as what the Europeans once did: America uses its might to plunder the land and resources of the world, leaving behind a trail of dead and destitute nonwhite peoples.

This brings us to the fifth and final tenet of anti-colonialism, which is that there is no end to this system of injustice without getting the colonizers out. This may occur peacefully or it may require violence, but either way it must occur. Fanon calls this "total liberation." But total liberation is not limited to taking down the foreign flags and sending the men in military uniforms home. Rather, it also requires purging the colonies of the enduring political and economic influence of colonialism. Here we have the crucial idea that colonialism does not necessarily end with national independence. Instead, anti-colonialists say, it can continue in subtle but powerful forms to dominate the life of supposedly free nations. Of the Western powers, Chinweizu writes, "Even now the fury of their expansionist assault upon the rest of us has not abated." The Indian social critic Gayatri Chakravorty Spivak deplores what she considers to be "the continuing success of the imperialist project."[17]

The idea that colonialism continues even after countries officially declare independence is called neocolonialism. In his book *Neocolonialism: The Last Stage of Imperialism*, Kwame Nkrumah, who became the first president of independent Ghana, argues that Africa's freedom was freedom only in name. That's because "in reality its economic system and its political policy is directed from outside." Nkrumah points to powerful Western corporations and other forces that, like puppet-masters, manipulate Africa's destiny. For Nkrumah, there is only one way to fight back: socialism. Nkrumah insists that state socialism on the part of the newly independent peoples can effectively stop the new threat posed by neocolonialism.[18]

Why is socialism the solution? How specifically are socialism and Marxism connected with anti-colonialism? Many people are surprised to discover that Marx was actually a defender of colonialism: he argued that it brought primitive societies into modernity and laid the foundation for industrialization and eventually communism. Marx predicted, however, that Communist revolution would occur first in the industrialized nations of Europe. That didn't happen, and it was a serious problem for Marxists. In the beginning of the twentieth century, an English author, J. A. Hobson, formulated the ingenious thesis that the Western capitalist countries had delayed their internal economic crisis by invading foreign countries and pirating their wealth. In effect, European colonialism was the way to postpone European capitalism's day of reckoning. In 1916, Lenin reformulated Hobson's thesis in his well-known tract,

Imperialism: the Highest Stage of Capitalism. As Lenin succinctly put it, "Capitalism has been transformed into imperialism."[19]

Notice the similarity between the titles used by Lenin and Nkrumah. Many anti-colonial leaders like Nkrumah embraced Lenin's analysis and became lifelong socialists. Many of them didn't even read Marx, but socialism was a way to position themselves against what they perceived to be an oppressive alliance between imperialism and capitalism. One of these anti-colonialists was Barack Obama Sr. Obama became an important figure in the Kenyan independence movement, but his greatest influence was not in Kenya. Rather, through an incredible osmosis, he was able to transmit his ideology to his son living in America. That man is today the president of the United States.

My argument in this book is that it is the anti-colonial ideology of his African father that Barack Obama took to heart. From a very young age and throughout his formative years, Obama learned to see America as a force for global domination and destruction. He came to view America's military as an instrument of neocolonial occupation. He adopted his father's position that the free market is a code word for economic plunder. Obama grew to perceive the rich as an oppressive class, a kind of neocolonial power within America. He began to detest corporations as institutional mechanisms for economic control and exploitation. In Obama's worldview, profits are a measure of how effectively you have ripped off the rest of society, and America's power in the world is a measure of how selfishly it consumes the globe's resources and how ruthlessly it bullies and dominates the rest of the planet.

For Obama, the task ahead is simple: he must work to wring the neocolonialism out of America and the West. First, he must rein in the military so that it does not conduct wars of occupation against other countries. Then he must use American leverage to restrict military adventurism on the part of America's allies, especially the former colonial powers in Europe. Even symbolic measures of humiliation are helpful in showing the former European colonialists that their day is now gone. In addition, Obama seeks to check American and Western consumption of global resources so that the former colonial (and now neocolonial) powers do not consume what belongs to others. Another objective for Obama is to bring the powerful sectors of American industry, such as the investment banks and health care, under government supervision and control. Obama seeks a large custodial state as a protection against the dangers of concentrated corporate power. Finally, Obama seeks to castigate and expose the rich, who are viewed as a neocolonial force within American society, so that they cease to be exploiters of the rest of the population.

It may seem shocking to suggest that this is Obama's core ideology, and that he believes it still. That is what I am saying. I am not suggesting that Obama has a comprehensive knowledge of anti-colonialism; a whole body of anti-colonial scholarship, associated with such names as Mario Vargas Llosa, Octavio Paz, V. S. Naipaul, and Derek Walcott seems unknown to him. Nor am I implying that anti-colonial views are the only determinants of Obama's beliefs. Certainly I admit that Obama must occasionally and pragmatically bend to the realities of a given situation or to the exigencies of politics. Still, Obama's anti-colonialism is deeply felt, and it suffuses his writings and speeches. In fact, it is the moral and intellectual foundation of his ideology. In a sense, I am saying nothing more than what Obama himself says: that his father's dream has become his dream. It is a dream that, as president, he is imposing with a vengeance on America and the world.

CHAPTER 3

OBAMA'S PRIVATE WAR

The best way to verify a theory is to test its explanatory power. Our theory, derived from Obama's testimony, is that he adopted his ideals from his father, and we know that his father's ideals were anti-colonial ideals. Based on this, we are in a position to examine the merits of our theory by checking it against what Obama is actually saying and doing. If the theory can account for Obama's major policies and enable us to predict what he is going to do in the future, then we are really onto something. But if the theory can also explain the little details about Obama, details that otherwise seem puzzling or mysterious, that would give our paradigm a degree of confirmation that very few comprehensive theories enjoy in politics.

So let's see if our working hypothesis fits the data available to us. We do this by putting on anti-colonial spectacles and viewing the world through those lenses. Events are reported in the press one way, but we are going to see them Obama's way. This approach not only has the benefit of giving us a radically different angle of vision. It also enables us to see how Obama, who obviously cannot reveal his true motivations, must constantly translate his ideology into terms that are accessible and palatable to the American people. In other words, our theory about Obama also predicts his mode of rhetorical delivery. If we are right about him, then he has to be careful about what he says.

He cannot say he hates the rich, so he has to talk about fairness and equality. He cannot say America is a nuclear menace to the world, so he has to say that he wants a nuclear-free world. He cannot say he thinks Wall Street is evil, so he must accuse the investment firms of not looking out for the interests of Main Street. Obama sometimes blows it; he doesn't always succeed with his anti-colonial marketing. Even his attempt, however, is impressive; this is a skill he has been honing for many years. Thus even as we verify our working theory about Obama's ideology, we can also admire the "translation" skills of a true political artist.

A good way to begin is with Obama's cool, detached temperament. Even typical liberal causes such as egalitarianism and the eradication of poverty don't seem to excite him. The minimum wage scarcely moves him as an issue, and he has never been known to show a passion for recycling. But Obama's voice rises in pitch when he condemns the scoundrels on Wall Street or gives a tongue-lashing to the CEOs of large banks or insurance companies. "The rich in America have little to complain about," Obama wrote in *The Audacity of Hope*. Recently in Illinois he condemned well-heeled executives for trying to earn as much as possible. Obama snapped, "I do think that at a certain point you've made enough money."[1]

This seems like an odd thing for a president to say. Isn't it good for America that Steve Jobs and Warren Buffett, who have more money than they can ever spend, still continue to do what they are doing? I am not concerned, however, with the merits of Obama's statement. Rather, I want to draw attention to what makes the guy irritable and mad, what makes him go bitter and sarcastic on us. The answer: big corporations and rich people.

Obama seems to have a longstanding prejudice against these groups. After graduating from college in 1983, Obama hoped to become a community activist. But first he went to work for a company to make some money. He described himself as "a spy behind enemy lines" in a "consulting house to multinational corporations" where he allegedly hung out with financiers and bond traders. "I had my own office, my own secretary, money in the bank." Dan Armstrong, a former work colleague, pointed out on his blog that Obama had no private office and no secretary. Nor was he employed by a major consulting firm, but rather as a copy editor for a small, low-paying newsletter company.[2] Obama's exaggeration is not important here; what is important is his attempt to portray even his service at this lowly outpost of capitalism as a kind of political espionage.

On May 13, 2009, Obama delivered the commencement address at Arizona State University where he told the graduating seniors, "You're taught to chase after the usual brass rings, being on this 'who's who' list or that top 100 list, how much money you make and how big your corner office is; whether you have a fancy enough title or a nice enough car. Let me suggest that such an approach won't get you where you want to go. It displays a poverty of ambition."[3] It may seem strange for a president to be lecturing students on the perils of economic striving in the teeth of a recession. But if you recognize that when Obama hears the word "profit," he thinks of neocolonial "exploitation," then all of Obama's stern rhetoric becomes comprehensible. Not that it makes sense, but we can see why he said it. Notice how artfully he puts it, though. "The poverty of ambition" is a typical Obama phrase. Obama criticizes ambition, but not in the name of modesty or restraint; rather, he implies that there is some higher form of ambition just waiting to be discovered by a new generation of young people. Could it be that this ambition is for organized activism against rich people and profit-making companies—Obama's own chosen vocation?

Now let's take up Obama's attitude toward Europe and specifically toward those former colonial powers, the French and the British. Obama visited Europe for around three weeks in 1988, before joining his father's family in Africa. For all its elegance and splendor, Europe didn't impress Obama; on the contrary, it alienated him. "By the end of the first week or so," he wrote in *Dreams from My Father*, "I realized that I'd made a mistake. It wasn't that Europe wasn't beautiful; everything was just as I'd imagined it. It just wasn't mine."[4] For Obama, Europe is a kind of distraction or delay from where he really wants to be, which is Africa. This may seem odd given that Obama's mother is white and therefore he has just as much claim to a European heritage as to an African one. Yet for all its wealth and grandeur—or perhaps because of it—Europe annoys him while Africa continues to exert its irresistible appeal.

By itself this admission may mean little, but now consider Obama's June 2009 visit to Paris, where he was invited to dinner by the French prime minister Nicolas Sarkozy and his model wife Carla Bruni. The Obamas declined. Their refusal was odd, given that they were staying at the residence of the U.S. ambassador just yards from the Sarkozy residence in the Élysée apartments. The French press noted the snub, but there wasn't much of a ruckus even among the usually prickly French. In fact, the Pew Research surveys show that the Europeans in general, and especially the French, remain enthusiastic about Obama.[5] How can this be explained if Obama has a streak that is anti-European and specifically anti-French?

The answer, of course, is that Obama has won over the French by criticizing his own country. The French are sensitive to snubs of their leaders, but this is a small price to pay for an American leader who comes to France and apologizes for American arrogance. It was in Strasbourg three months earlier that Obama delighted the French by saying, "In America, there's a failure to appreciate Europe's leading role in the world. Instead of celebrating your dynamic union and seeking to partner with you to meet common challenges, there have been times where America has shown arrogance and been dismissive, even derisive." Much is forgiven in Paris for an American leader who kowtows in this way.[6] Thus Obama can bash neocolonial America and stiff the prime minister of the old colonialists while at the same time basking in their adulation—quite a rhetorical feat indeed.

Obama's cold shoulder toward the French prime minister, however, was nothing compared to his treatment of the British. On March 7, 2009, then British prime minister Gordon Brown visited the White House. Obama presented him with a set of wrongly formatted DVDs. This was hardly an adequate response to what Brown gave the Obamas: an ornamental pen holder carved from the timbers of a British anti-slave ship from the 1880s. This was not an isolated lapse; only three weeks later, on April 1, 2009, the Queen came to visit. Obama gave her an iPod. Reporting on the incident, the London papers pointed out that the queen already owns an iPod. Not that Obama is incapable of graciousness; he was more than gracious—some said positively sycophantic—in bowing from the waist to the king of Saudi Arabia.

But the ultimate insult to the English was when Obama, right upon assuming the presidency, came upon a bust of Winston Churchill in the Oval Office and promptly decided to return it. Churchill, of course, is routinely quoted by American presidents, and the bust had been loaned to America from the British government's art collection. In a way it symbolized America's special relationship with Britain. Somewhat shocked by Obama's decision to remove the bust from the White House, British officials suggested that perhaps Obama could display it elsewhere. Obama declined. Chagrined, the British took it back, and the bust now sits in the residence of the British ambassador in Washington.[7]

Bizarre? It is if you think of Obama as just another socialist (why would a socialist have such a violent reaction to a Churchill statue?) or remember Churchill solely as the fellow who guided the British to victory in World War II. But with his anti-colonial background, Obama probably remembers Churchill as an imperialist who soldiered for the empire in India and Africa. Churchill was opposed to India's independence movement, and in 1942 famously said, "I have not become the king's first minister in order to preside over the liquidation of the British Empire." Even as late as 1954, when President Eisenhower raised with Churchill the idea of granting self-government to all remaining British colonies in Africa, Churchill responded that he was "skeptical about universal suffrage for the Hottentots."[8] In the 1950s, Churchill was prime minister during Britain's fight against the Mau Mau uprising in Kenya, the native country of Obama's father. So when we apply the anti-colonial hypothesis, we find that the inexplicable Churchill incident suddenly makes perfect sense.

Let's move from the symbols of European empire to those of American patriotism. If Obama is vehemently opposed to a world defined in America's image, to Pax Americana, then we would expect him to be cagey and defensive about displays of patriotism that convey America's leadership in the world. Sure enough, a *Time* photograph from the presidential campaign shows Obama at a fundraising event with several other Democratic politicians. The magazine noted that the national anthem was playing, but the photo shows that Obama does not have his right hand over his heart. And he's the only one: everyone else does!

Network video footage of the event confirmed that Obama was the lone holdout in this traditional display of patriotic allegiance.

Once again, this could be dismissed as an isolated episode, and was so dismissed by Obama's defenders. But a few months later, Obama announced that he would no longer wear a lapel pin with the American flag as had become customary for politicians and also many other public figures since the 9/11 attacks. "You show your patriotism by how you treat your fellow Americans," Obama said. The pin, he contended, had become "a substitute for true patriotism."[9] On the face of it Obama's comments are nonsensical; how can an American flag somehow undermine genuine patriotism? What Obama means of course is that patriotism of this sort is morally objectionable to him because of its associations with American invasions and American power. Obama clearly prefers the kind of patriotism that is not associated with the 9/11 attacks and America's subsequent actions in Afghanistan and Iraq. In Obama's ideology, we show our love for our country not through jingoistic flag-waving and foreign expeditions, but rather by agitating for domestic policies that take from the haves and give to those who don't have as much.

Obama's anti-colonialism, however, takes him far beyond the rejection of mere symbols; in some cases, he supports the release of terrorists who claim to be fighting wars of liberation against American aggression. In July 2010, reports surfaced in the British press that the Obama administration favored the release of Abdel Baset al-Megrahi, the Lockerbie bomber. This was an eye-opener, because when Scotland released Megrahi from prison and sent him home to Libya in August 2009, the Obama administration publicly protested the decision. Obama reaffirmed his position on Megrahi's release when British prime minister David Cameron came to visit in July 2010. The president's public sentiments seemed entirely appropriate: Megrahi, after all, had been convicted in connection with the 1988 bombing of a Pan Am Jet over Lockerbie, Scotland, killing 270 people, most of them American.

But a few days after Cameron departed, the British press obtained a letter that the Obama administration had sent a year earlier to the Scottish government. The letter seems to show that Obama's public outrage was contrived. In fact, the Obama administration took the position that releasing Megrahi on "compassionate grounds" was acceptable as long as he was kept in Scotland. This option, Obama said, would be "far preferable" to sending him back to Libya. Scottish government officials interpreted the letter to mean that U.S. objections to Megrahi's release were "half-hearted." So they let Megrahi go back to his own country, where he lives today as a free man.

While the American press has downplayed the story, the families of the Lockerbie victims now know about the Obama letter and want to see it. Yet the Obama administration refuses to make the letter public, probably because of its incriminating content. Now why would a U.S. president take such a benign view of a terrorist striking out against America? I cannot think of any possible explanation except one. On the anti-colonial explanation, it is because Obama views Megrahi as a resister who was striking out against U.S. imperialism. That is certainly how Megrahi portrayed himself at his trial.[10]

Now let's move to the issue of American exceptionalism and recall Obama's statement that America is no more unique than Greece or Britain or any other country. Why, I asked earlier, would he say this? The reason becomes clear when we examine the content of American exceptionalism. A good source text here is Alexis de Tocqueville, as fervent a champion of American exceptionalism as anyone, who announced to the Europeans that "all eyes are therefore turned toward the United States" because America was in the process of creating "a distinct species of mankind." Tocqueville's American is unique in his entrepreneurial zeal. "Choose any American at random and he should be a man of burning desires, enterprising, adventurous and above all an innovator." Tocqueville also finds that entrepreneurship produces a meritocratic society. "Natural inequality will soon make way for itself and wealth will spontaneously pass into the hands of the most capable."[11] Probably most people think these are true and fine things to say about America, but not Obama. For him, economic enterprise and meritocracy are, at a gut level, neocolonial code words for subjugating and taking advantage of others. He wants nothing to do with an exceptionalism that encourages such attributes.

Tocqueville's observations are updated in a more recent book, *American Exceptionalism*, by sociologist Seymour Martin Lipset. In it the author lists several features of contemporary America that are unique. Americans, he writes, are very patriotic—much more so than Europeans—and tend to view their country as superior to every other country. Moreover, Americans, almost uniquely, believe that the rest of the world would be much better off if it adopted the American way. Americans also think they are a providential nation, with God on their side. If this were not bad enough, from Obama's point of view, Lipset also remarks that Americans tend to agree with Calvin Coolidge when he said that "the business of America is business." In addition, Americans tend to look favorably on the rich because the rich are the ones who buy things and run companies and thus create jobs for the rest of society. Lipset says that while there have been vigorous socialist parties in Europe, socialism has never found a strong appeal in the United States. He observes that this may be because the ordinary guy has it pretty good in America. Lipset cites Werner Sombart's dictum that in America "all socialist utopias have come to grief on roast beef and apple pie."[12] Given Obama's hostility to what he regards as American militarism, as well as his antipathy to concentrations of wealth, it is easy to see why Obama decided to distance himself from American exceptionalism, even though his success in America is a clear illustration of it.

So far, we have been exploring the little incidents that show the relevance of Obama's anti-colonial ideology. Now let's use our theory to explain Obama's stance on some bigger issues. Here is the cover story from the June 26, 2010, *New York Times*: "In Deal, New Authority Over Wall Street." The article reports that the Obama administration has succeeded in convincing Congress to impose "an overhaul of the nation's financial regulatory system" that will "vastly expand the authority of the federal government." The legislation "imposes new rules" and also "levies hefty fees on the financial services industry, essentially forcing big banks and hedge funds to pay the projected $20 billion, five-year cost of the new oversight they will face. In addition, it empowers regulators to liquidate failing companies, fundamentally altering the balance between government and industry."[13] Now this can be read as a typical liberal or socialist-style attempt to redistribute the wealth, but that's not a very good explanation, because there's no redistributing going on here. This is about power, control, and bringing the money industry under the thumb of the federal government. This is about the federal government nailing the fat cats and making them cover the cost of the operation.

Two examples provide further evidence that this anti-colonial reading is on the right track. According to news reports, Obama took particular pleasure in personally approving the firing of General Motors CEO Rick Wagoner. This was the first time in American history that the president of the United States had essentially booted out the head of a private company. Sure, Obama had a pretext for doing so: GM was doing poorly, and the government had injected a big dollop of bailout money. I am not saying that Wagoner didn't deserve the boot. I am saying that the firing was a demonstration of Obama's desire to show big corporate CEOs in America who's boss. How exhilarating for an anti-colonialist to exercise such power against the regnant bigwigs! Another example: in the past year, several banks have attempted to pay back their stimulus money. But in some cases the Obama administration said no, we are not going to take it. Obama announced a "stress test" for banks in which he, not the banks, would decide whether they were financially sound and thus eligible to give the money back. In effect, Obama was saying: I want to maintain my control over you even when there is no reason to do so, even when you are ready to return the bailout money.

Next let's consider Obama's response to the devastating oil spill in the Gulf of Mexico. As torrents of black oil gushed toward southern shores, Obama sounded lethargic, almost bored, with what was going on and what needed to be done to stop it. Even Democratic strategist James Carville expressed amazement at Obama's personal and emotional remove from the situation. "I have no idea why they didn't seize this thing. I have no idea why their attitude was so hands off here." Listening to Obama talk on the subject, TV host Keith Olbermann responded: "It was a great speech if you were on another planet for the last 57 days."[14]

Finally, addressing the TV cameras on May 14, 2010, Obama managed to work up some enthusiasm. He condemned "British Petroleum"—an interesting term since the company long ago changed its name to BP. Given our anti-colonial theory, it's no surprise that Obama wanted to remind Americans of what BP used to stand for. He was equally outspoken in whacking the other oil companies for their "ridiculous spectacle" of "pointing fingers of blame." Actually these companies were not responsible for the spill, and the only blame, in addition to that of BP, belonged to the Obama administration for its Katrina-like incompetence in responding to the disaster.

Addressing the nation on the spill on June 15, 2010, Obama stressed that Americans "consume more than 20 percent of the world's oil, but have less than 2 percent of the world's resources." Obama went on to say that "for decades we've talked and talked about the need to end America's century-long addiction to fossil fuels." Unfortunately, "time and again the path forward has been blocked" by, among others, "oil industry lobbyists."[15] Now, on the face of it, this is a perfectly reasonable statement from a liberal politician who thinks this is what the American public wants to hear. But ask yourself, what does any of this have to do with the oil spill? Would the oil spill have been less of a problem if America consumed a mere 10 percent of the world's resources? Of course not. The point is that for Obama the energy and environmental issues reduce to a simple proposition: America is a neocolonial giant eating up more than its share of the world's resources, and in doing so America is exploiting the scarce fuel of the globe; consequently, this gluttonous consumption must be stopped. This is the heart of Obama's energy and environmental agenda: not cleaning up the Gulf or saving the environment in general, but redressing the inequitable system where the neocolonial West—and neocolonial companies like BP—dominates the use of global energy resources.

When Arizona passed a law in April 2010 authorizing state police to check the papers of people whom they had reasonable cause to suspect were illegal immigrants, Obama reacted with immediate disdain. "Being an American is not a matter of blood or birth, it's a matter of faith," he declared. The first part of this is right—American citizenship is not a matter of race, and immigrants can become citizens—but the second part seems absurd. Does Obama mean to suggest that a guy who lives in Mumbai or Mexico City and has no relationship with America can automatically become an American simply by having faith? "I have faith in America" automatically translates into "I have a right to U.S. citizenship"? Obama also said that the immigration problem cannot be solved "only with fences and border patrols." True, but fences and border controls could

well be part of the solution. Businesses, Obama said, should face consequences for employing illegal aliens. Once again corporate America is the
bad guy here, not the government which is negligent in controlling the
American border. Finally, under political pressure, Obama agreed to
deploy an additional 1,200 National Guard troops to the border, a woe-
fully inadequate response to an out-of-control situation.[16]

At the same time, the Obama administration filed a lawsuit against
Arizona to overturn the immigration control law on constitutional
grounds. So the federal government was basically taking Arizona to
court because of a state law that sought to accomplish what is already
required under federal law. Now laws do have to pass the constitutional
test, but the ACLU had already challenged the constitutionality of the
Arizona legislation. Some provisions of the law have been struck down,
and the litigation is likely to go on for some time. So why did Obama get
involved? Why would the president risk the political fallout on such a
controversial issue when it was already in the courts?

In his book *Culture and Imperialism*, the anti-colonial scholar Edward
Said (who turns out to have been one of Obama's professors at Columbia University) wrote that "the old divisions between colonizer and colonized have reemerged in what is often referred to as the North-South
relationship." Said notes that "Europeans and Americans now confront
large non-white immigrant populations in their midst," and these represent "newly empowered voices asking for their narratives to be
heard."[17] From this anti-colonial perspective, the nonwhites are the
descendants of the colonized, and they are now returning to claim their
rights and their lost territory. Not surprisingly, Obama will not settle for
federal inaction; he wants to make sure that his administration is on the
right side of this issue.

Obama's judicial nominations of Sonia Sotomayor and Elena Kagan
to the Supreme Court are also understandable in the context of the

anti-colonial theory. Sotomayor is the voice of the oppressed. Her controversial statement, "I would hope a wise Latina woman with the richness of her experience would more often than not reach a better conclusion than a white male who hasn't lived that life," probably commended her to Obama. Sotomayor was saying, in effect, that white male judges reflect one narrow point of view while nonwhite women reflect a quite different and superior perspective. The former can be seen to represent the colonizers and the latter the colonized. We're ready for your promotion, Sonia! The most controversial facet of Elena Kagan's career has been her decision as dean of the Harvard Law School to kick military recruiters off campus. During her hearings, Kagan insisted that her decision still permitted the military to recruit at Harvard, which was true, though they were limited in a way that other recruiters weren't. When Kagan, as dean, backed down from her original decision, it was done in order to avoid jeopardizing Harvard's eligibility for federal funds. But it would not be surprising if Kagan's hostility to military recruitment caught the approving attention of President Obama.

Let's turn to foreign policy and continue our application of the anti-colonial thesis to see how much it illuminates. In July 2010, Obama fired America's top commander in Afghanistan, General Stanley McChrystal, for his insubordinate remarks as revealed in a *Rolling Stone* interview. Whether or not the magazine used not-for-attribution quotations, as McChrystal's staff alleged, the firing in my view was justified because military commanders should not speak so disrespectfully of their civilian commander in chief.

Even so, the content of what McChrystal and his aides said is telling. Most of them were contemptuous of Vice President Joe Biden, regarding him a buffoon. McChrystal apparently found Biden's solutions for the region silly, saying they would lead to "Chaos-istan." The McChrystal team's reaction to Obama, however, was quite different. Obama frustrated them because they found him unreachable and impenetrable, basically uninterested in the facts on the ground and what the coalition forces were trying to do. McChrystal and his staff officer tried to explain the counterinsurgency strategy to the president, but Obama didn't seem to care. As a McChrystal aide put it, the president "didn't seem very engaged."[18] Now why would a president who has a big political stake in Afghanistan not care about proposed strategies to successfully prosecute the offensive and maybe even win the war? Short answer: Because he doesn't want to win. If Obama views Afghanistan as a war of colonial occupation, then his only concern is how fast he can get America out.

But wait a minute! Didn't Obama order an additional 30,000 troops to Afghanistan? Yes, but the Obama "surge" was a political necessity. Recall that Obama had campaigned on the position that Iraq was the "bad war" and Afghanistan was the "good war." We don't know at this point if Obama actually considered Afghanistan a good war; later I will show that he did not. At the time, however, Afghanistan was a convenient way for Obama to seem tough on terrorism while calling for an American pullout in Iraq. The rhetorical strategy worked; it helped Obama get to the White House with his anti-terrorist credentials intact. But then Obama, who might never have favored a victory in Afghanistan, was presented in 2009 by McChrystal with a strategy for success that required additional troops. Obama agreed to send them, but grudgingly—and he sent fewer than McChrystal said were necessary. As Thomas Friedman wrote in the *New York Times*, "The ugly truth is that no one in the Obama White House wanted this Afghan surge. The only reason they proceeded was because no one knew how to get out of it—or had the courage to pull the plug."[19]

But while announcing the surge, Obama also insisted that he would withdraw U.S. troops from Afghanistan in a year. "There's got to be an exit strategy," Obama said, and then added, going into his very subtle translator mode, "There's got to be a sense that this is not perpetual drift."[20] Obviously the withdrawal announcement undercut the surge, because enemies are likely to hold out more tenaciously even against a bigger force if they are assured that the whole operation will end in the not-too-distant future. As the *Economist* candidly noted, "There is almost no chance that Afghanistan will be transformed by the time of Obama's deadline."[21]

Obama's conservative critics treated this as just another Obama bungle, but it makes more sense to hold that Obama doesn't really care about whether Afghanistan is transformed or not. His goal is not success in Afghanistan; rather, it is how quickly he can get America out. His anti-colonial strategy doffs a hat to political reality, but also ensures, win or lose, a prompt pullout from a war he doesn't want to fight. Moreover, if America and NATO are seen to have "lost" Afghanistan, that would be a good thing, because from the anti-colonial point of view, such a defeat would discourage colonial military expeditions in the future.

Let's move our sights from Afghanistan to the Middle East. In recent months Obama caused a stir by allowing a public rift to emerge with the Israeli government over the building of additional settlements. Michael Oren, Israel's ambassador to the United States, charged that the rift was the worst political crisis between the two countries in more than three decades. Israel is so besieged around the world, even in Europe, that Washington usually takes extra care to be protective of her Middle Eastern ally. But not Obama. Sure, the Obama administration publicly denied the rift—Jews, after all, are a vital base of political and financial support for the Democratic Party—but no credible observer believes Obama's heart is with the Jewish state.

In July 2010, Israeli prime minister Benjamin Netanyahu appeared at a joint press conference with Obama and agreed to ease Israel's blockade of the Gaza strip; Netanyahu also pledged Israel's commitment to making peace with the Palestinians. He told Fox News he would put East Jerusalem on the negotiating table as a possible capital of a Palestinian state.[22] Obama welcomed Netanyahu's concessions, which seem to have been the necessary price to pay for Israel to mend fences with its most important ally and protector. Obama had humbled Netanyahu and he had also made his own feelings clear. Obama disapproves of Israel's actions, and he did not hesitate to warn the Israeli government that he is not Israel's uncritical cheerleader.

Obama, in fact, has a history of siding with Israel's opponents. During the presidential primary campaign, Obama stirred controversy by telling Democratic activists in Iowa, "Nobody is suffering more than the Palestinian people." In reality, lots of people in the world are worse off than the Palestinians; still, Obama's statement clearly indicated how strongly he felt about the Palestinian cause. While he was a state senator in Illinois, Obama befriended the scholar Rashid Khalidi, who has strongly defended the right of Palestinians to use armed resistance against Israel. The Muslim blogger Ali Abunimah wrote that he saw Obama a half dozen times at Chicago events organized by the Arab and Palestinian community. He recalled Obama attending a May 1998 fundraiser in which the keynote speaker was anti-colonial scholar and former PLO representative Edward Said. According to Abunimah, during the 2004 Senate campaign, Obama praised Abunimah's *Chicago Tribune* columns attacking Israel and urged him to "keep up the good work" for the Palestinian cause. Obama also added, "Hey, I'm sorry I haven't said more about Palestine right now but we are in a tough primary race. I'm hoping when things calm down I can be more up front."[23] Doesn't all of this make sense under the presumption that Obama regards Israel's occupation of the West Bank and Gaza as a war of colonial aggression?

In April 2010, Obama held a nuclear security summit in Washington, D.C., in which forty-seven countries agreed to a joint statement condemning nuclear proliferation. The highlight of the event was an announcement that, after months of bargaining, the United States and Russia had agreed to new, deep weapons reductions and updated verification rules that would see their strategic arsenals drop to 1,550 warheads, one-third below previously agreed levels. Many countries—including Canada, Chile, and Mexico—agreed to dispose of their stockpiles of enriched uranium and plutonium. Italy and Argentina promised they would install radiation detectors to check cargo for fissile material. All these initiatives were at the urging of the Obama administration; as one Obama official boasted, "We used the summit shamelessly as a forcing event to ask countries to bring house gifts."[24]

Which countries? Mainly they were America's friends and allies. Conspicuously absent at the summit were North Korea and Iran, the former country in possession of nuclear weapons, the latter energetically engaged in the process of acquiring them. Obama didn't seem concerned by their absence, and White House officials were even quoted saying they didn't want the issues of North Korea and Iran to "distract" from what was being accomplished at the summit. Obama treated the world to his impressive vision of how wonderful it would be if we could be rid of nuclear weapons, and then everyone went home.

Predictably, conservative columnists lambasted Obama, with Mark Steyn calling the president "dangerously delusional." Steyn asked his readers to imagine Britain convening a disarmament conference in 1938 and inviting America, France, Brazil, Liberia, and Thailand—but not even mentioning Germany or Japan. How likely would it be that then Germany or Japan, wowed by all the allied declarations of arms reductions, would agree to stop their own buildups? Charles Krauthammer, perhaps Obama's most trenchant critic, seconded these sentiments. Krauthammer scoffed at the U.S.-Russia deal and pointed out that "the number of warheads in Russia's aging and decaying nuclear stockpile is an irrelevancy now that the existential U.S.-Soviet struggle is over." Krauthammer also noted that nuclear weapons are not in themselves dangerous; what's dangerous is when they are in the hands of the bad guys. In this case, the bad guys had gotten off scot free. "The very notion that Kim Jong-il or Mahmoud Ahmadinejad will suddenly abjure nukes because of yet another U.S.-Russian treaty is comical."[25]

This criticism was cogent enough when you consider its underlying assumption about Obama: that his goal was to discourage North Korea from expanding its nuclear arsenal and Iran from building one. If this was indeed Obama's objective, then the critics are right—the man is an idiot! But here is where our anti-colonial hypothesis pays huge dividends. In fact, it shows that the joke is really on Obama's critics. Let's shift the underlying assumption and replace it with this one: Obama's goal is not to discourage Iran or North Korea but rather to limit the nuclear capability of the United States and its allies. Consider the possibility that Obama views America as the neocolonial titan in the world and its allies as support structures for Pax Americana. Now the summit can be viewed as an ingenious and completely successful effort to reduce American power in the world. In fact, the outcome is all the more brilliant because Obama was able to achieve this while posing as the champion of the worldwide eradication of nuclear weapons, thus enhancing his reputation as a Global Peacemaker.

So let's see where we are at this point. We have a powerful model—the anti-colonial model—that seems to make sense of many of Obama's actions. Other theories work like hammers: they have to beat away at Obama's statements and actions in order to fit them to some preconceived theory. This theory is not preconceived, but supplied to us by Obama himself. And it works like a nifty screwdriver that, with just a little effort and application, immediately gets the job done.

I now want to proceed in two stages: first, to examine how that anti-colonial ideology developed in Obama's life and mind; and second, to apply it in greater detail to Obama's policies. I intend to tell the remarkable story of Obama's life, showing at each stage how his ideas formed, how they progressed into a cohesive ideology, how the ideology found an effective implementation strategy, and finally how that strategy brought Obama into the Oval Office. After that, I intend to systematically examine Obama's key policies, both domestic and foreign, to expose what this man is doing to America. It's a riveting story, and told in a way you haven't heard before, but if you care about America's prosperity and security, I might as well forewarn you. Be very afraid.

CHAPTER 4

THE OUTSIDER

O n March 4, 2007, while campaigning for the Democratic nomination for president, Barack Obama stood in the pulpit of Brown Chapel A.M.E. Church in Selma, Alabama, and staked his claim to the civil rights heritage. "Don't tell me I don't have a claim on Selma, Alabama!" he chanted, as the crowd went wild. "Don't tell me I'm not coming home to Selma, Alabama."

Home? In fact, Obama was raised in Hawaii. Everyone knew that, so he had to make the connection. "Something happened back here in Selma, Alabama. Something happened in Birmingham that sent out what Bobby Kennedy called ripples of hope all around the world. Something happened when a bunch of women decided they were going to walk instead of ride the bus after a long day of doing someone else's laundry, looking after someone else's children. When men who had Ph.D.s decided that's enough and we're going to stand up for our dignity.

That sent a shout across oceans so that my grandfather began to imagine something different for his son."

Actually Obama's grandfather had no such imaginings; there is no indication that he had even heard of the American civil rights movement. Obama's father had studied in a missionary school and was working as a clerk in Nairobi. He was encouraged to come to America for further study by two missionary women, Helen Roberts and Elizabeth Mooney, who were living at the time in Kenya. In Obama's Selma narrative, this was made possible by the Kennedy family. "What happened in Selma, Alabama, and Birmingham also, stirred the conscience of the nation. It worried folks in the White House," he said. "The Kennedys decided we're going to do an airlift. We're going to go to Africa and start bringing young Africans over to this country and give them scholarships to study so they can learn what a wonderful country America is. This young man named Barack Obama got one of those tickets and came over to this country." Soon after that Obama got married and "Barack Obama Jr. was born. . . . So I'm here because somebody marched. I'm here because you all sacrificed for me."

Except that the Kennedys had nothing to do with Obama's father coming to America. As Obama's staff eventually acknowledged, Obama Sr. arrived here in 1959. John F. Kennedy was elected president the following year.[1] The two American teachers who had encouraged Obama Sr. to make the trip paid his travel costs and the bulk of his expenses. There was an airlift, organized by the Kenyan labor leader Tom Mboya with financial support from a number of American philanthropists. It brought several dozen African students to America to study, but Barack Obama Sr. did not come on that plane. Rather, he came on his own and enrolled at the University of Hawaii at Manoa.[2] Moreover, the march in Selma occurred in March 1965, while Obama Jr. was born in August 1961; Selma had nothing to do with the circumstances of Obama's birth.

I do not want to make too much of these details. Obama is not the first politician to weave a narrative that is not overly inhibited by the facts. He is, as his supporters might say, after the bigger picture. It is that bigger picture that I want to contest. Obama portrays himself as an African American who shared the transforming experience of racism and then the liberating involvement in the struggles of the civil rights movement. But Hawaii, where Obama grew up, is recognized by residents and scholars of ethnicity as a kind of multiracial paradise. Interracial marriages, for instance, were socially acceptable there long before they were even legal in some states on the mainland. When Obama's father Barack Sr. graduated from the University of Hawaii in 1962, the Honolulu *Star Bulletin* did a short profile on him. The newspaper reported that Barack Sr. "hasn't experienced any problems himself" with discrimination; in fact, he "expresses wry amusement at the fact that Caucasians in Hawaii are occasionally on the receiving end of prejudice."[3]

His son's Hawaii could hardly have been more idyllic; young Obama attended a prestigious private school, Punahou, which boasts a 75-acre campus with posh architecture and lush greenery. Among the distinguished graduates of Punahou are AOL founder Steve Case and eBay founder Pierre Omidyar. In Obama's time, the students at Punahou were a racial smorgasbord: Chinese, Japanese, Filipino, Samoan, Portuguese, and Italian, with many combinations in between. Obama was able to skip the long waiting list and gain admission to Punahou through his maternal grandfather's connections. This was indeed favoritism, but not of the racial kind.

While the issue of race is not a big deal in Hawaii, the issue of colonialism certainly is. I am referring here to the white European settlers who came to Hawaii, displaced the native population, and eventually dominated the political and economic life of the islands. Captain James Cook landed in Hawaii in 1779, an event that set off a hundred-year struggle for the fertile land, plentiful resources, and fabled beauty of the islands. When Queen Liliuokalani proposed a new Hawaiian constitution in 1893 that would restore the power of the Hawaiian monarchy, the planter aristocracy forced her to step down. Five years later, on July 7, 1898, U.S. president William McKinley signed a bill that authorized the annexation of Hawaii. All of this is widely talked about, even today. Remember that Hawaii became a state only two years before Obama's birth, and resentment over the historical events that led up to that was still raw when Obama was in school.

To envision the August 12, 1898, transfer of power from the local authorities to the American mainland, let's consider the account by Gavan Daws in his book *Shoal of Time*:

> This was the ultimate dispossession.... Two American warships were at Honolulu. Detachments of marines came ashore and were met by the Hawaiian National Guard.... The senior representative of the United States... read the resolution of annexation.... The Hawaiian anthem, "Hawaii Ponoi," was played for the last time as the song of an independent nation, and the Hawaiian flag was hauled down. The Stars and Stripes took its place, and the band played the Star Spangled Banner.... Hawaii was dead, but Hawaii-in-America had taken its first breath.[4]

How did I find out about Daws's book? I read about it in a required reading list that Obama was assigned at Punahou. According to journalists who have tracked his curriculum, Obama studied books documenting the white subjugation of native populations such as *Shoal of Time*, and also Dee Brown's *Bury My Heart at Wounded Knee*, about the American Indians of the Great Plains; and *Farewell to Manzanar*, an account of

Japanese American internment during World War II. I'm not sure if the course was titled "Oppression Studies," but you get the picture.

We know that this exposure influenced Obama's thinking. That's because in his autobiography Obama writes:

> Hawaii! To my family, newly arrived in 1959, it must have seemed as if the earth itself, weary of stampeding armies and bitter civilization, had forced up this chain of emerald rock where pioneers from across the globe could populate the land with children bronzed by the sun. The ugly conquest of the native Hawaiians through aborted treaties and crippling disease brought by the missionaries; the carving up of rich volcanic soil by American companies for sugarcane and pineapple plantations; the indenturing system that kept Japanese, Chinese, and Filipino immigrants stooped sunup to sunset in these same fields; the internment of Japanese-Americans during the war—all of this was recent history.[5]

Yet Obama seeks to integrate these anti-colonial themes into a larger narrative of race, and he does so by conjuring in his memory various racial slights that he suffered. At one point, he reports, a tennis coach at Punahou joked with Obama that he shouldn't touch the match schedule on the bulletin board because his color might rub off; Obama threatened to report him. Obama also recognized that there were few black heroes on his television at home and "there was nobody like me in the Sears, Roebuck Christmas catalog." This is pretty tame stuff. One of Obama's fellow students, Constance Ramos, who is of Filipino background, says she didn't even know Obama was black. "I never once thought of Barry as black. I still don't. . . . His skin tone is just about the same as mine, and nobody would call me black." Even the intense racial conversations that Obama reports having in school are, according to Keith Kakugawa—the student allegedly involved in those conversations—highly exaggerated. "The idea that his biggest struggle was race is bull," Kakugawa told the *Chicago Tribune*. "His biggest struggles were his feelings of abandonment."[6]

Abandonment. Obama confesses to this feeling of existential loneliness, and of being for many of his younger years a divided soul. Once again he seeks to cast the chasm in racial terms, speaking of "the ghostly image of the tragic mulatto trapped between two worlds." This is an evocation of the black scholar W. E. B. Du Bois' famous self-description: "One ever feels his two-ness—an American, a Negro; two souls, two thoughts, two unreconciled strivings; two warring ideals in one dark body, whose dogged strength alone keeps it from being torn asunder."[7] Obama wants us to believe that his loneliness and lack of place were caused by being suspended between a white world and a black world, the world of his mom and the world of his dad.

But no! There was a division, but hardly this one. The real division was between the comfortable but empty world that Obama inhabited and the dark, troubled world of the dad who caused that emptiness by being absent his whole life. This other world Obama had to recover through a persistent quest for his African father, and from a very young age his mother cultivated in him the indefatigable desire to pursue that quest. With a kind of photographic recall, Obama remembers multiple occasions where "sitting on the floor with my mother, the smell of dust and mothballs rising from the crumbling album, I would stare at my father's likeness—the dark, laughing face, the prominent forehead and thick glasses that made him appear older than his years—and listen as the events of his life tumbled into a single narrative."[8] Obama's supreme struggle is how to reconcile the two worlds in order to develop a cohesive sense of identity and place.

Obama's father is the central character of *Dreams from My Father*. This is odd, because for most of Obama's life his dad was absent. Still, his absence is palpable and continues to define the narrative, somewhat like the absence of Achilles defines the events of the *Iliad*. "Achilles absent, was Achilles still," Homer writes, and something similar can be said about Barack Obama Sr. Although he is away, he continues to inhabit and indeed overpower the mind of his impressionable son. Obama writes that "my fierce ambitions might have been fueled by my father—by my knowledge of his achievements and failures, by my unspoken desire to somehow earn his love, and by my resentments and anger toward him." Even in absentia, Obama confides, "my father's voice had nevertheless remained untainted, inspiring, rebuking, granting or withholding approval. You do not work hard enough, Barry. You must help in your people's struggle. Wake up, black man!"[9]

What kind of magnetism did his father have? Obama's aunt Zeituni told him about the time his father brought a young girl to the family hut in Kenya. This was before Obama was born. Barack Sr. was in his twenties, and the girl's name was Kezia. (Later she would become his first wife.) Obama's grandfather Onyango Obama was notoriously strict and, according to Zeituni, his hearing was very sharp. So when Barack Sr. lured Kezia into the hut, Onyango heard them and angrily confronted his son. Kezia fled. At this point, Zeituni said, she was sure Onyango would cane Barack Sr. But to Zeituni's astonishment, "Barack walked over to the old man's phonograph and started to play a record. Then he turned and shouted to Kezia, who was hiding outside: Woman! Come here! Right away Kezia came into the house, too frightened to refuse, and Barack took her into his arms and began to dance with her, around and around in the old man's house, as if he were dancing in a palace ballroom." No one, Zeituni said, had treated Onyango this way. For a long time the old man said nothing. Then he went to the door of the hut and shouted to his wife: Woman! Come here! Immediately the woman came, and Onyango began to dance with her. "Soon all four of them were dancing in the hut."[10] I grew up with people like Onyango, and I have to say that if this incident happened as Zeituni described, Barack Sr. was a man with a very forceful personality.

Obama begins *Dreams from My Father* in 1982, when a relative from Africa calls to tell him his father has been killed in a car accident. The death energizes Obama in his quest to find the man he never really knew. One of the highlights of Obama's autobiography is when his father comes to visit his 10-year-old son. Despite his tender age, Obama recalls the event with almost eerie clarity. But the meeting is brief; then the father is gone, and Obama never sees him again. Even so the son keeps searching, recovering through conversations with his mother and through study the shaping events of his father's life. Obama's narrative culminates in his month-long journey to Africa, where he talks to various relatives about who his dad really was, and then weeps at the man's grave.

It's powerful stuff. But at first glance it's a little hard for the reader to understand Obama's depth of allegiance. His dad was, after all, a complete jerk. He married Kezia in Kenya and had two children with her. Before the second child was born, he abandoned his family to come to America. There he met Obama's mother Ann, got her pregnant, and then married her, but without telling her he was already married. When Obama was two, his father abandoned him and his mother to go to Harvard; there he moved in with a teacher, Ruth Nidesand. Eventually he took Nidesand back to Africa, married her, and had two children with her. But he also rejoined his African wife, Kezia, and had two more children with her. Later in life he took up with still another woman, Jael Otieno, and impregnated her. The two of them planned to get married after the child was born, but the marriage never took place. By the time he was done, Barack Sr. managed a grand total of three wives, one wife-to-be, and eight children. He was a terrible husband and a worse father; he neglected virtually all his offspring, and one of his sons has accused him of domestic violence. In the words of Mark Ndesandjo, who is the son of Obama Sr. and Nidesand, "I remember situations when I was growing up, and there would be a light coming from our living room, and I could hear thuds and screams, and my father's voice and my mother shouting. I remember one night when she ran out into the street and she didn't know where to go."[11]

It's hard to imagine what could be so attractive about a man like this. Not surprisingly, his charms were lost on his mother-in-law, Barack Obama Jr.'s maternal grandmother Madelyn Dunham. She described her son-in-law as "straaaaaange." Yet by the testimony of many who knew him, Obama Sr. was quite a sophisticated charmer. He was an elegant dresser and wore a tie even to casual events. Obama's aunt Zeituni described him as a very good dancer. Frederick Okatcha, a family friend and now a professor at Kenyatta University, recalls that Obama Sr. "had everything with which to impress the girls, despite a different cultural background." He had a slight British accent and called himself "Doctor Obama," even though he was neither a medical doctor nor the holder of an academic doctorate. Obama recalls his father spouting off incomprehensible aphorisms: "Like water finding its level, you will arrive at a career that suits you." He was a smoker, as his son after him would be. At Harvard, he was also a heavy drinker. There he earned the nickname "Double Double" because he liked to order a double Scotch and tell the waiter, as soon as it was delivered, "Another double." Eventually Obama Sr. developed liver disease due to his excessive drinking. To make things worse, he was a reckless driver who often drove under the influence, getting into several accidents in which he killed at least one other person before finally getting into a fatal wreck himself.[12] Obama acknowledges that his father had liver trouble but says nothing about his alcoholism; he also neglects to say that his father was driving drunk when he got into the accident that killed him.

Heck of a guy to spend your life pursuing. What gave dignity and depth, however, to Barack Obama Sr. was that he was part of a much larger movement—the movement to build a free and independent Africa in the aftermath of colonial rule. We know that this history made an impact on young Obama because he tells us so. Obama was a shy, withdrawn child who was trying to find his place in the world. Before his father came to Hawaii, Barack Jr. would try and make himself important by boasting about his father to his friends. Listen to the way Obama describes it. "I explained to a group of boys that my father was a prince. 'My grandfather, see, he's a chief. It's sort of like the king of the tribe, you know...like the Indians. So that makes my father a prince. He'll take over when my grandfather dies.'" When the boys asked him if he was next in line, Obama responded, "Well...if I want to, I could. It's sort of complicated, see, 'cause the tribe is full of warriors. Like Obama... the name means Burning Spear. The men in our tribe all want to be chief, so my father has to settle these feuds before I can come."

Of course he knew it was all a lie. The lie was in danger of being exposed when Obama Sr. came to Hawaii to visit. One of Obama's teachers, Miss Hefty, invited Obama Sr. to come and speak about Africa to the class. The prospect filled the son with dread. "I spent that night and all of the next day trying to suppress thoughts of the inevitable: the faces of my classmates when they heard about mud huts, all my lies exposed, the painful jokes afterward. Each time I remembered, my body squirmed as if it had received a jolt to the nerves."[13]

The big day arrived. Obama's father came dressed in traditional Kenyan clothing, which gave his entrance the sense of drama. As Obama Jr. hesitantly took his seat in Miss Hefty's class, he heard some commotion, and then the math teacher, Mr. Eldredge, entered the room followed by thirty or so students from his class. "We have a special treat for you today," Miss Hefty told the two classes. "Barry Obama's father is here, and he's come all the way from Kenya, in Africa, to tell us about his country." Obama Jr. could barely endure his discomfort. "The other kids looked at me as my father stood up, and I held my head stiffly, trying to focus on a vacant point on the blackboard behind him. He had been speaking for some time before I could finally bring myself back to the moment."

Once Obama Jr. engaged with his father's presentation, he experienced something of a revelation. He describes the elder Obama's performance,

> He was leaning against Miss Hefty's thick oak desk and describing the deep gash in the earth where mankind had first appeared. He spoke of the wild animals that still roamed the plains, the tribes that still required a young boy to kill a lion to prove his manhood. He spoke of the customs of the Luo, how elders received the utmost respect and made laws for all to follow under great-trunked trees. And he told us of Kenya's struggle to be free, how the British had wanted to stay and unjustly rule the people, just as they had in America; how many had been enslaved only because of the color of their skin, just as they had in America; but that Kenyans, like all of us in the room, longed to be free and develop themselves through hard work and sacrifice.

Obama completes the story: "When he finished, Miss Hefty was absolutely beaming with pride. All my classmates applauded heartily.... The bell rang for lunch, and Mr. Eldredge came up to me. 'You've got a pretty impressive father.' The ruddy faced-boy who had asked about cannibalism said, 'Your dad is pretty cool.'"[14] Of course the most mesmerized person in the class that day was young Barack himself. He discovered that his father, whether or not he grew up in a mud hut, had a strange and talismanic power: the power to hold other people's attention, the power to convince. The son seems to have resolved right then that he should learn to be more like his father so that he too could have some of that power. Somehow by imbibing his father's personality—his talismanic secret—the withdrawn child could gain some of the confidence and persuasive power of his dad.

This was, by Obama's own account, a pivotal moment in his life. And how successfully Obama internalized his father's communication skills can be gleaned from an incident years later when Obama, now a young man, is courting the woman he will eventually marry, Michelle. She was not initially impressed by him. She said, "I had dated a lot of brothers who had this kind of reputation coming in, so I figured he was one of these smooth brothers who could talk straight and impress people. So we had lunch, and he had this bad sport jacket and cigarette dangling from his mouth, and I thought: oh, here you go. Here's this good-looking, smooth-talking guy. I've been down this road before." Then Obama took her to one of his talks at a Chicago church. I'll let Michelle pick up the story as she narrated it at the 2008 Democratic National Convention: "The people gathered there together that day were ordinary folks doing the best they could to build a good life.... And Barack stood up that day, and he spoke words that have stayed with me ever since. He talked about the world as it is, and the world as it should be. And he said that, all too often, we accept the distance between the two, and we settle for the world as it is, even when it doesn't reflect our values and aspirations." Michelle concluded that by the time he was finished, she was hooked. She took him to meet her family, and the two of them were eventually married.[15] From this episode, I conclude that the father's near-magical skill of communication had been fully transmitted to the son. Later we will see how other people besides Michelle became hooked.

Now let's get back to what made the senior Obama such an effective communicator. It wasn't just his persona; it was also what he said. Somehow he was able to integrate very primal themes—creation, the wilds of Africa, bringing down lions—with the grand themes of anti-colonialism and independence. It was one part *National Geographic*, one part "Out of Africa," and one part Nelson Mandela. A potent combination. Sure, Obama gave the students that day a crayon version of anti-colonial history, but the real history is no less exciting, and much bloodier. I defer the details of the bloodshed until later in this book because I want readers to discover them when Barack Obama Jr. discovered them, at an older stage of his life.

Here I want to focus on the excitement of independence, when African nations one by one threw off the colonial yoke and entered a new age of self-government. This happened not only in Obama's Kenya, but also in Nigeria, Congo, Togo, Mali, the Gold Coast, and elsewhere. The two big names in African anti-colonialism are Kwame Nkrumah, who led the freedom movement in Ghana, and Jomo Kenyatta, who spearheaded it in Kenya. "Spearheaded" is an appropriate word here because Kenyatta was known as the Burning Spear; evidently Obama Jr. had taken this appellation of the father of modern Kenya and assigned it to his own father.

Barack Obama Sr. was actually a political opponent of Kenyatta. This is worth noting because it shows two very different strains of anti-colonialism that developed in Kenya and in the Third World. Kenyatta was both pro-Western and a free market capitalist. In his book, revealingly titled *Suffering Without Bitterness*, Kenyatta argued that his

goal was for Kenya to embrace Western values, but to do so as an independent nation. Rebuffing those who were calling for socialism, Kenyatta wrote, "Those Africans who think that when we have achieved our
freedom they can walk into a shop and say this is my property, or go
onto a farm and say this is my farm are very much mistaken, because
this is not our aim."[16]

This, however, was the aim of many socialists, and quite possibly it
would have been supported by the senior Barack Obama. Obama Sr.
and Kenyatta were from different tribes. Kenyatta was Kikuyu, whereas
Obama Sr. was from the Luo tribe. Obama Sr.'s mentor was a fellow
tribesman—the labor leader Tom Mboya. Mboya had helped to organize Obama Sr.'s trip to America, and when Obama Sr. returned, Mboya
secured for him a series of government jobs, culminating in a position
at the Ministry of Economic Planning and Development. Mboya was a
socialist, but here again we have to be careful. There were two types of
socialists in Kenya at the time: the pro-Soviet socialists and the African
socialists. The leader of the pro-Soviet group was Oginga Odinga, and
the leader of the African group was Tom Mboya. The former group
wanted to follow the Soviet party line and promote international revolution; the latter wanted to develop an independent and distinctly
African form of socialism.

All the socialists, of course, rejected Kenyatta's free market approach.
Still, they could not agree with each other about what type of socialism
would work best in Kenya. Odinga was associated with the Lumumba
Institute which took its instructions from Moscow. Mboya was the
author of a paper called Sessional Paper No. 10 promoting for Kenya a
distinctive type of African socialism as an alternative both to Kenyatta's
free-market capitalism and to Odinga's Soviet-style socialism. Basically
Mboya was trying to find a method to promote redistribution in a way
that would not jeopardize economic growth. "Our task," he said,

"remains to try to achieve these two goals without doing harm to the economy itself and within the declared aims of our society."[17]

In July 1965, Obama Sr. published an article in the *East Africa Journal* examining the premises of Mboya's paper. The article was titled "Problems Facing Our Socialism," and it is signed "Barak H. Obama." From the article we get a rare direct look at the senior Obama's economic solutions in the aftermath of colonialism. Obama Sr. begins by asking some skeptical questions. What do we mean by socialism? Are we talking about Kenyan socialism or African socialism? If socialism means government ownership of the means of production—in other words, no private property—then why does Sessional Paper No. 10 make several references to private land and private industry? Clearly Obama Sr. is warming up, and we see his intelligence sparkle through the prose.

Then he gets to his main point: "The question is how are we going to remove the disparities in our country, such as the concentration of economic power in Asian and European hands, while not destroying what has already been achieved and at the same time assimilating these groups to build one country?" For starters, Kenya must "break our dependence on other countries politically and economically." In addition, through taxation and regulation the government must bring down the foreigners who still dominate the Kenyan economy. "One need not be a Kenyan to note that nearly all commercial enterprises ... and industries are mostly owned by Asians and Europeans. One need not be a Kenyan to note that when one goes to a good restaurant he mostly finds Asians and Europeans, nor has he to be a Kenyan to see that the majority of cars running in Kenya are run by Asians and Europeans."

Despite his references to Asians and Europeans, for Obama Sr. this is not an issue of race; rather, it is an issue of power. To put it bluntly, certain groups have the power concentrated in their hands, and therefore the power has to be taken from them by force. "We need to eliminate power structures that have been built through excessive accumulation so that not only a few individuals shall control a vast magnitude of resources as is the case now." The senior Obama proposes that the state seize private land and turn it into "clan cooperatives" for growing food and manufacturing goods. He also proposes that taxes be raised, and no level of taxation is too high as long as "the benefits derived from public services by society measure up to the cost in taxation." In order to italicize the point, Obama Sr. insists that "theoretically there is nothing that can stop the government from taxing 100 percent of income so long as the people get benefits from the government commensurate with their income which is taxed." Obama Sr. contends that these solutions are justified by the circumstances in which Africans find themselves. "We have to give the African his place in his country and we have to give him this economic power if he is going to develop." The article ends on a resounding note. "Is it the African who owns this country? If he does, then why should he not control the economic means of growth in this country?"[18]

Barack Obama Jr. has never mentioned this article, either in his books or in any of his public statements, but given his exhaustive research into his father's history, it is hard to believe that he is not closely familiar with it. Living today in Obama's America, we can recognize several themes that the son seems to have derived from his father. First there is the idea that the ordinary African is deprived because the rich people at the top—people who are not like us—control most of the wealth and use it to exploit society. A second theme is that the country belongs to everyone, not just to the upper crust; therefore, the state must intervene to take from the undeserving haves in order to give to the deserving have-nots. There is no level of taxation—not even 100 percent—that is unacceptable as long as it serves the purpose of taming the plutocrats and yields revenues that are justified in terms of the benefit to society.

One of the most interesting features of Obama Sr.'s paper is that it shows how socialism emerges within the framework of anti-colonialism. Socialism is hardly a necessary outgrowth of anti-colonialism. This is shown by Kenyatta's approach, which was manifestly anti-colonial but also pro-capitalist. Obama Sr., however, rejected the Kenyatta way. He wasn't a pro-Soviet socialist, but he was an African socialist. As an African socialist he was to the left of Mboya: while Mboya sought to preserve private property and still claim the socialist label, the senior Obama wanted more state confiscation, more economic redistribution. All of this may help us understand why President Obama is so often accused of being a socialist. He does have socialist leanings or tendencies, but those have grown out of his commitment to his father's broader anti-colonial ideology.

There is a bitter postscript to the senior Obama's story. His fortunes plunged as he came into increasing conflict with Kenyatta and also with Kenyatta's future successor, Daniel arap Moi. Obama Sr. lost his government job and could not find another one. Even Mboya could do little to protect him, and with Mboya's assassination in 1969—allegedly by a man with ties to the government—Obama Sr.'s career was finished. Ultimately he fell into desperate poverty. No doubt these reversals exacerbated his drinking problem, which in turn led to his liver disease and several car crashes. In one accident Obama was so badly injured that both his legs had to be amputated and replaced with iron limbs. Still, he continued to drink and drive. In his final journey he staggered out of a Nairobi bar, drove his car off the road into the stump of a gum tree, and died instantly. This was on November 24, 1982. But—as we will see—his memory as well as the central tenets of his anti-colonial ideology are alive and well three decades later in the White House.

What about Barack Obama Jr.'s mother? She too was a strange one, and her strangeness derives, in part, from her own parents, Stanley and Madelyn Dunham. One indication of the eccentricity of her parents is that they hoped for a son and so when they got a daughter they named her "Stanley." Yes, Stanley was Obama's mother's first name. The poor thing continued to be called Stanley until she got to college, where she switched to her middle name, Ann. Stanley—or perhaps I should call her Ann—grew up in Kansas where, like Dorothy, she developed a fascination with the great big world out there. Years later, when the family moved to Hawaii, she found her own Wizard of Oz in the form of Barack Obama Sr. She never lost her devotion to him. Even though Obama Sr. lied to her about his African marriage and abandoned her when he went to Harvard, she cultivated in her son Barack Jr. an almost mystical reverence for his absentee father. Obama writes that whenever he raised an issue about his dad, or expressed frustration or hostility toward him, Ann would defend Obama Sr. She would explain and justify his actions and inform her son that his father was a great man, a true son of Africa. "You have me to thank for your eyebrows," she once told Obama. "But your brains, your character, you got from him." Obama writes that "the stories I heard about my father painted him as larger than life, which also meant that I felt I had something to live up to."[19] She, as much as he, was responsible for Obama's lifelong fascination with his father.

Ann had an evident romantic attraction to everything that was dark and strange and unlike her white-bread upbringing in the Midwest. One of her friends, Julia Suryakusuma, later remarked that "Ann was really, really white. I think she just loved people of a different skin color." Obama recalls that whenever a black man or woman came up in conversation, no matter what the context, she praised that person extravagantly. "Every black man was Thurgood Marshall or Sidney

Poitier; every black woman Fannie Lou Hamer or Lena Horne."[20] This undiscriminating judgment is part of the reason, but only part of the reason, that Ann fell so gullibly for Obama's father. Once he left her, she soon took up with an Indonesian student named Lolo Soetoro. They married in 1966, and a year or so later they took young Barry to Jakarta. There Ann had a child with Soetoro, whom they named Maya, and she also developed an anthropological interest in peasant blacksmithing.

Obama Jr. spent around four years in Indonesia with his mother. Then, in a surprise move, she dispatched him back to Hawaii to live with his grandparents. Although Obama likes to describe himself as raised by a single parent, in fact he grew up without either his father or his mother for several years. When her marriage with Soetoro dissolved in 1972, Ann stayed in Indonesia to do field work. She also took extensive trips to Thailand, Nepal, India, Bangladesh, Pakistan, and China. Remarkably, she never returned to the United States to live with her son. Eventually she contracted ovarian cancer and came to America for medical treatment. But Obama Jr. did not visit her, nor was he present when she died in Hawaii in 1995. Recently Duke University Press published her dissertation on "village industry in Indonesia." Scholars say it is a useful contribution to a little-known subject.

Lolo Soetoro's influence on Obama has been largely ignored, even though Obama himself says he learned a lot from his Indonesian step-father. Part of the reason for the neglect is that many of Obama's critics have focused on Soetoro's Muslim background and on whether Obama converted to Islam during his high school years. All of this gets both Soetoro and Obama completely wrong. Neither of them was in any serious way religious. Soetoro's life was far more defined by growing up in the harsh circumstances of colonial Indonesia and then in the equally grim aftermath of Dutch withdrawal from that country.

Soetoro was born in Bandung, Indonesia. Today Bandung is mostly remembered as the site of the famous Bandung Conference. That took place in 1955, when Lolo was twenty years old. There, in Lolo's hometown, the heads of state and senior officials of twenty-nine newly independent Asian and African countries met to consider their future. President Sukarno of Indonesia was the host, and in attendance were Jawaharlal Nehru from India, Kwame Nkrumah from Ghana, and Jomo Kenyatta. The main thrust of Bandung was a joint declaration that these countries did not want to align with either the West or the Soviet Union; they wanted to go their own way, sometimes called the "third way." Bandung gave rise a few years later to the so-called Non-Aligned Movement.

Soetoro would surely have sympathized with the objectives of the Bandung Conference. As a child he grew up under colonialism, and his parents endured the hardship and humiliation of an especially severe form of forced labor imposed by the Dutch. The historian K. M. Panikkar writes in *Asia and Western Dominance*, "The Dutch alone of the European nations in the East carried out a policy which systematically reduced a whole population to the status of plantation labor, without recognizing any moral or legal obligation to them."[21] His father and oldest brother were killed during the revolutionary struggle, when the native Indonesians fought for freedom from the Netherlands, and the Dutch army burned Soetoro's family home.

Eventually the war ended, and the Soetoros returned to rebuild their home. Like Barack Obama Sr., Lolo Soetoro got a basic education in his homeland and then came to Hawaii to study; the two ended up at the same university and married the same woman. Soetoro was recalled to Indonesia in 1966 when the Sukarno government decided it needed the services of its citizens living and studying abroad. A year later Soetoro's new wife, Ann, joined him in Jakarta with her son.

Soetoro became a kind of surrogate father to Obama, who writes affectionately about him. "With Lolo, I learned how to eat small green chili peppers raw with dinner . . . and, away from the dinner table, I was introduced to dog meat . . . snake meat . . . and roasted grasshopper. . . . Lolo explained that a man took on the powers of whatever he ate. One day soon, he promised, he would bring home a piece of tiger meat for us to share."[22] This was Obama's Indonesia, exotic, unpredictable, a feast for the senses. The family lived in a Jakarta neighborhood that was more like a village than today's sprawling metropolis. While the Soetoro family lived in a brick house with a tiled roof, many of the houses were bamboo huts, and electricity had just arrived a few years earlier.

We know Soetoro shared with Obama his sufferings at the hands of the Dutch, because Obama writes about it. Soetoro also taught Obama that one should be tough in the world and not whine about one's situation. Obama was a bit of a whiner. Contrary to the lean, trim Obama that we now see, Obama as a young boy was rather round and overweight, and he was often teased in school not so much for being dark-skinned (many Indonesians are just as dark-skinned), but mostly for being fat. Obama was sensitive to being overweight, and when the kids brought that to his attention, he would yell back, "Curang! Curang!" The word in Indonesian means "cheater," and what Obama was saying, in effect, was, "No fair!" Obama has subsequently portrayed himself as fluent in Indonesian, but his friends at the time recall that he could barely speak the language; one of the few words that he knew was "Curang."[23] Obama's stepfather Lolo knew how tough it was to grow up in Indonesia, and he informed Obama about the importance of learning the arts of combat and survival, how to make one's way in a cruel world. For Soetoro this meant learning how to throw a punch and also how to make compromises and cut deals when one had to.

Paradoxically, Soetoro's anti-colonial experience took him in a very different direction than that of Barack Obama Sr. Over time, Soetoro became more pro-American and anti-Communist. When the left-leaning Sukarno was overthrown in a coup by the right-wing General Suharto, Soetoro joined the military in its campaign against Communist rebels in the countryside. Then Soetoro took a job in the oil business, and he relocated the family to a nicer neighborhood. Dutch colonists used to live there, and many Japanese moved in during their occupation of Indonesia in the Second World War. When the Soetoros moved in, the area was full of diplomats, Indonesian businessmen, and white Europeans and Americans living abroad. Soetoro began to hang out with these white expats.

All of this alienated Soetoro's bohemian wife, Obama's mother. She admired Sukarno for his decision to nationalize the major industries and hated Suharto for his pro-Western and pro-American inclinations. Ann was particularly offended at the way the rich foreigners of Soetoro's acquaintance talked about their servants and showed no interest in the indigenous cultural traditions of Indonesia. As Obama writes, "She taught me to disdain the blend of ignorance and arrogance that too often characterized Americans abroad." In time she began to view her second husband as a kind of sellout, somehow lacking the authenticity that she continued to admire in Obama's father. Basically she fell in love with the old anti-colonial Lolo and came to detest the new pro-American Lolo.

Is this speculation? I'll let Obama tell the story.

> She had expected it to be difficult, this new life of hers. Before leaving Hawaii, she had tried to learn all she could about Indonesia...the history of colonialism, first the Dutch for over three centuries, then the Japanese during the war, seeking control over vast stores of oil, metal and timber; the fight

for independence after the war and the emergence of a freedom fighter named Sukarno as the country's first president....A poor country, underdeveloped, utterly foreign—this
much she had known. She was prepared for the dysentery
and fevers, the cold water baths and having to squat over a
hole in the ground to pee, the electricity going out every few
weeks, the heat and endless mosquitoes. Nothing more than
inconveniences, really... and anyway, that was part of what
had drawn her to Lolo after Barack had left, the promise of
something new and important, helping her husband rebuild
a country in a charged and challenging place beyond her parents' reach.... Still, something had happened between her
and Lolo. In Hawaii he had been so full of life, so eager with
his plans. At night when they were alone, he would tell her
about growing up as a boy during the war, watching his father
and eldest brother leave to join the revolutionary army, hearing the news that both had been killed and everything lost,
the Dutch army setting their house aflame, their flights into
the countryside, his mother's selling her gold jewelry a piece
at a time in exchange for food. Things would be changing
now that the Dutch had been driven out, Lolo had told her;
he would return to teach at the university, be a part of that
change.[24]

The problem, Obama writes, is that "he didn't talk that way anymore."
He had sold out to power. "Power. The word fixed in my mother's mind
like a curse." She became convinced that "power had taken Lolo" and
that "power was taking her son." Obama tells us that she sent him back
to Hawaii because she wanted the time and the freedom to finish her
dissertation. Also there were greater opportunities for her son in America.

But Obama's own account gives us a different reason. After all, she was quite willing to deprive her son of opportunities by bringing him to Indonesia. The main reason she sent him back to America was to prevent him from being corrupted by Lolo. She considered Lolo a sellout to the power structure, and she wanted to prevent her son from making the same compromise. In fact, she wanted her son to be influenced not by her second husband but by her first. Now we see how Obama's biological father, even in absentia, had so much influence: his influence was in large part transmitted by the mother. She was Obama Sr.'s first convert.

More speculation? Not according to Obama Jr. He describes fights between his mother and Lolo, with her accusing him of being a sellout and Lolo pleading that there was nothing wrong with hanging out with the white people because "these were her own people." Obama writes that "my mother's voice would rise to almost a shout: They are *not* my people." And at that point, Obama tells us, Ann began to run down Lolo to her son. Incredibly she started comparing Lolo unfavorably with Barack Sr. I say "incredibly" because Barack Sr. was the one who abandoned his son who was being raised without complaint by Lolo.

Obama writes that when his mother's frustration mounted with Lolo, "She had only one ally in all this, and that was the distant authority of my father. Increasingly, she would remind me of his story, how he had grown up poor, in a poor country, in a poor continent; how his life had been hard, as hard as anything that Lolo might have known. He hadn't cut corners, though, or played all the angles. He was diligent and honest, no matter what it cost him. He had led his life according to principles that demanded a different kind of toughness, principles that promised a higher form of power. I would follow his example, my mother decided. I had no choice. It was in the genes."[25] Not surprisingly, Ann soon divorced Lolo, who eventually married an Indonesian woman. Lolo died in Jakarta in 1987.

Barack Obama was ten when he returned to Hawaii to live with his grandparents. It was here that Barack Obama Sr. made his one and only visit to see his son and dazzle him and his classmates. Both Obama's African father and his Indonesian stepfather were products of the great anti-colonial struggles of their day. But they went in different directions, and Obama's mother made sure that for her son she chose the direction of his biological father. And her preference sunk in. Obama writes, "I realized, perhaps for the first time, how even in his absence his strong image had given me some bulwark on which to grow up, an image to live up to, or disappoint."[26] It is obvious that these youthful experiences made an intense and vivid impression, because the memories were just as powerful many years later when Obama wrote about them. It seems obvious that they still continue to stir his heart and guide his actions. We are, even now, living with the consequences.

CHAPTER 5

AFRICAN IN AMERICA

T his chapter traces the process by which Barack Obama became black. We know that Obama wants to be known as African American; he said so himself by checking the box on the 2010 U.S. Census form marked "Black, African American or Negro."[1] How, then, did Obama become black? Surely not by appearance; the man is lighter skinned than I am, and I'm not black. Nor did Obama become black through skin treatments, whether discovered through imaginary issues of *Life* magazine or elsewhere. Writing in the *Washington Post*, Marie Arana informs us that Obama "is not our first black president. He's our first biracial, bicultural president." The same point was made by political maverick Christopher Hitchens on the BBC program *Newsnight*.[2]

In an Associated Press article, "Many Insisting that Obama is Not Black," the position articulated by Arana and Hitchens is rebutted by an appeal to the "one drop rule." This is the infamous rule according to which a single drop of black blood makes a person officially black. But the one drop rule is an American phenomenon that doesn't really apply to Obama. On the liberal website *Salon*, Debra Dickerson noted that "black in our political and social vocabulary means those descended from West African slaves." That's not Obama, as African American columnist Stanley Crouch points out. "Obama's mother is of white U.S. stock. His father is a black Kenyan." Crouch's article was titled "What Obama Isn't: Black Like Me."[3]

In American history, the one-drop rule traces back not to slavery but to segregation; it was a way for Southerners to enforce segregation laws and prevent mixed-race persons from "passing" as white. (In the antebellum period, slave status passed through the mother and had nothing to do with whether one looked light or dark.) But of course Obama has no roots in American slavery and neither did he grow up in the South. His childhood experience, as we have seen, is scarcely comparable to that of most blacks in the United States. So we're back to the question of how Obama became black.

Certainly Obama recognized from early adolescence that he needed to be black. There were psychological reasons for this: Obama knew that he was different, and during his teens and early twenties, blackness was a way to understand and express that difference. The choice of blackness made sense because he wanted to identify with his African father. His father wasn't around, however, and the surrogates whom he found happened to be black Americans. Another reason is political. As a young man who aspired to politics, Obama knew that he would have to count on a group that he could call his own, one that he could rally and that would rally behind him. "Kenyans in America" is not a large constituency, so Obama wisely chose African Americans as his home team.

Obama's strategy for becoming black was both simple and ingenious. Through laborious effort, he familiarized himself with the literature and rhetoric of the American black experience, and then he found a way to fit that black experience into the anti-colonial experience. In other words, he came to see the situation facing African Americans as analogous to the one facing native peoples around the world in their struggles with Western domination. Here is a sample of how Obama routinely makes the connection. "I know, I have seen, the desperation and disorder of the powerless: how it twists the lives of children on the streets of Jakarta or Nairobi in much the same way as it does the lives of children on Chicago's South Side. I know that the response of the powerful to this disorder...is inadequate to the task."[4] In this way, the son of a Kenyan immigrant and a white woman from Kansas is successfully able to "pass" as a black American.

We know the strategy has worked because Obama has always gotten away with it, and it helped to carry him to the White House. When Obama worked as a community activist in Chicago, his boss gave him a copy of Taylor Branch's *Parting the Waters*, a history of Martin Luther King and the civil rights movement. Obama said, "This is my story."[5] In reality, this wasn't his story, but he made it his story. When Obama spoke during the presidential campaign in the church in Selma, he shared the stage with his Democratic rival Hillary Clinton. She was married to the man whom novelist Toni Morrison dubbed the first black president. Obama had to beat out Hillary and claim that title for himself, winning the endorsement of John Lewis, Joseph Lowery, and the other civil rights leaders in the audience. And he did: they embraced him as one of them.

Historically, Obama's strategy of passing into blackness via a Third World route is not such a strange move. Many black leaders have attempted to draw parallels between the American black experience and that of the peoples of Africa and the Third World. In 1957, Martin Luther King was invited to Ghana to witness the transfer of power from the British to the new president Kwame Nkrumah. The transfer took place on midnight of March 5, and King was deeply moved by it. King saw that Nkrumah didn't come dressed as a ruler or prince, but rather wearing the prison cap assigned to him when he was jailed by his colonialist captors. "Before I knew it," King said, "I started weeping. I was crying for joy."

In a private reception with Nkrumah, King said, "I want you to come to visit us down in Alabama where we are seeking the same kind of freedom Ghana is celebrating." King subsequently said, "There is no basic difference between colonialism and racial segregation," and "this event, the birth of this new nation, will give impetus to oppressed peoples all over the world—not only in Asia and Africa, but also in America." King preached a sermon on that topic the following month at Dexter Avenue Baptist Church in Montgomery, Alabama. He rallied American blacks to resistance, saying that oppressors never give in without a fight. Then he promised that victory would come for blacks in America as it had come for the subject people of Ghana. "An old order of colonialism, of segregation, of discrimination is passing away, and a new order of justice . . . is being born."[6]

In the mid-1960s, Malcolm X traveled to Africa where he visited more than a dozen countries, including Egypt, Sudan, Ethiopia, Kenya, Tanzania, Nigeria, Ghana, Liberia, and Algeria. He had meetings with several of the new rulers of Africa, including Kenyatta in Kenya, Nkrumah in Ghana, Milton Obote in Uganda, and Julius Nyerere of Tanzania. "You can't separate the African revolution from the mood of the black man in America," Malcolm X said in a subsequent interview with two leaders of America's Young Socialist Alliance. "You can't separate the militancy that's displayed on the African continent from the militancy that's displayed right here among American blacks. Since Africa has gotten its independence through revolution, you'll notice the stepped-up cry against discrimination in the black community." And in 1971 Jesse Jackson drew the same connection in a typically Jesse Jackson way. Upon hearing that the United Nations was providing funds for poor, developing countries, Jackson submitted a request that the United Nations fund black America through his own group, Operation PUSH. Jackson's appeal was based on the idea that blacks in America constituted a kind of poor, developing nation within the United States, and since he was the spokesman for black America, he was a deserving recipient of UN money. The UN declined to provide any funds, but hey, you can't blame Jackson for trying.[7]

While these civil rights leaders all drew the parallel between anti-colonialism and the American black struggle, they were basically trying to fit the anti-colonial model into the civil rights model. In effect, they were saying: what matters most to us is our struggle in America, and now let's show how our struggle over here is really part of this bigger struggle that's going on around the world. Obama makes the same transition, but in the opposite direction. He figures out how to fit the civil rights model into the anti-colonial model. In effect, Obama is saying: what matters most to me is this big struggle between the rulers and the subject peoples across the globe, but I can understand and identify with the black struggle in America as a local skirmish within that larger conflict.

Even before he went to the Punahou school in Hawaii, Obama was introduced to the black American experience by his mother. She brought home audio recordings of Martin Luther King speeches and the music of Mahalia Jackson. At school Obama remembers reading James Baldwin, Ralph Ellison, Richard Wright, Langston Hughes, and W. E. B. DuBois. He was especially impressed with Malcolm X, and probably got from him what he calls his "bad-assed nigger pose." And it was a pose. With fine self-perception Obama writes of putting on a racial "costume" and "living out a caricature of black male adolescence." He even tries to attribute his drug use to this rebel stance, although drugs were easily available in Hawaii and socially cool to try at Punahou, and perhaps no further explanation is needed than that.[8]

Obama's racial posturing reached its zenith the day his grandmother Madelyn Dunham came home and asked that her husband drive her to work the following week. She complained that an aggressive bum had hassled her at the bus stop. "I gave him a dollar and he kept asking." Weirdly, Obama's grandfather accused his wife of only wanting him to drive her because the bum was black. "And I just don't think that's right!" he declared pompously. Now one might expect the grandson to at least attempt to defend his grandmother, who was working in large part to pay for his schooling. His grandfather was barely working at the time, so it was hardly an imposition for him to make the drive.

Instead, Obama responded thus to his grandfather's accusation: "The words were like a fist in my stomach, and I wobbled to regain my composure. . . . I knew that men who might easily have been my brothers could still inspire their rawest fears."[9] But of course Obama's reaction depends entirely on the pretense that aggressive bums are no cause for female alarm. Most likely Madelyn's fears would not have been provoked had she been joined at the bus stop by a black man in a suit. Her anxiety, in other words, was not the product of baseless prejudice but rather a reasonable conclusion based on the facts of the situation. Even so, her grandson treats her like a kind of closet bigot. This shameful episode is partly excused by Obama's youth, although, as we will see, Obama brought it up again in his mature years. On that occasion he much more inexcusably exploited it to obtain political cover for himself.

Obama discussed his grandmother's alleged fear of blacks with one of his grandfather's buddies, a black radical and secret member of the Communist Party named Frank Marshall Davis. During the presidential campaign some conservatives highlighted Davis's Communist ties.

This provoked John Edgar Tidwell, who has edited a volume of Davis's writings, to protest what he termed the "McCarthy-era smear tactics" against Davis. Tidwell's protests are in vain; in the book's introduction, he himself admits that Davis was in fact a Communist for at least part of his career.[10] Still, we will discover that this was not the most important thing about Davis as far as Obama was concerned.

Davis, like Stanley Dunham, was from Kansas, and since Davis had a white wife, Stanley evidently thought he qualified as an excellent multiracial role model for his grandson. Grandfather would take Obama to Davis's cottage where Obama would sit on the ground and watch the two men smoke, drink, play Scrabble, and talk. While discussing grandma's racism, however, Davis spoke to Obama only in Stanley's absence. Davis told Obama that no white person could understand blacks. "Maybe some of these Hawaiians can, or the Indians on the reservation. They've seen their fathers humiliated. Their mothers desecrated. But your grandfather will never know what that feels like." Therefore, Davis concluded, "Your grandma's right to be scared. She understands that black people have a reason to hate." Once again Obama responds in dramatic fashion: "The earth shook under my feet, ready to crack open at any moment. I stopped, trying to steady myself, and knew for the first time that I was utterly alone."[11]

Davis is important because he ameliorated that loneliness and became a kind of surrogate father for Obama, at least while he stayed in Hawaii. (Recall that Obama did not at this time live with either of his natural parents.) Even later Obama remembered Davis fondly, and when he quit his job as a financial researcher to become a community organizer, Obama wrote, "It made me smile, thinking back on Frank and his old Black Power, dashiki self." Hawaiians who remember Davis say the man was just as likely to sport cut-offs and Aloha shirts. More important, Davis's biographer points out that "his editorial philosophy connected...white supremacy and imperialism."[12] A recent book, *Writings of Frank Marshall Davis*, clearly demonstrates the centrality of anticolonialism to the man's writings.

Davis's early work is focused on Black Power. He grew so frustrated with what he perceived to be the inherent bigotry of American life that when he saw the black actor and activist Paul Robeson praising Hawaii as a multiracial paradise, he packed up and moved there. In Hawaii, Davis was impressed by the absence of anti-black sentiment. In his column "Land of Ethnic Hash," Davis writes, "You soon learn that in Hawaii you can't tell an individual's ethnic origin by looking." There were prejudices, but "these are much more complex than those on the mainland.... Out here many dark Puerto Ricans are insulted if they are mistaken for Japanese; the Portuguese bitterly resent being called *haole* or mainland white; many Koreans will let you know right away that they are not Chinese." So Davis's philosophy became less black-centered, in fact less racial, and began to incorporate what he saw as wider currents of oppression and subjugation.

I was particularly struck by Davis's three-part series examining the fate of the world in the aftermath of World War II. Davis asked: would an international institution like the United Nations insist that all the major countries—including Russia and China—have an equal say, or would Britain and America dominate the postwar economic and political order? Davis focused his critical lens on a single man, Winston Churchill, whom Davis accused of seeking Anglo-American supremacy. Davis argued that since Britain was no longer powerful enough to hold its empire on its own, Churchill was pushing for America to join Britain in sustaining and indeed extending the old British empire. In Davis's view, Churchill had a plan to use "strong arm tactics to bludgeon all other countries into submission," and thus Britain and America could establish their joint sway over the whole world. Davis termed this prospect "super-imperialism."[13]

Obama makes no reference to any of Davis's writings and merely calls him "a poet named Frank." But given Davis's worldview, it is easy to see his appeal to young Obama. And given Davis's antipathy for Churchill, a man whose colonial history Davis knew well, we can see where Obama learned this other side of the scourge of the Nazis. Perhaps we have a source here for why Obama removed that Churchill bust from the White House. But Davis wasn't finished with Obama in Hawaii. Before Obama left home in 1979 to enroll at Occidental College in Los Angeles, Davis warned him about "leaving your race at the door, leaving your people behind." Obama should beware of the establishment, Davis said, because "they'll train you so good, you'll start believing what they tell you about equal opportunity and the American way and all that shit." Davis counseled Obama to be on his guard and "stay awake."[14]

At Occidental, Obama hung out, as he put it, with "the more politically active black students. The foreign students. The Chicanos. The Marxist professors and structural feminists and punk-rock performance poets. We smoked cigarettes and wore leather jackets. At night, in the dorms, we discussed neocolonialism, Frantz Fanon, Eurocentrism, and patriarchy." In one of his classes Obama read Joseph Conrad's *Heart of Darkness*. He commented to a friend, "See, the book's not really about Africa. Or black people. It's about the man who wrote it. The European. The American. A particular way of looking at the world. So I read the book to help me understand just what it is that makes white people so afraid. It helps me understand how people learn to hate."[15]

As an analysis of Conrad's novella, this is rather jejune—young Obama doing his best impression of Chinua Achebe. Achebe is the Nobel Prize in Literature nominee from Nigeria who wrote a famous critique of *Heart of Darkness*. Achebe's analysis was much more subtle. He recognized that Conrad was a Polish expatriate who viewed colonialism from an angle much more distant and skeptical than that of British writers like Rudyard Kipling. Yet while Achebe found Conrad innocent of the charge of condoning imperialism, he found him guilty of the charge of condoning racism: "Conrad saw and condemned the evil of imperial exploitation but was strangely unaware of the racism on which it sharpened its iron tooth."[16]

The case against Conrad, however, is far from settled, even when it is advanced by a figure of Achebe's stature. One of Conrad's leading characters, Marlow, observes that "the conquest of the earth, which mostly means the taking it away from those who have a different complexion or slightly flatter noses than ourselves, is not a pretty thing when you look into it too much."[17] Marlow is European, and obviously he's speaking from the European point of view. Even so, he makes very clear his distaste for the whole enterprise of declaring other people inferior so that their land can be plundered. Racism in this framework is not about "what makes white people afraid" or about "learning to hate," as Obama would have it. Rather, when you overpower other people and take their possessions, racism enables you to justify the appropriation by declaring those others to be inferior. Conrad recognizes the role that racism plays: it justifies Kurtz's ivory-trading post. We shouldn't be too hard on Obama for his C-plus analysis of Conrad; in later years he would receive much better and more personal lessons in the reality of colonial conflict and oppression.

At Occidental, Obama became active in the student campaign to divest university funds from South Africa. This was Obama's first involvement in student politics, and he spoke at a divestment rally on February 18, 1981. "There's a struggle going on. It's happening an ocean away. But it's a struggle that touches each and every one of us. A struggle that demands we choose sides. Not between black and white. Not between rich and poor. It's a choice between dignity and servitude. Between commitment and indifference."[18] Those who listened carefully to Obama's words that evening would have realized he was speaking a different political language than the other speakers.

They viewed South Africa through the prism of American racial conflict. Presuming a close analogy between Southern segregation and South African apartheid, they interpreted the South African struggle in civil rights terms. And this is how several scholarly studies such as George Fredrickson's *White Supremacy* have typically treated the subject. But Obama's perspective was wider: he recognized that the South African struggle was only incidentally an issue of black and white. Primarily it was a struggle between the colonizers and the colonized.

South Africa had been settled by white Europeans, the Dutch in the seventeenth century and the English in the nineteenth century. In the twentieth century, the Afrikaners (the descendants of the Dutch and French Huguenot settlers) herded much of the majority black population into separate homelands called Bantustans. Apartheid was established not merely for social and political separation, but also to enable the Afrikaners to exploit cheap black labor. This was how Obama viewed the issue, as the anti-colonial resistance struggle of his own day. For Obama the racism issue could be understood from inside the larger issue of colonial subjugation. Given the anti-colonial significance of the South Africa debate, it's easy to see why Obama seized upon this issue, ignoring other hot-button issues of the time such as campus bigotry and affirmative action.

Two of Obama's closest friends at Occidental were Pakistani students Mohammed Hasan Chandoo and Wahid Hamid. "I think that one of the reasons he felt comfortable with us," Hamid subsequently told a journalist, is that "we didn't come with a lot of predispositions about

race. We weren't carrying that American baggage. We were brown . . .
and we got along with people who were white and black." In the summer of 1981, Obama visited his mother and half sister Maya in Indonesia, but before that he visited Chandoo and Hamid in Pakistan.
Chandoo's girlfriend at the time, Margot Mifflin, said that Obama
returned from Pakistan "amazed at how the peasants bowed to the
landowners in respect as they passed." Hamid added, "We went to rural
Sindh . . . where the feudal system is still strong. Barack could see how
the owner lives and how the serfs and workers are so subservient."[19]
Surely these dichotomies contributed to Obama's developing perspective on the world.

    That fall, despite his mediocre grades at Occidental, Obama trans-
ferred to Columbia University. Oddly, not much is known about Obama
at Columbia. Graduates of Columbia from that period say they never
encountered Obama either in their classes or socially. The *New York
Times* attempted to track down people who knew Obama at Columbia
but without success. The *Times* reported that Obama himself "declined
repeated requests to talk about his New York years, release his Columbia transcript, or identify even a single fellow student, co-worker, room-
mate or friend from those years."[20]

    We do know a couple of people who taught Obama at Columbia; one
of them was Edward Said. Before his death in 2003, Said was the leading American champion of the Palestinian cause. As a consequence of
his advocacy of armed resistance against Israel, the magazine *Commentary* dubbed him "Professor of Terror." Said is also the author of influential anti-colonial works such as *Orientalism* and *Culture and
Imperialism*. He seems to have had a lasting influence on Obama: some
of Obama's writings are highly resonant with Said's themes and arguments. Also, as I mentioned in an earlier chapter, during his rising years
in Chicago politics, Obama attended a Palestinian event in Chicago at

which Said was the dinner speaker. Even so, nowhere does Said's name appear in any of Obama's writings or speeches. As far as public Obama is concerned, Said does not exist.

At Columbia, Obama wrote an article in a student weekly, *Sundial*, calling for an end to the U.S. military industrial complex. Obama's article was a response to the so-called nuclear freeze movement that was sweeping American campuses at the time. As an undergraduate at Dartmouth in the early 1980s, I remember well the paranoia of the freeze activists, who seemed convinced that the world was about to end unless their nuclear freeze solution was immediately implemented. Calling as it did for a reciprocal freeze in U.S. and Soviet nuclear arsenals, the freeze was a liberal cause, but apparently not liberal enough for Obama. For him the issue came down to the big, bad military industrial complex and its irrational, insatiable desire for more costly weapons. "Generally the narrow focus of the freeze movement as well as academic discussions of first versus second strike capabilities suit the military industrial interests, as they continue adding to their billion dollar erector sets."[21]

Obama's arrival at Harvard Law School in Cambridge, Massachusetts, in the fall of 1988 followed brief stints of community organizing work in New York and Chicago. Wonder why Obama went to Harvard? Here is a clue: it is the leading academic institution in America. And here's another: his father went there. By the time Obama went to Cambridge, he was twenty-seven and older than his peers; this maturity helped Obama win the election for editor of the *Harvard Law Review*. It was a densely packed contest, and Obama was one of many candidates jostling for the position. The story goes that Obama won by convincing the conservatives to vote for him. The conservatives were impressed because here was a black American who did not seem preoccupied with race. They got a glimmer, but probably did not fully appreciate the extent to which Obama's central concern wasn't race but power; he was merely playing along with black identity politics in order to fit in and find a constituency for himself.

Still, Obama applied a certain work ethic to the task of being black. He joined the board of directors of the Black Law Students Association. He presented himself to his professors as a champion of the African American cause, earning major brownie points and inspiring one of his teachers, the legal scholar Laurence Tribe, to later proclaim Obama the "best student I ever had." One of his professors, civil rights advocate Charles Ogletree, said Obama "came well steeped in the history of the civil rights movement and wanted to know even more."[22]

Obama's eagerness to make common cause with African Americans even moved him to get involved in the bizarre Derrick Bell controversy. Bell threatened to resign from the Harvard law faculty if the university didn't increase minority hiring; Bell specifically demanded the immediate recruitment of a woman of color. At a time when blacks could do virtually no wrong at Harvard—when the university was doing pirouettes and backward somersaults to please blacks—Bell somehow convinced himself that "racism is an integral, permanent and indestructible component of this society" and that Harvard was a big part of the problem. What was Bell's evidence for this? Actually, he had none. So instead Bell drew on his imagination. One of his stories, "The Space Traders," envisioned hordes of whites seeking to round up blacks and subject them to a Holocaust. Some blacks survive, however, and they are chased down to be sold into slavery to aliens from outer space.[23]

Crazy stuff. Obama must surely have recognized the fatuousness of Bell's claims, especially at Harvard. Even so, he spoke in measured tones in defense of Bell. Nobody recalls precisely what he said, but Rosa Parks was mentioned, and everyone present concluded that Obama was a regular soul brother. Harvard went to considerable lengths to placate Bell, but he could not be placated and left Harvard for New York University.

Still, Obama saw how Bell's antics were taken with utmost seriousness by everyone on campus. Obama seems to have recognized that race was now a source of power in American society. Somehow whites had been shamed by the nation's past into conceding to blacks a kind of unquestioned moral superiority.

The Tunisian writer Albert Memmi makes a similar point in *The Colonizer and the Colonized*. Memmi's argument is that, over time, colonization wears down the conscience of the oppressor. "He is a privileged being and an illegitimately privileged one; that is, a usurper. Furthermore, this is so not only in the eyes of the colonized but in his own as well."[24] Something analogous can be said about racism: it has convinced whites, no less than blacks, that whites have been the beneficiaries of unearned privileges. Thus whites now recognize blacks as America's de facto racial experts, and anything blacks say, however preposterous, is typically agreed to or at least greeted with deference. Here was a source of power that a clever fellow could later exploit.

Although Obama schmoozed all the liberal professors at Harvard, his real mentor was Roberto Mangabeira Unger. Born in Rio de Janeiro to a Brazilian mother and a German father, Unger is perhaps the leading anti-colonial scholar in the field of legal studies. A few years ago, Unger took a leave of absence from Harvard to serve in the executive office of Brazilian president Lula da Silva. Lula was reputed to be anti-American and also a socialist, but when he turned out to be pro-American and a moderate, Unger called for Lula's impeachment. Not surprisingly, Lula sent Unger back to Harvard. This was in 2009.

While Obama was at Harvard in the late 1980s, Unger was associated with the Critical Legal Studies movement. These scholars were dubbed "Crits." According to the Crits, law pretends to be fair and neutral, but it is really a sham; it is politics by other means; legal structures are merely a camouflage for keeping entrenched interests in power. What's needed is to topple these interests and replace them; and law can serve this transformative end as well. There were several Crits at Harvard, though Unger eventually broke with the movement because he considered its approach too limited and ineffective.

Unger's own vision was much more comprehensive and revolutionary. He calls his perspective "total criticism." Basically this means using the law to pull down the existing power structures and replace them with alternative power structures more reflective of Third World and minority interests. One of Unger's proposals, which he advances in the name of "empowering democracy," is for the government to seize all private capital and place it into a capital fund that would be allocated by teams of workers and citizens.[25] Come to think of it, Unger's proposal sounds a lot like the 1965 paper of Barack Obama Sr.

Obama took two of Unger's courses, one on Jurisprudence and another on Reinventing Democracy. Obama's attraction to Unger's work is obvious. Obama said he went to Harvard Law because it was the "perfect place to examine how the power structure works." Unger showed him not only how to examine it, but also how to dismantle it through the instrument of law. So what does Obama say about Unger in his speeches and writings? Nothing. Like Edward Said, Unger has simply disappeared from Obama's official record, and not because his influence was minor; in fact, quite the opposite. Even after Obama left Harvard, leaving his other admiring liberal professors behind, he continued to communicate with Unger, all the way up to the presidential campaign. One or two enterprising reporters did find out about Unger and attempted to contact him. Unger, however, refused to talk to anyone in the press about his pupil and protégé, giving David Remnick his "simple reason." Unger confessed, "I am a leftist, and by conviction as well as by temperament, a revolutionary. Any association of mine with Barack Obama in the course of the campaign could do only harm."[26]

By the early 1990s, Obama was a very different man from the impressionable, "bad assed" kid who had come to the East Coast from the Western shores of Hawaii and California. Still, his background and his memories shaped him. His understanding had been heightened by leading anti-colonial thinkers such as Edward Said and Roberto Unger. But now he had an additional plus: he had found a way to pass as a black American, and to integrate himself into the civil rights experience. This was hardly his experience, but even that worked to Obama's benefit: his distance gave the impression of intellectual detachment and objectivity, and thus was interpreted by others as "maturity." As the first black president of the *Harvard Law Review*, Obama even enjoyed a minor celebrity, which brought him his first book contract. Thus having studied the world, Obama was now ready to go out and change it.

CHAPTER 6

BECOMING BARACK

"Becoming part of the Third World," writes Shiva Naipaul in *Black and White*, "is to some degree a psychological process, a quasi-religious conversion. It is, at bottom, a mode of being, a state of mind. That state of mind spreads like an infection and begins, after a while, to create its own political, social and personal realities."[1] And so it is with our man in the White House. Here we examine how Obama went from being Barry to being Barack, in other words, how he formed his adult identity and the core of his ideological convictions.

In a way, we can see the transition in his name itself. At Punahou, he was always Barry. At Occidental, a girl he liked inquired about his given name and he said it was Barack, which meant "blessed" in Arabic. The girl, Regina, thought that sounded cool and asked if she could call him Barack. He agreed, but everyone else still called him Barry. Then Obama met an older student, Eric Moore, who told him he had been to Kenya and worked in a rural clinic near Lake Victoria, not far from where Barack Sr. was born. Excited to find someone who had actually been to his father's country, Obama asked Moore to tell him everything about Kenya. Later Moore said, "In some ways I knew more about him than he knew about himself at that point." Moore, who was African American, asked Obama, "What kind of a name is 'Barry' for a brother?" Obama told him his real name was Barack. Moore responded, "That's a very strong name." Moore made it a point to call him Barack, and so did some of his close friends. Still, it was not until Obama transferred to Columbia University that he made the transition from Barry to Barack. This was around 1982, the year his father died.[2]

That name change is symbolic of a deeper change in Obama, but we cannot discover that change by tracking Obama's career as a community organizer. Obama did move to Chicago to gain political experience as a young activist. He worked for a church-based outfit that used the techniques of the Chicago radical Saul Alinsky. And Obama was able to ride his activist credentials to the state house, getting himself elected state senator when the frontrunner was disqualified on a technicality. But Obama's early political career is largely inconsequential, because he accomplished very little. As a state senator, he usually showed up, listened to the debates on the various issues, and robotically voted "present." (He voted "present" more than 100 times.) He made an abortive run for Congress in 2000 and lost badly in the Democratic primary. No one at that point would have predicted Obama's future. Obama himself was biding his time, going through the motions; the real action of his life was indeed elsewhere.

Before we get to that action, it is helpful to spell out an important choice that Obama had to make about what kind of black politician he was going to be. Recall from the previous chapter Obama's recognition that white America had been shamed by its history of slavery and racism, and this shaming had resulted in an accumulation of white guilt. This white guilt has in our day become a fund of political and financial capital for blacks to draw on. But a certain degree of black "acting out" is required to capitalize on this opportunity. In Chicago, where these thespian techniques had been virtually perfected, Obama realized that he had three options.

The first option was black nationalism. In Chicago, where Obama encountered it, this took the shape of the Nation of Islam. In *Dreams from My Father*, Obama relays his conversations with a black nationalist named Rafiq al Shabazz. In this case, as with other characters, the real Rafiq, whose name is Salim al Nuriddin, turns out to be somewhat different from the character Obama depicts. Even so, Obama's Rafiq is over the top, a bit of a cartoon character; Obama has little difficulty resisting his militant rhetoric. Obama's real problem with black nationalism emerges when he discusses Louis Farrakhan's solution for the African American community: economic self-help. Obama notes that Farrakhan's newspaper *The Final Call* had been thick with "promotions for a line of toiletries—toothpaste and the like—that the Nation had launched under the brand name POWER, part of a strategy to encourage blacks to keep their money within their own community." Over time, however, "the ads for POWER products grew less prominent in *The Final Call*; it seems that many who enjoyed Minister Farrakhan's speeches continued to brush their teeth with Crest."[3]

This is the sole moment of humor in Obama's book, and it emerges from his contempt for a strategy that seeks black uplift through black self-financing. Obama's objection seems to be not merely that blacks aren't loyal to black products; it is also that, in America, by and large blacks are not where the money is. This brings us to Obama's second option, which is the Jesse Jackson option, otherwise known as the shakedown. Unlike Farrakhan, Jackson knows exactly where the money is.

Over the years Jackson has figured out how to approach corporations, from Coke to NASCAR, threaten them with public accusations of racism, and then blackmail them into paying off Jackson's Operation PUSH, hiring blacks whom Jackson recommends, and diverting a percentage of their business to minority businesses of Jackson's choosing. Jackson has flourished through his godfather position at the head of a kind of black mafia; what makes the operation especially impressive is that, unlike the real Mafia, Jackson can get his results without having to break heads, and moreover, he can look like he's doing a lot of good for society while he is doing very well for himself.[4]

Obama is very careful in discussing the Jackson option in his book. He doesn't want to alienate Jackson, and neither does he want to offend the Chicago political machine, run at the time by such racial scam artists as Chicago mayor Harold Washington and U.S. Senator Carol Moseley Braun of Illinois; that machine also operated on race-based patronage. Still, despite their recognition that whites are the ones who have the money, the shakedown artists have a problem which Obama was quick to discern. The problem is that people who are intimidated into paying up are likely to be very resentful of the person who shakes them down. Besides, they are forking over only a small portion of their funds. So a relatively small monetary gain comes with a big loss of white political support. Jackson may fly around in a private jet, courtesy of some CEO who provided it to beat the racism rap. But notice that Jackson tried twice to run for president and did not even come close to winning the nomination; most likely today he could not be elected to any statewide office.

Therefore Obama turned to a third option, and this is the one that has worked well for him. It is the non-racial option, the option of seeking to organize on a community basis in order to advance himself politically. Not that Obama was against the idea of a shakedown; it's just that he wanted a bigger, more effective shakedown. What could be better than getting people to give voluntarily, even happily? Saul Alinsky helped Obama see how he could get whites to become accessories in such a large-scale project. Alinsky's *Rules for Radicals* is dedicated to a most unusual figure, who is credited with being "the very first radical." That figure is Lucifer, otherwise known as Satan. Not content with having Satan on his side, Alinsky also acknowledges his debts to Niccolo Machiavelli, but with one distinction. "*The Prince* was written by Machiavelli for the Haves on how to hold power. *Rules for Radicals* is written for the Have-Nots on how to take it away." Alinsky's context was American, yet his rules could easily be adapted to Obama's anti-colonial outlook: Alinsky could show him how, working on behalf of the wretched of the earth, he might bring down the Haves and seize power.

Despite his book's title, the most important aspect of Alinsky was not his radicalism; it was his pragmatism. Alinsky argued that blacks cannot succeed without the support of whites; more broadly, the folks at the bottom of society cannot win without making an alliance with, or at least manipulating, the folks in the middle and even some folks at the top. Even if all the low-income blacks, Mexicans, Puerto Ricans, and even poor Appalachian whites come together, the coalition would fail because it would not have enough power to make a real change. Alinsky's point was to call for a politics that transcends race and even class. He did so not to fulfill some multicultural vision, but simply because of the political reality that no radical change—radical in the sense of going to the root of things—was possible without including the white middle class in such a coalition.

Alinsky admitted that the white middle class was provincial, selfish, and often antagonistic to immigrants and minorities. Still, with careful crafting it was possible to devise a message that would bring these folks on board. Basically you have to create alienation, to cut this group from the power bases in society, to intensify its feelings of hopelessness and frustration. "Go in and rub raw the sores of discontent," Alinsky advised. "We'll give them a way . . . to exercise their rights as citizens and strike back at the establishment that oppressed them." This, Alinsky concluded, was the way to sell the middle class majority on a politics that would normally be alien and unpalatable.[5] For Obama, here was an unforgettable lesson in political packaging and marketing.

While Alinsky was an important instructor in tactics, another figure—and this time quite a character—played a crucial role in solidifying Obama's core identity. Approximately two decades ago, while he was working as an activist in Chicago, Obama came to the Trinity Church in order to hear its pastor Jeremiah Wright. Obama was not particularly religious; in fact, when pastors asked which church he attended, he typically hemmed and hawed. But, in *The Audacity of Hope*, Obama writes, "I was drawn to the power of the African American religious tradition to spur social change."[6] Trinity, Obama had heard, was that kind of church. Obama's interest was sharply boosted when he saw a sign spiked into the grass outside the church building: FREE SOUTH AFRICA. In the Reverend Wright, Obama encountered a man who frequently wore a dashiki or other African garb. A charismatic figure who was also an intellectual, Wright was capable of moving between the First World and the Third World, and of blending literary and political references with his biblical themes.

The sermon Obama heard that first day was called "The Audacity of Hope." It was a cosmopolitan address: Wright spoke of hardship in America, but he also spoke of Sharpeville, South Africa, and Hiroshima. Wright said, "The world . . . seems on the brink of destruction. Famine ravages millions of inhabitants in one hemisphere, while feasting and gluttony are enjoyed by inhabitants of another hemisphere." Obama reproduces the following passage as one that especially struck him. "It is this world, a world where cruise ships throw away more food in a day than most residents of Port-au-Prince see in a year, where white folks' greed runs a world in need, apartheid in one hemisphere, apathy in another hemisphere.... That's the world!"[7] The anti-colonial themes are obvious here: North versus South; rich, white Europeans versus the poor, dark-skinned people of Africa and the Caribbean. These were the themes of Obama's life, and he was drawn in from the start.

Since Wright's name surfaced during the presidential campaign, there has been much speculation about why Obama picked Trinity as his home church. After all, there were plenty of others to choose from, including several large churches that would also have served as a strong political base for Obama, and others that were closer to the South Side of Chicago where Obama lived. Many conservative critics of Obama pointed to Wright's controversial statements—such as his chant of "God damn America!" or his insistence that the U.S. government was deliberately spreading AIDS in the black community— and asserted that Obama must have agreed with them. Obama himself said he never heard those statements, and his liberal supporters suggested that perhaps he didn't quite know what Wright was all about.

None of this makes any sense. Certainly it is preposterous to suggest that Obama shared Wright's crackpot conspiracies about AIDS and the government. Nor can I envision Obama himself joining with Wright in chanting "God damn America." On the other hand, it is equally absurd to claim that Obama was clueless about Wright's real views. He attended the church for two decades. Throughout this time, the Obamas supported the church financially, and in 2007 they donated $22,500 to Trinity, their single largest charitable contribution.[8] Wright presided over Obama's wedding and baptized his two children. Even more telling, just as Obama took his father's name Barack as a tangible sign of his identification with him, so too Obama took the title of Wright's sermon

"The Audacity of Hope" and made it the title of his second book. Some have suggested that Wright became a kind of surrogate father for Obama, and that with his several thousand church members, Wright was perceived by Obama as having succeeded where his own father had failed. If this is the case, then Wright would be Obama's third paternal surrogate, following in the train of Lolo Soetoro and Frank Davis. In any event, over time Obama and Wright developed a close relationship. And clearly an intelligent man like Obama knew who Wright was and what he stood for; in fact, those were his main reasons for choosing Trinity and staying there.

What was it about Wright that appealed so much to Obama? Here we must distinguish between the many faces of Jeremiah Wright. Wright is a character who could easily have appeared in one of Mark Twain's novels, right alongside the Duke and Dauphin. The man is one part civil rights activist, one part Afrocentrist, one part anti-colonialist, and all parts opportunist. He rails against the rich while he himself lives in an affluent, gated community. He met his wife Ramah in a rather unusual way: she had been married to someone else, but when she came to him for counseling he coaxed her into his bed, ultimately convincing her that she would be better off with him than with her husband.[9]

Who knows whether Obama was aware of any of this? He certainly did know some of Wright's Afrocentric preoccupations: the "white value system" and the "black value system," Cleopatra was black, Jesus was black, everyone who invented anything was black, and so on. Most leading anti-colonial thinkers dismiss Afrocentrism as a foolish diversion. "No," admits Aimé Césaire with a hint of impatience, "we've never been Amazons or the Kings of Dahomey, nor princes of Ghana with 800 camels." The Nigerian Nobel laureate Wole Soyinka has written sarcastically that Negroes no more need to prove their Negritude than tigers need to prove their tigritude.[10] My guess is that, in line with this thinking,

Obama dismissed all of Wright's Afrocentric nonsense. He didn't care about it because, in his view, on the really crucial issue, Wright was 100 percent right.

The crucial issue was anti-colonialism, and this is a central theme in Wright's sermons, but it's been ignored because hardly anyone has taken what the man says seriously. Yet Wright has been stressing this theme all along. Asked about his affiliation with black liberation theology on Sean Hannity's show, Wright said there was nothing specifically black about it; indeed, he claimed to have been influenced by the Sandinistas in Nicaragua, and by "Asian theologians and Hispanic theologians." Speaking at the National Press Club, Wright showed how his reading of the Bible gave rise to anti-colonialist themes. "In biblical history, there's not one word written in the Bible between Genesis and Revelation that was not written under one of six different kinds of oppression, Egyptian oppression, Assyrian oppression, Persian oppression, Greek oppression, Roman oppression, Babylonian oppression. The Roman oppression is the period in which Jesus is born.... It sounds like some other governments I know."[11]

Here is an extended quotation from "The Day of Jerusalem's Fall," a sermon that Wright gave on September 16, 2001, a few days after 9/11:

> We took this country by terror away from the Sioux, the Apache, the Iroquois, the Comanche, the Arapaho, the Navajo. Terrorism. We took Africans from their country to build our way of ease and kept them enslaved and living in fear. Terrorism. We bombed Grenada and killed innocent civilians, babies, non-military personnel; we bombed the black civilian community of Panama, with stealth bombers, and killed unarmed teenagers and toddlers, pregnant mothers and hard-working fathers. We bombed Qadaffi's home

and killed his child. Blessed are they who bash your children's
heads against the rocks. We bombed Iraq; we killed unarmed
civilians trying to make a living. We bombed a plant in Sudan
to pay back an attack on our embassy. Killed hundreds of
hard-working people, mothers and fathers who left home to
go that day, not knowing they would never get back home.
We've bombed Hiroshima, we've bombed Nagasaki, we've
nuked far more than the thousands in New York and the Pentagon and we never batted an eye. Kids playing in the play-
ground, mothers picking up children after school, civilians,
not soldiers, people just trying to make it day by day. We have
supported state terrorism against the Palestinians and black
South Africans, and now we are indignant. Because the stuff
we have done overseas is now brought back into our own
front yard.[12]

I have left out the part that was most widely reported in the media, the
Reverend Wright's insistence that 9/11 was a case of "America's chickens coming home to roost." Forget about that line, which is in any case
lifted from Malcolm X. The point is that Wright's remarks are consistent and well thought out; there is an ideology here. Notice that Wright
does exactly what Obama was training himself to do. He took the slavery issue but then incorporated it into a larger pattern that included the
whole world: he fits the civil rights issue into the larger anti-colonial
issue. This is the core of Wright's thinking, and it was entirely in line
with Obama's own thinking. And that, I believe, is why Obama felt right
at home at Trinity.

But now it is time to leave American shores and join Obama on the
most important journey of his life. This was his first trip to Kenya, which
he took in 1988, when he was twenty-six years old. Obama's chapter on

Kenya takes up 130 pages of *Dreams from My Father*, and it represents the culmination of his quest for self-identity. As we will see, it was a kind of pilgrimage, complete with its scenes of trial, redemption, temptation, and vindication. Obama emerges from Kenya "born again," not in the religious sense, but rather ideologically. From that point on Obama is already made, or self-made, and the rest of our study will be devoted to seeking an application of Obama's ideology to his presidential run as well as to his domestic and foreign policy.

"At the time of his death," Obama said of his dad, "my father remained a myth to me, both more and less than a man." Obama's half-sister Auma visited him in New York while he attended Columbia. She told him for the first time about how humiliated and degraded their father had become, dropping from one low post to another even lower. Auma vividly described how Barack Sr. would stagger into her room drunk at night and rage about how he had been betrayed by the world. Obama's reaction shows how hard he took this news. "I felt as if my world had been turned on its head; as if I had woken up to find a blue sun in the yellow sky; or heard animals speaking like men. . . . To think that all my life I had been wrestling with nothing more than a ghost!"[13]

Obama intended his African odyssey to find out the truth about his father for himself, and it's worth following it in some detail. Like Marlow in Conrad's *Heart of Darkness*, Obama pushes deeper and deeper into the heart of Africa, seeking in this case not an ivory empire but a different kind of treasure—a truth to guide his life. On the flight to Nairobi, Obama sits next to a young Englishman who is on his way to South Africa. "The rest of Africa's falling apart now, isn't it?" he informs Obama. "The blacks in South Africa aren't starving to death like they do in some of these godforsaken countries."[14] Obama glares at him while the man drops off to sleep. In this anonymous Englishman, Obama has his first experience of the neocolonial mentality.

At the Nairobi airport, Obama is met by Auma and his aunt Zeituni, and the aunt makes a strange statement to Auma. "You take good care of Barry now. Make sure he doesn't get lost again." Auma explains that "lost" in this context doesn't just mean that someone hasn't seen you in a while. Rather, it refers to native Africans who have gone abroad and have never been heard from again. They are lost in the sense of being cut off from their own people, their own roots. Later, one of Obama's half-brothers will explain to him that he has not just returned home; he has returned to "Home Squared." For people who go abroad, Roy Obama explains, "there's your ordinary home" and there's your "true home." Your true home is your ancestral home, which is home twice over, and therefore Home Squared. Obama finds this whole concept quite profound.[15]

Having lunch with Auma at the New Stanley Hotel, Obama takes note of the tourists. "They were everywhere—Germans, Japanese, British, Americans—taking pictures, hailing taxis, fending off street ped-dlers, many of them dressed in safari suits like extras on a movie set." In Hawaii, Obama found the tourists amusing "with their sunburns and their pale, skinny legs." Not so in Kenya. "Here in Africa the tourists didn't seem so funny. I felt them as an encroachment, somehow; I found their innocence vaguely insulting. It occurred to me that in their utter lack of self-consciousness, they were expressing a freedom that neither Auma nor I could ever experience, a bedrock confidence in their own parochialism, a confidence reserved for those born into imperial cul-tures." Notice that Obama, despite his privileged background, despite Columbia and Harvard, identifies not with the American tourists but with the native people of Africa, and he lumps American tourists into "those born into imperial cultures."

An American family sits down to eat, and the waiters spring into action. Since Auma and he were there first, Obama is outraged at being passed over for service. The waiters ignore his beckoning gestures. Indignant, Auma and Obama leave, and Auma comments that even in Africa, African women are treated like prostitutes. "The same in any of these big office buildings. If you don't work there, and you are African, they will stop you until you tell them your business. But if you're with a German friend, they are all smiles. 'Good evening, miss,' they'll say." Kenya, Auma concludes, "is the whore of Africa, Barack. It opens its legs to anyone who can pay."

Obama reflects bitterly that "not all the tourists in Nairobi had come for the wildlife. Some came because Kenya, without shame, offered to re-create an age when the lives of whites in foreign lands rested comfortably on the backs of the darker races." And he's not finished. "Did our waiter know that black rule had come? Did it mean anything to him?"[16] Through an act of reflection, Obama converts his poor treatment at a restaurant into a case study in the workings of neocolonialism. If all of this seems like multicultural mind games, we have to realize that Obama does not see it that way at all. To him these episodes are all part of a grand drama.

At one point Obama finds himself turning onto Kimathi Street. He knows the name: Kimathi was one of the leaders of the Mau Mau rebellion. Of course! Obama has read his history. He tells us he read a book about Kimathi back in Chicago and can still recall the man's dreadlocks. And now he can feel only anger because no one else seems to know who Kimathi is. He was a guerilla fighter. "Kimathi had been captured and executed.... Kenya became the West's most stalwart pupil in Africa, a model of stability...Kimathi became a name on a street sign, thoroughly tamed for the tourists."[17] And here, to see what Obama is getting at, we need a little bit of history. We need to plumb into the gory details of the Mau Mau uprising, one which scarred Kenya and also Obama's family.

Historians wonder why the British were so brutal in suppressing the Mau Mau. The reason is obvious: by the end of the nineteenth century, the small island of England controlled a worldwide empire. It had to maintain this empire through a very small distribution of soldiers and settlers living abroad, outnumbered in every case by the natives. Edward Said points out that in 1879 there were 180,000 British soldiers defending an empire that spanned four continents and one that "was frequently in turmoil throughout India, Afghanistan, and southern and western Africa."[18] Even through the first half of the twentieth century, the British maintained vast regions of colonial territory with only the tiniest contingents of British military and administrative personnel.

This meant that British settlers living abroad had very little protection provided by British soldiers and policemen. Mostly they had to rely on locals hired by the colonial administration, locals who were regarded as cagey and unreliable. So when trouble started, the settlers typically panicked and began to shriek for protection: the natives are revolting! And in Kenya a faction of the Kikuyu people did spawn a rebellion that was conducted in the name of *ithaka na wiyathi*—land and freedom. They had a point: the British had seized the fertile lands of the Kikuyu and turned them into lavish plantations. The rhythms of Kikuyu life were severely disrupted. So the Kikuyu launched a campaign of murderous assaults not only against English settlers, but also against Africans and fellow Kikuyu who did not side with them. At its peak, this guerilla insurgency had around 20,000 insurgents, and it was led by three men: Waruhiu Itote (also known as General China), Stanley Mathenge, and Dedan Kimathi. Each of these three proved to be a savage and elusive opponent, and one, General China, actually survived the conflict and became a hero in post-independence Kenya.

As the rebellion gathered support, it drew on the system of kinship oaths among the Kikuyu. The Mau Mau oaths, which became notorious for the gruesome rituals that accompanied them, were professed to swear loyalty to each other and to kill all white Europeans they could get their hands on. The preferred method of assassination was to kill entire families with the machete and then to mutilate their bodies. As these massacres were discovered one after another, a massive cry for help and immediate action arose from the settler community. There were shrill calls to the British government to wake up to the threat of the Mau Mau.

Even today the term "mau mau" is used to suggest fear and intimidation, as in Tom Wolfe's *Radical Chic and Mau-Mauing the Flak Catchers*. The Mau Mau revolt in Kenya was portrayed by the international press as a kind of primitive African uprising in which jungle savages were cutting people into pieces simply as an expression of their native barbarism. As white public opinion both in Kenya and Britain hardened against Mau Mau attacks, the British government went into action and brought in the Royal Air Force as well as several thousand crack troops to destroy the rebels and put down the uprising.

The centerpiece of the British strategy was Operation Anvil, in which Nairobi was placed under martial law, and army troops searched the city rooting out Mau Mau guerillas and their protectors. The presumption of the British, according to historian Wunyabari Maloba, was that every Kenyan was a Mau Mau sympathizer unless he could prove himself innocent. Maloba writes that families were separated as husbands who couldn't demonstrate their innocence were locked up in detention camps, and their wives and children sent to congested reserves.[19]

From the perspective of curtailing the Mau Mau, however, Operation Anvil was an unqualified success. It drove the rebels out of the city and into the forests of Mount Kenya and the Aberdare mountain ranges. Then the British expanded Operation Anvil into a broader campaign that targeted the entire Kikuyu community. Historian David Anderson estimates that "at the peak of the emergency the British held more than

70,000 Kikuyu supporters of Mau Mau in detention camps . . . the vast majority were held without trial." Altogether some 150,000 Kikuyu were confined over the course of the rebellion. Historian Caroline Elkins, in her own controversial book on the subject, notes that while the men were in official camps the women and children were herded into enclosed villages surrounded by barbed wire and patrolled by guards. "Once I added all of the Kikuyu detained in these villages to the adjusted camp population, I discovered that the British had actually detained some 1.5 million people, or nearly the entire Kikuyu population."[20]

Elkins terms this system of confinement the "Kenyan gulag." Anderson doesn't use this term, but he notes that during the worst years of the Mau Mau suppression, "Kenya became a police state in the very fullest sense of the term." Some 1,500 Kenyans were sentenced to be hanged for collaboration with the Mau Mau in this period, and more than a thousand were sent to the gallows. "In no other place and at no other time in the history of British imperialism was state execution used on such a scale as this."[21] And from cases that Elkins studied we find horrible accounts of rape and torture in the detention camps. In some cases Kenyans were subjected to electric shock treatments; in others, people had their private parts severed with a pair of scissors or pliers. Elkins spares us none of the details. And even when the British campaign against the Mau Mau finally ended, its aftermath is heartbreaking. It was not uncommon for men to come home to discover that their wives had been raped and had given birth to other men's children during their time of confinement.

As for Dedan Kimathi, he was eventually hunted down by the British. The soldiers, many of them recruited from the Kikuyu, surrounded Kimathi's hiding place, and wounded and captured him. After a brief trial, he was hanged on February 18, 1957, and his body thrown into an unmarked grave. With Kimathi's death the Mau Mau rebellion was finished. Yet remarkably, although Kenya became independent only a few years later in 1963, few people remember the Mau Mau rebellion today. Jomo Kenyatta wanted no association with Mau Mau, telling the Kenyan people, "We shall not allow hooligans to rule Kenya. Mau Mau was a disease which has been eradicated and must never be remembered again." Not surprisingly, the British didn't want to talk about what had happened in the camps. India had become independent in 1947, and when the country's first prime minister Nehru heard about the British atrocities in Kenya, he complained to the former British governor general in India, Lord Mountbatten. Nehru's complaint made its way up to the prime minister, Winston Churchill, but Churchill had no interest in opening up an investigation into British abuses in Kenya, and so the book on colonial atrocities against the Mau Mau was officially closed for the moment.[22] At this point we can better understand Obama's determination to get that Churchill bust out of the White House.

While the literature on the Mau Mau crackdown makes for gruesome reading, in a sense it is not unique, because colonial powers have always used their power to crush such revolts. In India, for example, the British brutally suppressed the so-called Sepoy Rebellion in 1857–1858. But that was 150 years ago, while the Mau Mau suppression ended in 1960, only a year before Obama was born. It is one thing to read about these atrocities, and quite another to experience them. For Obama, these were not academic wars or war crimes for classroom debate. They were real wars and war crimes whose scars were endured by his grandfather and father.

Obama's grandfather Hussein Onyango Obama served as a cook for the British army in Myanmar (then called Burma) and Sri Lanka (then Ceylon); later he provided domestic help in Kenya in various British households. The British often called him "boy" and "coolie" and subjected him to routine insults. He may even have suffered greater indignities: historian David Anderson writes, "Kenya's settlers regulated their African labor through a version of the old English master-and-servants laws, and defended their right under this legislation to administer corporal punishments to their domestic staff and farm laborers." Anderson writes that flogging was common in Kenya, while it was very rare in neighboring British colonies like Uganda or Tanganyika.[23]

Onyango was arrested by the colonial authorities in 1949, just as the Mau Mau rebellion was starting. He was accused of being a rebel sympathizer. The charge was prima facie dubious; Onyango belonged to the Luo tribe, and the Luo were not on good terms with the Kikuyu. Even so, there were some Luo who were part of the Mau Mau rebellion. We read, for instance, in B. A. Ogot and W. R. Ochieng's *Decolonization and Independence in Kenya* that "the Mau Mau raiders of Athi River prison in 1953 included a contingent of Luo combatants."[24] Still, that was four years after Onyango's arrest, so he could not have been one of the collaborators. According to one of his wives, Sarah Obama, Onyango was beaten until he confessed that he was, in fact, a Mau Mau collaborator. At this point Onyango was left without food for days, and occasionally British soldiers showed up to poke him with sharp objects or squeeze his genitals between metal rods. Onyango saw some of his fellow prisoners die from torture. Others simply disappeared and were never heard from again. When Onyango finally returned home, according to Sarah, "I saw that he was now an old man."[25]

One might expect that Obama Jr. would sympathize with his grandfather Onyango, especially upon discovering his abuse at the hands of the British. Interestingly, Obama has no such reaction and treats his grandfather with scathing contempt. The reason emerges soon enough. Sarah Obama—whom Obama calls "granny"—tells him that once Onyango was released, he left the city and became a rural farmer and goat-herder. There he began to speculate on the source of the white man's power. "What your grandfather respected was strength," Granny says. Onyango began to tell his family and friends that superior knowledge was the source of the white man's effectiveness. He would even suggest that whites had conquered the world because they were better organized and more competent with technology than blacks. "The white man alone is like an ant," Onyango liked to say. "He can be easily crushed. But like an ant, the white man works together.... Black men are not like this.... That is why the black man will always lose." Africans, he feared, were headed nowhere because of the inherent lethargy and stupidity of the native people. "The African is thick," Onyango would sometimes say. "For him to do anything, he needs to be beaten."[26]

It is not hard to see that, after Obama heard this, he was basically done with grandpa. Obama writes, "I had imagined him to be an independent man, a man of his people, opposed to white rule." But now Obama had a totally different perspective. "What Granny had told me scrambled that image completely, causing ugly words to flash across my mind. Uncle Tom. Collaborator. House nigger."[27]

Ironically, Obama's sympathies are entirely reserved for his father, even though Obama Sr. only experienced colonialism as a child. Obama is deeply touched to hear about his father walking miles to school, proudly bringing his grades back home to his parents, and eventually moving to the port city of Mombasa where he became active in politics. In 1952 Obama Sr. was briefly jailed during the emergency declared by the British to deal with the Mau Mau uprising. After his release, Obama Sr. made his connection with Mboya and continued his involvement in the anticolonial cause. Then, thanks to the two missionary women, he got his big chance to go to America. For Obama Jr. this was the great moment, his father's chance to make a difference and change his country and the world, but tragically the promise was never fulfilled, and his father died a broken man. One might attribute this to his father's chronic carelessness and irresponsibility, both with himself and with others, but Obama Jr. views those characteristics as themselves shaped by colonial victimization. Somehow the badge of inferiority and humiliation, somehow the sharp currents of history that no one talks about—these are responsible for denying Barack Obama Sr. his rightful dream.

For Obama the dream is non-negotiable; it is everything; anyone who denies it is beneath contempt. In Nairobi, Obama is happy to commune with his relatives, most of them doing nothing with their lives, the men looking for government benefits, the women for men who will provide for them. But then he encounters one of his own half-brothers, Mark. Mark, the son of Barack Sr. and Ruth Nidesand, seems a lot like Obama. He received his undergraduate degree from Brown and his masters from Stanford, both in physics. Mark then lived and worked in the United States. (Since then he got his MBA from Emory and is now a business consultant living in China.)

In another sense, however, Mark could not be more different from his half-brother Barack. He professes no real attachment to Kenya— "just another poor, African country"—and when Obama asks, "You don't think about settling here?" Mark replies, "There's not much work for a physicist, is there, in a country where the average person doesn't have a telephone." Mark has also changed his last name from Obama to Ndesandjo, relinquishing his own dad's name and taking the name of the man who married his mother after she divorced Barack Sr. Surprised by Mark's indifference, not only to Kenya but also to his own father, Obama persists: "Don't you ever feel like you might be losing something?" Mark replies, "You think that somehow I'm cut off from my roots, that sort of thing. Well, you're right. At a certain point, I made a decision not to think about who my real father was. He was dead to me even when he was still alive. I knew he was a drunk and showed no concern for his wife or children. That was enough."

Shocked by Mark's disdain for his idol, Obama presses him. "That doesn't bother you? Being numb, I mean?" Mark compounds the offense. "Towards him, no. Other things move me. Beethoven's symphonies. Shakespeare's sonnets. I know—it's not what an African is supposed to care about. But who's to tell me what I should and shouldn't care about? Understand, I'm not ashamed of being half Kenyan. I just don't ask myself a lot of questions about what it all means. Who knows? What's certain is that I don't need the stress. Life's hard enough without all that excess baggage." At this point Obama is done with Mark. "Outside we exchanged addresses and promised to write, with a dishonesty that made my heart ache."[28] Obama doesn't want to see his brother again. The temptation has presented itself—the temptation to deny his father and his African homeland—and he has successfully resisted it.

In the climax to his narrative, Obama visits the burial mounds of his father and grandfather. This scene is absolutely pivotal for Obama's development. Obama himself recognizes this, and he leads up to it with a sense of drama and trepidation. First he describes going out into the wilderness past a group of painted Masai. What follows is virtually biblical.

> We came upon a tribe of hyenas feeding on the carcass of a wildebeest. In the dying orange light they looked like demon dogs, their eyes like clumps of black coal, their chins dripping with blood.... It was a savage scene, and we stayed there for a long time, watching life feed on itself, the silence interrupted only by the crack of bone or the rush of wind.... I thought to myself: This is what Creation looked like. The same stillness, the same crunching of bone. There in the dusk, over that hill, I imagined the first man stepping forward, naked and rough-skinned, grasping a chunk of flint in his clumsy hand, no

words yet for the fear, the anticipation, the awe he feels at the sky, the glimmering knowledge of his own death.[29]

Why is Obama raising the issue of creation? Because his narrative is really about his own death and rebirth. Next Obama describes his granny braiding hair as she sits him down outside their family hut and tells him about himself. This is Obama's book of Genesis, and so predictably he writes, "I asked Granny to start from the beginning." Granny's beginning has a very familiar tone: "First there was Miwiru. It's not known who came before. Miwiru sired Sigoma, Sigoma sired Owiny, Owiny sired Kosodhi, Kosodhi sired Ogelo, Ogelo sired Otondi, Otondi sired Obongo, Obongo sired Okoth, and Okoth sired Opiyo."[30]

Granny describes the idyllic times before colonialism.

> This is the time before the white man came. Each family had their own compound, but they all lived under the laws of the elders. Men had their own huts, and were responsible for clearing and cultivating their land, as well as protecting the cattle from wild animals and the raids of other tribes. Each wife had her own vegetable plot, which only she and her daughters would cultivate. She cooked the man's food, drew water, and maintained the huts. The elders regulated all plantings and the harvests.... The children did not go to school but learned alongside their parents. The girls would accompany their mothers and learn how to grind the millet into porridge, how to grow vegetables and pack clay for the huts. The boys learned from their fathers how to herd and work *pangas* and throw spears.[31]

As Obama hears his family history, he is moved into a kind of reverie. "How to explain the emotions of that day? I can summon each moment in my mind almost frame by frame . . . .It wasn't simply joy that I felt in each of these moments. Rather, it was a sense that everything I was doing, every touch and breath and word, carried the full weight of my life; that a circle was beginning to close, so that I might finally recognize myself as I was, here, now, in one place."[32]

Obama takes the great Kenyan railroad from Nairobi to Kisumu. Obama knows his colonial history.

> The railway had been the single largest engineering effort in the history of the British empire at the time it was built—six hundred miles long, from Mombasa on the Indian Ocean to the eastern shores of Lake Victoria. . . . It seemed like ancient history. And yet I know that 1895, the year that the first beams were laid, had also been the year of my grandfather's birth. . . . The thought made the history of the train come alive for me, and I tried to imagine the sensations some nameless British officer might have felt on the train's maiden voyage, as he sat in his gas-lit compartment and looked out over miles of receding bush. . . . I tried to imagine the African on the other side of the glass window, watching this snake of steel and black smoke passing his village for the first time.[33]

Before he visits the family gravesite, Obama is given some small but priceless mementos of his own ancestry. He gets a *Domestic Servant's Pocket Register* that his grandfather once possessed, along with some of the old man's letters. More valuable, he gets a stack of letters that his own father wrote to various American colleges—Morgan State, Santa

Barbara Junior College, San Francisco State—seeking admission. "Dear
President Calhoun," one letter begins. "I have heard of your college from
Mrs. Helen Roberts of Palo Alto, California, who is now in Nairobi here.
Mrs. Roberts, knowing how much desirous I am to further my studies
in the United States of America, has asked me to apply to your esteemed
college for admission." And so on. Obama cannot believe what he is
holding in his hands. "This is it," he writes. "My inheritance."[34]

Finally Obama visits the grave where both his grandfather and father
are buried. Briefly, he recalls his grandfather, but then

> the picture fades, replaced by the image of a nine-year-old
> boy—my father.... How lucky he must have felt when his
> ship came sailing in. He must have known, when that letter
> came from Hawaii, that he had been chosen after all; that he
> possessed the grace of his name, the *Baraka*, the blessings of
> God. With the degree, the ascot, the American wife, the car,
> the words, the figures, the wallet, the proper proportion of
> tonic to gin, the polish, the panache, the entire thing seam-
> less and natural, without the cobbled-together, haphazard
> quality of an earlier time—what could stand in his way? He
> had almost succeeded, in a way his own father could never
> have hoped for. And then, after seeming to travel so far, to
> discover that he had not escaped after all!

At this point Obama is simply overcome with emotion.

> I dropped to the ground and swept my hand across the
> smooth yellow tile. Oh, Father, I cried. There was no shame
> in your confusion.... No shame in the fear.... There was only
> shame in the silence fear had produced. It was the silence that

betrayed us. If it weren't for that silence, your grandfather might have told your father that he could never escape himself, or recreate himself alone. Your father might have taught those same lessons to you. And you, the son, might have taught your father that this new world that was beckoning all of you involved more than just railroads and indoor toilets and irrigation ditches and gramophones.

Obama continues, "For a long time I sat between the two graves and wept." And from that weeping came something new, something that wasn't there before.

> When my tears were finally spent, I felt a calmness wash over me. I felt the circle finally close. I realized that who I was, what I cared about, was no longer just a matter of intellect or obligation, no longer a construct of words. I saw that my life in America—the black life, the white life, the sense of abandonment I'd felt as a boy, the frustration and hope I'd witnessed in Chicago—all of it was connected with this small plot of earth an ocean away, connected by more than the accident of a name or the color of my skin. The pain that I felt was my father's pain.

A light rain begins to fall, and Obama feels a tap on his arm. His half-brother Bernard says, "They wanted me to see if you were okay." Obama smiles. "Yeah, I'm okay."[35]

Finally he is okay. As Obama's writing shows, he has moved into a higher mode, suspended as it were above the plane of mundane reality. For the second time, Obama has had a transforming experience with his father. The first time was when Barack Sr. came to speak at his school in

Hawaii. That's when the son resolved to imbibe his father's personality, his magnetic charm, his persuasiveness. But here, at the family tomb, Obama receives something more fundamental. In Obama's own words, "I sat at my father's grave and spoke to him through Africa's red soil."[36] In a sense, through the earth itself, he communes with his father and receives his father's spirit. It is here that Obama takes on his father's struggle, not by recovering his father's body but by embracing his father's cause. And so he makes his decision. Where Obama Sr. failed, Obama Jr. will succeed, but he will succeed calmly, strategically, using the panache and persuasiveness that he also got from his father. Obama Sr.'s hatred of the colonial system becomes Obama Jr.'s hatred; Obama Sr.'s failed attempt to set the world right becomes Obama Jr.'s objective for the future. As Obama himself puts it, the dreams of the father forge the dreams of the son, and through a kind of sacramental experience at the family grave, the father's struggle becomes the son's birthright.

CHAPTER 7

PUTTING ON
THE MASK

B arack Obama returned from his father's grave in Kenya a
changed man. If our account is right, at this point in his life he
was filled with hatred, but it was a calm hatred, an ideological
hatred. This hatred derived from the debris of the anti-colonial wars and
their impact on his family and especially his father. These anti-colonial
wars now raged in Obama's mind, and he seems to have resolved to
become an anti-colonial warrior himself, taking up the cause and seeing
the fight to the finish; his father's dream had truly become his own. This
was not about settling individual scores—about going and finding the
men who had harmed his father and holding them to account. Nor was
it a matter of rescuing relatives like poor George Obama. No, this was
about systems, social hierarchies, and the movement of history. The
colonial wars themselves were over, but they had been replaced by
something else, a neocolonial subjugation that defined the world of the
twenty-first century. It was this world that Barack Obama resolved to

change, and that is how he could be true to the largeness of his father's liberationist dream.

But right away, we can see, Obama faced a problem. Actually, two problems. The first is the difficult question of what to do about all this. In other words, how to realize his father's dream? This is a problem of ideology and of policy. The second problem, equally daunting, is one of politics and marketing. How does a man obsessed with events so far away return to America and sell that vision to others who don't share it? How does a man like Obama get elected in a country which has virtually no awareness of the defining events of his life, no concern for the injustices that move him, and consequently no sense of urgency about the need to put the resolution of the colonial problem at the forefront of the national agenda? It is here, we will discover, that the creativity and indeed political genius of Obama really show themselves.

Obama is a miracle story in American politics. How do you go from local politics in Illinois in 2004 to being a United States senator from that state and a national celebrity at the Democratic convention that same year, and president of the United States four years later? Not only did Obama impress by winning; it was the way he did it. In a sense, he rose above the field. He became a genuine national and indeed global celebrity, a status that very few men—Gandhi and Mandela come to mind—have achieved on the world stage. He flummoxed his critics, who flailed against him, and he stirred powerful emotions in his supporters, emotions that even they could not fully account for. He inspired giddy excitement in the mainstream media; much of the coverage of his campaign read like press releases issued by his campaign. It is Obama who is responsible for creating the Obama Choir, those hypnotized followers who routinely suspend their rationality when it comes to this political rock star. Somehow the man consumed by the wars and hatreds of a world far away became, in a very different context, the embodiment

Young Obama with his mother Stanley Ann in an undated photo taken in Honolulu, Hawaii. She was Barack Obama Sr.'s first convert.
Photo: UPI Photo/Obama Press Office

Obama, age 10, is shy and pudgy and clearly devoted to his father, Barack Obama Sr. This is the only time the absentee father came to visit, but a single incident at Obama's school proved to be the first defining moment of young Obama's life.
Photo: Newscom

Obama's stepfather Lolo Soetoro, shown here with Ann and their young child Maya, taught the timid, withdrawn Barry Obama how to survive in a harsh world. Undated photo taken at the Soetoro home in Jakarta, Indonesia. *Photo: Newscom*

Obama with his elementary school class in Jakarta, Indonesia. Everyone tries to fit Obama into American history. But this is Obama's history. *Photo: AFP Photo/Ho*

Obama, age 26, carries a large sack of corn to the hut of his "granny" Sarah Obama. Actually Sarah isn't Obama's real granny, but one of the other wives of Obama's grandfather Onyango Obama. Photo taken sometime in 1988. *Photo: Newscom*

During his first visit to Kenya in 1988, Obama sits outside his ancestral hut where he learns that his original home in Africa is "Home Squared," the home that matters most. *Photo: Newscom*

Obama's "granny" Sarah recounted for him the life of his grandfather Onyango Obama, whom Obama scorned as a "house nigger," and also of his father Barack Obama Sr., whom Obama idolized and sought to emulate. *Photo: Pete Souza/Chicago Tribune/MCT*

The British brutally crushed the Mau Mau rebellion in Kenya, leaving deep scars on Obama's grandfather, who was held without trial in a detention camp. *Photo: Getty Images*

Kenya's first president Jomo Kenyatta answers questions at a press conference; with him is the labor leader Tom Mboya, who was partly responsible for Barack Obama Sr. coming to America. Obama Sr. allied himself with African socialism in opposition to Kenyatta's free market capitalism.
Photo: Newscom

When Obama was elected president, a statue of Young Obama was erected in a public park in Jakarta. But in response to 50,000 signed petitions by Indonesians saying that Obama has done nothing for Indonesia, the statue was recently taken down. *Photo: AFP Photo/Adek Berry*

When President Obama came across a bust of Winston Churchill in the Oval Office, he promptly returned it to the British. For Obama, Churchill is not remembered as the sustainer of Britain during World War II; rather, he is remembered as the obstinate defender of British colonialism and as the prime minister who was responsible for the arrest of Obama's father and grandfather.
Photo: Newscom

When Barack Obama Jr. visited his father's grave, he wept. "I saw that my life in America—the black life, the white life, the sense of abandonment I'd felt as a boy, the frustration and hope I'd witnessed in Chicago—all of it was connected with this small plot of earth an ocean away." This is the second turning point in Obama's life, his political born-again experience.
Photo: Newscom

George Obama sitting outside his hut in Nairobi, Kenya, where he was reportedly living on pennies a day with no help from his millionaire half-brother.
Photo: © Stephen Morrison/epa/Corbis

LEFT: Edward Said, Obama's teacher at Columbia and a former
spokesman for the Palestine Liberation Organization.
Photo: Newscom/Richard B. Levine

RIGHT: Roberto Mangabeira Unger, Obama's teacher at Harvard,
didn't want to harm Obama's presidential chances so he refused
all interviews. *Photo: Newscom*

LEFT: Jeremiah Wright's Third World theology with its denunciations
of American empire is the key to understanding why Obama stayed in
his church for two decades. *Photo: AFP Photo/Mandel Ngan*

RIGHT: Bill Ayers, like Ho Chi Minh, saw himself as an anti-colonialist
fighting against American imperialism in Vietnam. *Photo: Newscom*

Young Indians in a call center exploiting "the advantage of backwardness." Globalization and free trade have lifted more poor people in the world out of poverty in a decade than foreign aid programs did in half a century. *Photo: Newscom*

The cities in China, such as the Shanghai skyline shown here, are bigger and glitzier than anything in America and the West. Unless America gets its act together, China will become the world's largest economy, and America's moment of leadership will be short-lived. Oddly, Obama doesn't seem to care. *Photo: AFP Photo/Philippe Lopez*

of hope and aspiration for tens of millions of people who cheered for him and voted for him. How did he do it?

Let's begin by acknowledging one of Obama's great achievements, an achievement that even Obama's critics would have to concede. Obama has transformed the landscape of race relations in America. He has done this not by anything that he has said or done, but by what he stands for and what he represents. Not everyone, of course, is happy with the change. During the presidential campaign, Jesse Jackson said something revealing about Obama without realizing that the microphone was on. He said, "I want to cut his nuts off."[1] The reason for Jackson's pique is pretty obvious. It is that Obama has, in a sense, cut Jackson's nuts off by delegitimizing the whole racial shakedown model. Sure, many of the race hustlers are still at it, but now somehow their mission has lost its moral luster; the nation seems to have moved beyond it; making a living today by crying "racism" has become tawdry and disreputable.

One race hustler who might be getting out of the business is Al Sharpton; he has found a better gig. Sharpton has become Obama's link to the black street and also, in a way, Obama's defender in the African American community. When black activists like Tavis Smiley and Michael Eric Dyson pummel Obama for not being sufficiently attentive to black concerns, Sharpton fires back. "We need to try to solve our problems and not expect the president to advocate for us." Sharpton adds, "It's interesting to me that some people don't understand that to try to make the president do certain things will only benefit the right wing, which wants to get the president and us."[2] Sharpton has even made the sartorial transition, going from his brightly colored track suits and gold medallions to now wearing tailored business suits. Evidently even Sharpton has figured out that the old shakedown routine is losing its effectiveness, and it's time for a new assignment. Sharpton has adapted; Jackson still hasn't.

The premise of the race hustlers is that America owes blacks in a big way because America continues to be a racist society. What makes Obama different is that he doesn't seem to believe a word of it. Naturally he recognizes America's history of slavery, segregation, and racism. And he occasionally does pay homage to the civil rights constituency by mumbling something about how racism is still an issue in America. In *The Audacity of Hope*, Obama argues that "for all the progress that's been made in the past four decades, a stubborn gap remains between the living standards of black, Latino and white workers."[3] Echoing the civil rights orthodoxy, Michelle Obama recently told Steve Kroft on *60 Minutes* that despite his education and success, her husband was a black man who was still in danger of being beaten up or shot in the street.[4] But I doubt that Obama deep down would agree with this. Surely Obama knows that educated, successful blacks are much more likely today to be beaten up or shot by a black gangbanger than by a white person.

Obama's specific achievement is to restore the credibility of the color-blind ideal in America. "The unavoidable fact," writes Andrew Kull in *The Color Blind Constitution*, "is that over a period of some 125 years the American civil rights movement first elaborated, then held as its unvarying political objective, a rule of law requiring the color-blind treatment of individuals." From Frederick Douglass to Martin Luther King, black leaders pressed for America to get beyond race and treat people based on who they are, not on how they look. Race was considered "the painted face," in the words of civil rights activist Morris Dees, something that should be socially and morally irrelevant.

Somehow, as Kull notes, "The color-blind consensus, so long in forming, was abandoned with surprising rapidity."[5] Just when America accepted it—and passed a series of laws, such as the Civil Rights Act of 1964, which institutionalized it—the very people who pushed for color-blindness decided that color-blindness was not enough. They now became champions of affirmative action and racial preferences. The new orthodoxy was summarized by the title of one of Cornel West's books, *Race Matters*. West's point was not merely that race is a social reality, but that race ought to matter: race-conscious solutions are required to combat persistent inequalities. Still, despite its abandonment among today's civil rights leadership, the color-blind ideal has endured as a true reflection of American ideals and aspirations.

Obama has brought us a giant step closer to realizing these ideals and aspirations. This makes Obama sound like a descendant and disciple of Martin Luther King. Is he? The answer, surprisingly enough, is no. If we have made any progress to this point in understanding Obama, we can see that Obama's politics arise from a very different source than Martin Luther King's dream. It is not that he opposes King's dream; but it is irrelevant to his worldview. Obama often quotes Martin Luther King on "the fierce urgency of now." What Obama means is that we should all act now to do what he wants. This reference has nothing to do with King's vision that America become a society where race does not matter. That's not a primary concern with Obama; as we are about to discover, his representation and implicit advocacy of the color-blind ideal are largely tactical. He has found a way to benefit politically not just from being black but also from being a certain kind of black leader: a non-Jesse Jackson, and in some ways an anti-Jesse Jackson. This is an important source of his appeal to America's white majority.

Let's come back to Obama's two challenges: what to do about his father's dream today and how to sell that vision to America. Here we can understand Obama more deeply by delving into the writings of a man Obama studied carefully: the anti-colonial activist and writer Frantz Fanon. Obama acknowledges Fanon in *Dreams from My Father*, and the book is suffused with themes drawn from Fanon. Recall that it was Fanon's *Black Skin, White Masks* that seems to have been the actual source for Obama's made-up *Life* magazine story about the black man who was desperately taking medication to whiten his skin.

Yet Fanon is absent from Obama's later book *The Audacity of Hope*, and even Fanon's influence seems hard to locate there. In a way, the two books show Obama's transition from the real Obama to the political Obama. Fanon, I believe, is the man who helped pave the transition. He is the one who helped Obama to put on his mask, the mask that would enable Obama to translate his anti-colonial ideas into the language and imagery of modern American politics. Even so, Obama is no rote follower of Fanon: as we will see, he agrees wholeheartedly with Fanon in one respect while completely inverting Fanon's teaching in another. Drawing on Fanon but going beyond him, Obama has come up with his own distinctive vision and strategy.

Fanon's appeal to Obama had two sources. First, Fanon was by profession a psychiatrist, and his work consistently spells out the psychology of anti-colonialism. This suited Obama's own interior cast of mind; he found in Fanon a fellow militant seeking a way to give his introspective rage a revolutionary expression. Second, Fanon wasn't a mere theoretician of anti-colonialism; he was an anti-colonial fighter. He didn't just complain about oppression; he tried to do something about it. This too fit Obama's own practical plans to take action against the enemy.

Born in the Caribbean in 1925, Fanon studied in France and then joined the Algerian liberation movement, the FLN, contributing to its underground newspaper *al-Moujahid*. In 1957 the French authorities expelled him from Algeria, so he moved to Tunisia to continue his FLN work. The Algerian war of independence was especially brutal, killing thousands of French and hundreds of thousands of Algerians. Fanon was a leading voice calling for independence, not only for Algeria but for all of Africa. He died in 1961, a few months before Algeria became free and in the same year that Obama was born. Fanon's work enjoyed a vogue in the West in the late 1960s and through the 1970s, especially in schools and universities where young people were mobilizing against the Vietnam War. No wonder Obama discovered Fanon and absorbed his ideas. It solidified his worldview and confirmed his intense hatred for colonialism and neocolonialism.

Fanon argued that colonialism and neocolonialism are total systems that are, in their inherent structure, evil. The form of colonialism may vary, but even so "exploitation, tortures, raids, collective liquidations . . . take turns at different levels in order literally to make of the native an object in the hands of the occupying nation." Addressing French liberals who defended colonialism but condemned its excesses, Fanon wrote, "Torture in Algeria is not an accident, or an error, or a fault. Colonialism cannot be understood without the possibility of torturing, of violating, of massacring."

Racism, Fanon argued, was a characteristic feature of colonialism. Not that colonial systems required it; but typically they found it a convenient way to rationalize why the occupiers were on top and the rest were at the bottom. Racism enabled the bad guys to feel good about being bad; to enjoy a sense of entitlement to their violent and exploitative behavior. Recall that this analysis of racism is very similar to the one we derived from Joseph Conrad's *Heart of Darkness*. Even so, Fanon recognized that "racism . . . is only one element of a vaster whole: that of the systematized oppression of a people."

Fanon also insisted that colonialism could not be reformed; it had to be totally overturned and eliminated. Fanon wrote that "every Frenchman in Algeria is at the present time an enemy soldier," even if that Frenchman did not work for the colonial authorities and considered himself uninvolved in colonial oppression. In other words, you are either on the side of oppression or on the side of liberation; there is no middle ground. This is a war to the finish: one side must win and the other must lose. "The struggle is at once total and absolute.... Liberation is the total destruction of the colonial system."

Fanon's strategy for eliminating colonialism was violence. "The native is ready for violence at all times," Fanon wrote. Only through a "murderous and decisive struggle" could colonialism be overthrown. Fanon said that "colonized man is an envious man." He wants to destroy the colonial system, or to wring the neocolonialism out of every institution of society. In Fanon's view, the hidden desire of the colonized is to replicate the crimes of the colonizer. "The native is an oppressed person whose permanent dream is to become the persecutor."[6]

Is this also Obama's dream? I think it is, and this helps to explain Obama's friendship and association with the radical activist Bill Ayers. As a member of the Weather Underground, Ayers participated in the bombings of the New York City Police Headquarters in 1970, the Capitol building in 1971, and the Pentagon in 1972. Ayers, now a professor of education at the University of Illinois at Chicago, held a fundraiser for Obama at his apartment in 1995 when Obama made his first run for the Illinois State Senate. The two formed an acquaintance, which deepened into a friendship when they served jointly on the board of an educational foundation called the Woods Fund. Ayers and Obama also worked together for six years, from 1995 to 2001, on a multimillion dollar educational grant program called the Chicago Annenberg Challenge.

During the presidential campaign, Obama's media spokesmen poohpoohed the idea that Obama bore any responsibility for what Ayers did in the early 1970s when Obama was only a child. Yet the issue wasn't what Ayers did then, but how he feels about it now. A few years ago, Ayers told the *New York Times* that "I don't regret setting bombs. I feel we didn't do enough." Asked if he might do it again, he answered, "I don't want to discount the possibility."[7] Even so, Obama counted Ayers a supporter and a friend. Surely this is not because Obama himself would contemplate bombing the Pentagon! That would be quite a first for a U.S. president. So what's going on here?

In a letter to the *Times*, Ayers said that his actions must be understood in the context of the Vietnam War. The story of his activism, he said, "begins literally in the shadow of Hiroshima and comes of age in the killing fields of Southeast Asia." Read Ayers's memoir *Fugitive Days*, and the anti-colonial themes jump out at you. Of the Weathermen, Ayers writes, "We had been insistent in our anti-Americanism, our opposition to a national story stained with conquest and slavery and attempted genocide." Vietnam, Ayers writes, was the cause that spurred him to action. "What kind of a system is it that allows the U.S. to seize the destinies of the Vietnamese people?"

Today we think of the Vietnam War as America's attempt to stop communism. But that's not how Ho Chi Minh saw it, and that's not how Bill Ayers saw it either. For Ho and Bill, this was an anti-colonial struggle. Vietnam was a French colony, and when the French encountered guerilla resistance in that country, they solicited and received American aid. In 1954, in the wake of the disaster at Dien Bien Phu, the French pulled out, and the Americans stepped in to fill the gap. Ayers accurately notes that Americans tended to view Vietnam as a domino: "If Vietnam falls . . . all of Indochina will follow in short order." Ayers accepted the logic of dominoes but read it in the other direction. If America is permitted to impose neocolonialism on Vietnam, soon it will take it upon itself to occupy the rest of Southeast Asia, and who knows what after that?[8] Ayers believed he was using violence in a noble cause, the cause of halting American neocolonialism in Vietnam.

With this background information, it is easy to see why Obama should admire Ayers—they are fellow anti-colonial warriors—even if Obama himself eschews violence. Obama, of course, made the same intellectual compromise with Fanon, embracing his anti-colonial cause while rejecting his call to violence. Fanon advocated violence on the grounds that oppressors never concede power without a fight. He was all in favor of the oppressed exchanging places with the oppressor and giving the bad guys a taste of their own medicine. At the same time, Fanon insisted that the colonized should not imitate the racism or even the race-consciousness of the oppressor. In Fanon's view, colonialism was rooted in racism, but anti-colonialism needed to transcend tribal and racial boundaries.

Fanon's reason for rejecting race and color-consciousness was eminently practical. Since the colonizers had incomparably greater resources and also the best weapons, the colonized needed massive numbers to make up for what they lacked in resources and firepower. Fanon called for the unity of the oppressed: he sought initially to unite the various African tribes and nationalities into a joint African resistance. Ultimately he envisioned the possibility of the black, brown, and yellow races coming together in a global front against white European supremacy. Fanon even saw the possibility of a few white European sympathizers who might join the liberationist cause. In Fanon's case the most prominent was the philosopher Jean-Paul Sartre, who wrote the introduction to Fanon's *The Wretched of the Earth*.

Obama embraced Fanon's call for a transracial and even nonracial politics of resistance. But he seems to have seen a possibility that Fanon missed, or perhaps one that was not available in Fanon's time but became available in Obama's. This was the possibility that went beyond forming a coalition of the oppressed. It involved winning a substantial number—perhaps a majority—of whites over to the cause of anti-colonial politics. If this could be done, it would eliminate the need for violence. Indeed it would be a feat of political diplomacy, to be able to recruit your enemy to participate in his own overthrow!

Still, how to do this? Curiously, Obama may have found the answer in Fanon, right in the very same passages where Obama pirated his *Life* magazine story. In *Black Skin, White Masks*, Fanon spoke of laboratories that were searching for a "denegrification" serum, a serum that would turn black people white. He also wrote of West Indian black women who were determined to marry a white man with blue eyes, in part so they could have lighter children. Fanon called this phenomenon "lactification."

The term, which comes from milk, means whitening. Fanon's point wasn't merely that blacks sought greater social prestige by being associated with a lighter skin color; rather, it was that lactification was a metaphor for the way in which colonized people deny their own heritage and seek to copy the ways of their oppressors. Fanon mocked the Africans and West Indians who learned without irony French poems about "our ancestors, the Gauls." For Fanon, lactification doesn't just refer to looking white; it also refers to acting white, to people with "black skin" who seek to put on "white masks." As Fanon put it, "The more the colonized has assimilated the cultural values of the metropolis, the more he will have escaped the bush. The more he rejects his blackness and the bush, the whiter he will become."[9]

Here Obama seems to have had an original idea that turned Fanon on his head. Obama's idea was: what's wrong with putting on the white mask? Let's clarify the difficulty facing Obama. In the last chapter we saw how Obama benefited from Saul Alinsky's transracial strategy to assemble an effective coalition. Alinsky's goal was for the activist to reach America's white middle class because, as he put it, "that is where the power is." Alinsky had nothing but contempt for left-wing activists who treated the white middle class as a bunch of square, sexually uptight, gun-toting, small-minded racists. Yes, Alinsky wrote, the middle class is mighty screwed up. But it has become that way because it's desperate; its economic condition is deteriorating and so people turn to guns and religion to give them consolation. (Sound familiar?)

Alinsky advocated that a successful activist must not disdain the middle class but rather join it. Certainly he wasn't calling for an embrace of the provincial values of the middle class. Rather, he urged that activists adopt the style and attitude of the middle class. If the middle class is "square," then be square. Don't wear the black leather jacket and the hippie bandana; wear a suit and tie. Don't come across as an angry misfit; come across as a nice young man who is only upset because of manifest injustice. Smile a lot; smiles are a great way to disguise rage and contempt. In this way, Alinsky argued, the activist could build a rapport with ordinary Americans and mobilize them on behalf of radical causes.[10]

Obama's genius was to figure out a simple but effective way to achieve both Fanon's goal of advancing the anti-colonial vision and also Alinsky's goal to win over mainstream America. Obama knew from his experience at Columbia and at Harvard that there was an immense fund of white racist shame that had given rise to an equally large fund of white racial guilt. This guilt was ready to be tapped, and in Chicago Obama saw how it was being tapped by Jesse Jackson and his fellow shakedown artists. But what if it could be tapped in a much bigger and more consequential way?

Author Shelby Steele, one of America's most insightful commentators on race relations, notes that whites have been looking for some time for a black leader who has credibility within the black community and yet can offer whites racial absolution. This should not be taken too cynically. Many whites genuinely espouse an idealism that seeks to move beyond race, and they recognize that it's going to take a black spokesman to make this case on a national level and help to get us there. Steele notes bluntly that this idealism cannot be divorced from a powerful sense of white racial guilt. We have to get beyond race because America's past racial history has become such an embarrassment.

Now the black leader that whites are looking for does not actually have to issue indulgences in the manner of the medieval papacy; rather, by his words and deeds, he can signal to white America that whites are no longer on the hook for past racism. In Steele's view, whites have been eagerly, hungrily awaiting the black leader who would give them a chance, through their support of his leadership, not merely to say to others but to feel, in their innermost being, "Whew, I am not a racist." Steele speculated that whites may be willing to pay heavily both in money and in political support if such a candidate appeared on the horizon. He would truly be the anointed one.[11]

Obama's ingenuity was to recognize that this unique opportunity required a black man of a kind not seen in American politics before. Such a man would have to look black but act white. His general demeanor would resemble that of Colin Powell far more than that of Al Sharpton. Ideally such a man would have close-cropped hair, a Midwestern accent, and dress in preppie fashion. He would speak in a measured tone—no angry black man routines—and project mainstream interests and mainstream values. Ideally he would locate himself in the middle of the political spectrum, equidistant from extremes, a kind of unifier and healer. Yes, this was the formula. Obama realized that he might be able to reach the political heights by being the first black man in American politics who really knows how to play the white man.

Call it the triumph of lactification. Finally Obama had hit upon a technique to achieve the kind of persuasive success that as a 10-year-old boy he had witnessed his father demonstrate in his classroom. The appeal of Obama senior was the appeal of the strange, wise African who was embroiled in some of the most exciting anti-colonial struggles of the day. The son, however, could not use the same self-presentation; he was operating in a very different milieu and would have to market himself in a different manner. He needed a different sales pitch and now he had found one. He would become Black America's great historical representative, perhaps even the first black president of the United States. Paradoxically he would achieve that status by lactification, by social and cultural whitening, by becoming White America's All-Time Favorite Black Man.

Obama's lactification strategy had two elements. The first is to avoid as much as possible the race issue, to project a nonracial image. Obama has in general been very good at this. The only time he slipped was about six months into his presidency, when he intervened in the arrest of the Harvard scholar Henry Louis Gates. The police were responding to reports of a break-in. As it turned out, Gates was trying to get into his own house, but rather than cooperate with the authorities, he became abusive and told the arresting officer, "This is what happens to black men in America," and "you don't know who you're messing with." Asked about the incident, Obama commented publicly that "the Cambridge police acted stupidly." Boldly, the police department fired back at Obama, demanding that he familiarize himself with the facts. Recognizing that public support was mobilizing behind the cops, Obama quickly backtracked, taking back his criticism of the police department and inviting both Gates and the officer to the White House for an amicable reconciliation.[12]

The Harvard incident shows that, in private, Obama is not quite the race-neutral figure that he projects himself to be in public. Still, Obama has consistently upheld his public indifference to race both in his presidential campaign and so far in the Oval Office. Obama writes in *The Audacity of Hope*, "I reject a politics that is based solely on racial identity . . . or victimhood generally," and he has lived up to that statement. In that book, Obama even calls for a modification of affirmative action programs so that they are based on need and benefit all races. During his presidential campaign, Obama kept what his staffers called "radioactive" blacks at a safe distance. As president, Obama has been refreshingly unwilling to blame racism for his political problems. Even as his approval ratings have fallen, Obama has consistently denied that this is due to white racism, pointing out that "I was actually black before the election."[13]

The second part of Obama's lactification strategy was to present himself as part of the cultural mainstream. Not completely: Obama knew the benefit of maintaining a residue of cultural strangeness in order to confirm his credibility as an outside guy who embraces mainstream values. That's why Obama so often campaigned by calling himself the "black man with the funny name." Obama pretended that this was a terrible political liability that he would just have to live with. But in fact it was a considerable asset. I discovered something similar myself many years ago. When I first graduated from college and began to publish articles, I considered changing my name. I told a friend and fellow writer, "I'm thinking about writing under my middle name. I'm going to go by Joseph, not Dinesh." He responded, "Are you crazy? Who can forget a name like Dinesh? Joseph is a boring name. Dinesh is very different, very cool. Stick with Dinesh." And I did. Obama stuck with his name not only because of his bond with his father, but also because his name marked him as different, and this was a large part of his appeal to white America.

Of course Obama couldn't be too different: he certainly didn't want to show up in an African outfit or sound foreign. (I too have jettisoned the sing-song Indian accent and the characteristic Indian head-wobble.) Obama knew that he needed to sound more like Tom Brokaw than like Nelson Mandela. As he told *New York* magazine, "The fact that I conjugate my verbs and speak in a typical Midwestern newscaster voice— there's no doubt that this helps ease communication between myself

and white audiences." At the same time, Obama understood that lacti-
fication allowed for an occasional fallback into the Ebonics mode.
Obama added, "There's no doubt that when I'm with a black audience
I slip into a slightly different dialect."[14]

The right cadence, however, was not enough; there was also the matter of content. Obama recognized that he had to deliver radical and even
revolutionary themes in a bland, anodyne way so that they could cross
the threshold of political acceptability. Here Obama knew that he would
have to become the Translator, someone who could almost mechani-
cally convert anti-colonial politics into a rhetoric that sounds harmless
and even beneficial to the people who are the targets of that politics.
This was not an easy challenge, yet Obama was entirely up to it.

The approach that Obama developed is really quite simple. On a
given issue, Obama begins by contrasting two extreme positions, and
then he presents his view as the rational and middle-of-the-road solution, even if there is nothing rational or middle-of-the-road about it. For
instance, if Obama wants to argue for confiscatory taxes, he insists that
there are some in society who don't think the rich should pay any taxes
at all. There are others who say that the rich should give up all their
income in taxes. Obama, ever the mediator of these differences, then
declares that he will settle for the rich paying their fair share—say 40 or
50 percent. In this way Obama's outrageously high taxation comes to
seem sensible against the backdrop of two extreme positions, even
though no one really holds those positions.

I am caricaturing Obama's approach a little, but only a little. Here is
an actual example from *The Audacity of Hope*. Obama considers the
stance of his Republican opponents who hold to "the absolutism of the
free market, an ideology of no taxes, no regulation, no safety net."[15] Do
you know anyone who actually espouses this view? Neither do I. But this
is Obama's perfected technique: he invents outrageous positions and

attributes them to his critics so that his own positions always come out sounding centrist and sensible. If you listen to him carefully, you can easily detect his bogus framework of "two extremes with me in the middle." Now when I hear him go at it on various issues, I simply chuckle and tell myself I am listening to the lactification man.

It has certainly worked for him. Not only was Obama elected senator of a major state, he won that office by decisively winning the white vote. Then he trounced Hillary Clinton for the Democratic nomination, overcoming the Clinton political machine. He was elected president with more votes that any Democrat had received in a generation, and he also won states like Virginia, North Carolina, Indiana, Florida, and Ohio that had traditionally voted Republican. Not only did Obama win close to 100 percent of black voters, he was the first Democrat to also win a majority of rich white voters. Among Americans who earn more than $200,000 a year, Obama beat out McCain by six percentage points.[16] As president, he has successfully launched a juggernaut of new legislation. In less than two years he has made remarkable progress in implementing his agenda—an agenda that prior to his election seemed completely outside the bounds of political possibility.

Certainly Obama had his share of luck, even more luck than the lead character in *Slumdog Millionaire*. After he entered a crowded Democratic primary in the 2004 Senate race, the front-runner Blair Hull was accused of beating his wife. That cleared the way for Obama to win the nomination. Then, in a sort of twofer, the Republican standard-bearer Jack Ryan became embroiled in his own sex scandal when his former wife made allegations involving strip clubs. When Ryan exited the race, his party nominated an out-of-state eccentric who kept attacking Obama for being out of step with God. Obama was elected by an overwhelming margin to the Senate. Interrupting his first term to challenge Hillary Clinton for the Democratic nomination for president, Obama discovered he could count on a huge reservoir of repressed disgust for the Clintons. Earlier, Democrats had held back their emotions, not wanting to help out the Republicans, but now they abandoned Hillary in droves and went for her unknown but uncontaminated rival. Obama, having won the Democratic nomination, then faced in John McCain a Republican who did not command the full support of his party. Moreover, the economy went into a nosedive a few weeks before the election, turning McCain's one selling point—experience—into a liability, because it was the guys with experience who seemed to have gotten us into this mess. Few people in American politics have enjoyed what Obama himself at an earlier stage of his career termed his "almost spooky good fortune."[17]

Even so, Obama could never have exploited these opportunities without his lactification strategy. Interestingly, a few people noticed the strategy during his various campaigns. When he ran for Senate, the *Chicago Tribune* published an article in its Sunday magazine called "The Skin Game" which asked: "Do white voters like Barack Obama because he's not really black?" And during the presidential campaign it was the unperceptive Joe Biden, now Obama's vice president, who put his finger on the source of Obama's appeal. During the Democratic primaries, Biden said, "I mean, you got the first mainstream African-American who is articulate and bright and clean and a nice-looking guy."[18] This was a gaffe by columnist Michael Kinsley's definition of the term: a gaffe is when a politician accidentally tells the truth. Biden was promptly chastised for his racial insensitivity and he apologized. Actually Biden was simply saying what many people believe but are afraid to say. And Biden's point wasn't racist: he wasn't saying that it's rare for a black person to be bright and articulate. Rather, he was saying that Obama's political attractiveness derives not merely from his blackness but also from the fact that he happens to be a particular kind of black guy, a black guy who sounds—well, pretty white.

It was at the 2004 Democratic National Convention that Obama's lactification strategy paid its first big dividend. The audience at the convention, and in the media, and around the nation, was electrified not only by what was said, but also by who was saying it. The messenger in this case was just as important as the message. Here, for the first time, we saw the emergence of the Obama Choir. One of the founders of that movement is surely columnist Anna Quindlen, who described her reaction to Obama as one of the "solitary lunatic... standing up and cheering at the TV." Actually Quindlen had no idea that she was a dupe of Obama's lactification strategy. He had virtually handed the woman a racial absolution certificate, and she was cheering him for making her feel good about herself. Despite her sense of solitary ecstasy, Quindlen was no isolated lunatic; she had lots of company in the mainstream media. As one of Obama's media aides Julian Green put it, "We actually have fans among the media. I've never run across that for any other politician."[19]

Obama's lactification technique also came to his rescue during the Jeremiah Wright controversy. This was a very dangerous scandal for Obama. It threatened to expose him as a radical masquerading as a mainstream centrist, an anti-colonial revolutionary posing as an "aw shucks" all-American. Let's see how Obama got out of that one. Remarkably no one in the mainstream media had paid much attention to Wright; in fact, hardly anyone bothered to investigate Obama for anything. While the *New York Times* ran a long—and as it turned out false—article accusing John McCain of having an affair with an aide, Obama's personal life was completely taboo. The mainstream media thoroughly checked out McCain's vice presidential pick Sarah Palin, even reporting on her daughter's sex life and her husband's drunk driving citation from two decades earlier. It was the conservative media—notably Sean Hannity of Fox News Channel—that first began to report on Wright. Even when the Wright scandal broke, the networks and major newspapers pretended not to notice. The *New York Times* refused to report Wright's incendiary comments for more than two months, and then bowdlerized them to make them sound tame. Here is how the *Times* portrayed Wright's remarks about 9/11: "Mr. Wright said the attacks were a consequence of violent American policies."[20] That's it. Nothing about God damn America or chickens coming home to roost!

On March 18, 2008, Obama delivered his now-famous speech addressing the race question at the National Constitution Center in Philadelphia. The speech was, from start to finish, a masterpiece of obfuscation. "I suppose the politically safe thing would be to move on from this episode and just hope it fades into the woodwork," Obama said. This is just what the *New York Times* and other Obama Choir outlets had been trying to accomplish for their man, but by this point the attempt had failed. Obama had to face the issue. So he was not doing the brave thing, only the politically necessary thing. Obama continued, "The fact is that the comments that have been made and the issues that have surfaced . . . reflect the complexities of race in this country that we've never really worked through—a part of our union that we have yet to perfect." Pure diversion. The comments of Obama's preacher were about American foreign policy and how America was the primary force for evil in the world. Obama sought to deflect attention from the content of Wright's explosive words by pretending that they were part of some kind of ongoing national seminar on race relations.

Finally Obama pretended that Wright's denunciations of America were news to him, and that Wright was just not the fellow that he'd known for twenty years. These whoppers were topped off with Obama's high-minded excuse for not disowning Wright. "I can no more disown him that I can my white grandmother—a woman who helped raise me . . . but a woman who once confessed her fear of black men who passed by her on the street, and who on more than one occasion has uttered racial or ethnic stereotypes that made me cringe."[21] Now stereo-types are basically generalizations, and generalizations can be false or true; which cringe-inducing stereotypes his grandmother held, Obama did not say. Somehow, in Obama's mind, Madelyn Dunham's occa-sional use of these stereotypes and her understandable desire not to be hassled by a black panhandler put her in the same category as the hate-filled, paranoid Jeremiah Wright. Once again making himself equidis-tant from two unacceptable extremes, Obama even-handedly said he could no more throw Jeremiah Wright overboard than he could throw grandma overboard (although later the irrepressible Wright was indeed given the heave-ho).

Far from calling Obama on these shameful evasions and bogus equiv-alences, the mainstream media went into an orgy of congratulation. Typical was the *New York Times*, which compared our Artful Dodger's speech to the orations of John F. Kennedy. An accompanying *Times* edi-torial made the message even more explicit. It was titled, "Obama's Pro-file in Courage." On television, the sycophantic Chris Matthews claimed Obama's remarks constituted the "best speech ever given on race rela-tions in this country," one that was "worthy of Abraham Lincoln" and should be required reading in classrooms around the country.[22] With media obeisance like this, you know that you are virtually unstoppable.

Election night was an eerie moment—at least for Obama. Put your-self in his place. Here you are, the insecure, rotund kid who grew up in Hawaii and Indonesia. Your life has been shaped by a father you barely knew, a man who grew up in a hut and had multiple wives and drank himself to death. Your ideology, inherited from that strange man, could scarcely be more remote from what most Americans care about. Yet here you are, right in the center of everything, just elected forty-fourth president of the United States, the most powerful man in the world. What a feat! What a consummation! Now, finally, the dream can become a reality. Now, at last, the rage can find its true object. Putting on his calmest expression, Obama promised the American people that "change has come to America."[23] He wasn't kidding.

CHAPTER 8

HUMBLING THE OVERCLASS

I f we want to understand what kind of change has come to America, we should begin with Barack Obama. No, not *that* Barack Obama. I mean Barack Obama Sr. If we consider the senior Obama's anti-colonial philosophy, and once again take up his 1965 paper on African socialism, we will find ourselves with a very useful guide to the current goings-on in the White House. The ideology of the father is the key to the public policy actions of the son. So let's consider how the senior Obama might view the challenges and opportunities of the American presidency. In a word, what would this Luo tribesman do if he were making decisions in the Oval Office?

In this chapter we focus on economic change. For Barack Obama Sr. that would raise the issue of neocolonialism. Recall that neocolonialism is the situation facing a country when actual colonialism has ended; neo-colonialism is the economic exploitation that remains even after political independence. Barack Obama Sr. would have agreed with the anti-colonial writer Amilcar Cabral that "national liberation exists when and only when the national productive forces have been completely freed from all kinds of foreign domination." And he would have seconded Frantz Fanon's contention that "colonialism and imperialism have not paid their score when they withdraw their flags and their police forces." Rather, these oppressors have to realize that "the wealth of the imperial countries is our wealth too.... For in a very concrete way Europe has stuffed herself inordinately with the gold and raw materials of the colonial countries.... Europe is literally a creation of the Third World." This awareness, Fanon concludes, produces a "double realization: the realization by the colonized peoples that it is their due and the realization by the capitalist powers that they must pay."[1]

These anti-colonial writers were focused on Europe as the colonial power, as it was in their time. But when Barack Obama Sr. came to America, he recognized that all of this was changing. Even in the 1950s, the United States was becoming the power to be reckoned with; American domination has only increased in the ensuing decades. Applying the senior Obama's anti-colonial model to the United States, we would expect him to have advocated that everything possible be done to weaken the economic hegemony of America, to achieve a more equitable world where the weaker nations become stronger and the strong ones weaker, and he would have supported massive transfers of wealth from America to formerly colonized nations.

The critique of neocolonialism espoused by Obama's father operates on the conviction that Western banks, investment houses, insurance companies, oil and mineral companies, and—we can add for good measure—the automobile and the pharmaceutical industries, are owned and operated by rich fat cats. This group—let's call it the overclass— achieves its position by exploiting the weak and the poor. As he argued in his paper, Obama Sr. sought to use the power of the state to bring down this overclass. Certainly the senior Obama's socialism wasn't doctrinaire. While the hard-line socialists wanted to abolish private property and equalize wealth and income, Obama Sr.'s goals were narrower: subduing neocolonial institutions mattered more to him than making everything equal. Obama Sr. would have attempted to wring the colonialism out of American society by curbing the wealth of the overclass and by bringing corporate America under state control. Let us examine how all of this squares with the agenda of the younger Obama—our President Obama.

I'd like to begin with a story from the August 18, 2009, issue of the *Wall Street Journal.* The headline reads, "Obama Underwrites Offshore Drilling." Did you read that correctly? You did. The Obama administration supports offshore drilling. But it's drilling off the shore of Brazil. With Obama's backing, the U.S. Export-Import bank offered two billion dollars in loans and guarantees to Brazil's state-owned oil company Petrobras to finance exploration in the Santos Basin near Rio de Janeiro. Apparently Petrobras would like even more money, and so the Obama administration is considering increasing the amount. Note that Obama is not funding Brazilian exploration so that the oil ends up in the United States; he is funding Brazilian exploration for the oil to stay in Brazil.

Now consider the fact that the Obama administration has been working overtime to block offshore drilling in the United States. First Obama issued a decree outlawing all drilling below a depth of 500 feet—in other words, the majority of all new offshore drilling in America. When a federal court judge blocked this order, the Obama administration got around the ruling by issuing a new decree banning all drilling from floating platforms. Actually this was an even more sweeping ban than the one that the court had struck down. The effect of Obama's offshore drilling ban is not only to put thousands of Americans out of work, but also to force drilling companies to move their assets to other parts of the world.

The entire American energy infrastructure has been harmed by Obama's drilling moratorium.

Given these facts, the editorial writers at the *Wall Street Journal* are baffled by Obama's subsidy for Petrobras. They write, "Americans are right to wonder why Obama is underwriting in Brazil what he won't allow at home."[2] This seems like a double standard, but usually behind every double standard is a single standard waiting to be uncovered. In this case the bafflement disappears when we apply the senior Obama's anti-colonial perspective. This model predicts that President Obama would do everything he can to transfer wealth from the colonizers to the colonized. Evidently Obama wants America to curtail its energy consumption so that developing countries like Brazil can enjoy greater access to cheap energy. The issue, you see, has nothing to do with drilling per se or even protecting the environment; it's all about shifting the balance of energy consumption away from the West and toward the developing world.

I admit it is a little frightening to contemplate the prospect of a U.S. president assiduously working to reduce America's standard of living. But as we'll see, it's part of a consistent pattern that we can now begin to chart. Obama's Petrobras decision is part of his broader energy and environmental policy. The cornerstone of that policy is his cap and trade legislation. Obama's proposal is for the government to sell carbon permits that would restrict carbon emissions by making companies pay for the right to release carbon into the atmosphere. The House has already passed a version of Obama's cap and trade legislation, although it is stalled in the Senate. Obama seems determined to make this a major initiative if he can move the Senate to change its mind. Obama's energy secretary has already declared carbon a "pollutant," even though without carbon no life forms on earth would exist. But this way Obama can achieve through regulation what Congress has so far refused to approve through legislation, and the net effect of this would be to put strong curbs on America's energy production and consumption.

Obama is also directing the U.S. government to invest billions of dollars in solar and wind energy. In addition, he is using bailout leverage to compel the Detroit auto companies to build small, "green" cars, even though no one in the government has investigated whether consumers are interested in buying small, "green" cars—the Obama administration just believes they should. All these measures, Obama recognizes, are expensive. The cap and trade legislation is estimated to impose an $850 billion burden on the private sector; together with other related measures, the environmental tab will exceed $1 trillion. This would undoubtedly impose a significant financial burden on an already-stressed economy.

These measures are billed as necessary to combat global warming. Yet no one really knows if the globe is warming significantly or not, and no one really knows if human beings are the cause of the warming or not. For years people went along with Al Gore's claim that "the earth has a fever," a claim illustrated by misleading images of glaciers disappearing, oceans swelling, famines arising, and skies darkening. Apocalypse now! Now we know that the main body of data that provided the basis for these claims appears to have been faked. The Climategate scandal showed that scientists associated with the Intergovernmental Panel on Climate Change were quite willing to manipulate and even suppress data that did not conform to their ideological commitment to global warming.[3] The fakers insist that even if you discount the fakery, the data still show.... But who's in the mood to listen to them now?

Independent scientists who have reviewed the facts say that average global temperatures have risen by around 1.3 degrees Fahrenheit in the past 100 years. Lots of things could have caused that. Besides, if you project further back, the record shows quite a bit of variation: periods of warming, followed by periods of cooling. There was a Medieval Warm Period around 1000 A.D., and a Little Ice Age that occurred several hundred years later. In the past century, the earth warmed slightly from 1900 to 1940, then cooled slightly until the late 1970s, and has resumed warming slightly since then.

How about in the past decade or so? Well, if you count from 1998, the earth has cooled in the past dozen years. But the statistic is misleading, since 1998 was an especially hot year. If you count from 1999, the earth has warmed in the intervening period. This statistic is equally misleading, because 1999 was a cool year. This doesn't mean that temperature change is in the eye of the beholder. It means, in the words of Roy Spencer, former senior scientist for climate studies at NASA, that "all this temperature variability on a wide range of time scales reveals that just about the only thing constant in climate is change."[4]

Isn't Obama supposed to be in favor of change? Well, not in this case apparently. He wants the earth to stop changing like this. Perhaps he is right and man-made global warming is a problem. But even if it is, the question to consider is whether it's worth spending the money to try to stop the warming, or whether we should learn how to adapt to it. Human life on earth is not likely to be jeopardized if the planet is a few degrees warmer one hundred or two hundred years from now. Eminent scientists such as Freeman Dyson of Princeton and Richard Lindzen of MIT have pointed out that living creatures have adapted to all kinds of temperature variations in the course of history. It also seems likely that people living fifty or one hundred years from now will be much richer than we are and have much better technology to deal with the possibility of global warming.

How does Obama view the issue? Speaking before the United Nations Summit on Climate Change in September 2009, Obama did his best Al Gore imitation. "Rising sea levels threaten every coastline. More powerful storms and floods threaten every continent. More frequent drought and crop failures breed hunger and conflict.... The security and stability of each nation and all peoples—our prosperity, our health, our safety—are in jeopardy. And the time we have to reverse this tide is running out." Obama did not offer a shred of evidence that any of this is imminent.

Rather, Obama's goal seemed to be one of whipping up frenzy for the purpose of...well, here is where it gets interesting, and where the Obama agenda and the Gore agenda diverge. Gore basically wants everyone in the world to curb their standard of living to save the planet. That's not going to happen, but at least it's consistent. Obama has a different idea. He certainly wants America to make significant sacrifices to combat global warming. Not only does he seek to raise business costs, but he recognizes that those costs are likely to be passed on to the consumer. Carbon taxes are going to make most everything cost more because nearly all goods and services require energy to produce. Obama acknowledges that Americans are likely to have "doubts and difficulties" about such a course, especially because "we seek sweeping but necessary change in the midst of a global recession." Still, Obama is determined to move ahead. "Difficulty is no excuse for complacency." And Obama wants the European countries to join America in this project.

Given Obama's emphasis on America and the West, one might think that America was the largest carbon dioxide emitter in the world. But no. The *New York Times* reports that in 2007 China overtook the United States as the world's leading producer of carbon dioxide. In fact, China accounted for two thirds of the growth in the year's global greenhouse gas emissions.[5] Of course China needs more energy because of its fast-growing economy. In this respect it is joined by India, whose demand for energy is also rapidly increasing. Economist Martin Feldstein pointed out the obvious implication: whatever America does to reduce carbon emissions is likely to prove useless because it will be more than canceled out by increased emissions in China and India.[6] So what does Obama intend to do about Chinese and Indian emissions? Well, he intends to give them both some stern advice. They should, he tells the United Nations, "do their part." Actually India's environmental minister Jairam Ramesh has already informed the U.S. State Department that India has no interest in abiding by carbon emissions targets.

But this isn't just about the big countries like India, China, and America. Other poor and developing nations are also trying to improve their standard of living, and this requires that they raise—not curtail—their energy consumption. Obama stressed to the UN that it would be hard for the poorer countries of the world to do anything by themselves for the environment. Therefore, "we have a responsibility to provide the financial and technical assistance needed to help these nations adapt to the impacts of climate change and pursue low-carbon development."[7]

This isn't just talk: the agreement coming out of the UN Summit proposed that the West fork over $100 billion to developing countries in exchange for those countries agreeing to some limits on their carbon use.[8] The Obama administration supports this measure, although Congress has so far refused to go along. During his time in the Senate, Obama attempted an even bigger transfer of wealth: he sponsored the Global Poverty Act that would have committed the United States to spending over $800 billion over a decade or so to eradicate poverty in the Third World and also to enable Third World countries to follow Western environmental standards.[9] Obama seems convinced that there is a "climate debt" that rich nations owe poor nations. When it comes to combating global warming, he is determined to ensure that the rich nations pay not only their share but also the share of the poor nations.

What's the effect of all this? Obviously it is to make the rich nations poorer and the poor nations richer. See how this fits neatly into the anti-colonial paradigm? Obama's basic assumption is that America and the West are using up too much of the planet's resources. This is a huge theme with Obama; he never stops talking about it. In a 2008 appearance on *60 Minutes*, for instance, Obama told interviewer Steve Kroft, "This has been our pattern. We go from shock to trance. You know, oil prices go up, gas prices at the pump go up, everybody goes into a flurry of activity. And then prices go back down again and suddenly we act like it's not important, and we start, you know, filling up our SUVs again. And, as a consequence, we never make any progress. It's part of the addiction, all right. That has to be broken. Now is the time to break it."[10]

For Obama, the high oil prices aren't the problem; America's level of consumption is the problem. America's energy "addiction" is presumed to be a new form of neocolonial exploitation: the planet has limited resources, and the greedy West is taking a disproportionate share. So Obama's cap and trade policies are aimed at taxing America and using some of that money to subsidize the wretched of the earth. He is raising the cost of doing business for the colonizers in order to give an economic advantage to the colonized. Who cares whether the planet is actually getting hotter or colder? As long as Obama achieves this transfer of income from the big guys to the little guys, he will most likely consider his environmental and energy policies a success.

In focusing on Obama's energy and environmental policy I have, in a sense, gotten ahead of myself. So let's back up a bit and examine how Obama's anti-colonial agenda began with the very first days of his presidency—days he spent not undermining the overclass and the big banks but bailing them out. Actually, Obama began both by attacking the big banks and by rescuing them from apparent financial ruin. Previously the Bush administration had approved a multibillion dollar bailout plan for Wall Street and the banks. For many, that may not come as a surprise: Republicans are known to be friendly to Wall Street and the bankers.

But from the beginning Obama went along with this plan, actually expanding it along the way. Now why would he do that?

In the months leading up to the 2008 presidential election, the economy went into a free-fall. The free-fall began with a Wall Street financial crisis that involved major investment firms—Lehman Brothers, Bear Stearns, Merrill Lynch—as well as the nation's largest mortgage companies, Fannie Mae and Freddie Mac, and also the nation's largest insurance company, American International Group (AIG). All were going down, and taking the stock market with them. The Dow Jones average plunged 2,500 points from 11,000 in September to around 8,500 in October. Economic activity virtually froze, and a panicked Bush administration prepared plans for a massive $700 billion bailout, paid for with taxpayer money.

For the hapless Bush team, already in the process of cleaning out their desks, this was a basic issue of saving a legacy. But from the outset Obama wholeheartedly supported the bailout. The reason for this is suggested in something that Obama's adviser, and later his chief of staff, Rahm Emanuel said. "You never want a serious crisis to go to waste. What I mean by that is it's an opportunity to do things you could not do before."[11] But what is it that Obama wanted to do? At first glance it seems that he must have wanted to save the economy. Maybe he thought that in order to save Main Street you have to save Wall Street. But Obama usually portrays the interests of Wall Street as opposed to those of Main Street. Moreover, while it's clear that the financial sector was suffering a liquidity crisis, it's not clear that it was suffering a bankruptcy crisis. Panics can cause people to act hastily, but in retrospect it's not obvious that a bailout of this magnitude was even necessary.

For Obama, however, the bailout was an opportunity to rescue Wall Street and the banks even while lambasting the financial sector for getting the country into this mess. This drumbeat has continued for two years. To get a small whiff of Obama's rhetoric, in late 2009 he blasted "fat cat bankers on Wall Street" who had not displayed "a lot of shame" and "still don't get it" about why the public was infuriated with them. In January 2010, Obama said his determination to regulate the financial sector "is only heightened when I see reports of massive profits and obscene bonuses." In April 2010, he scolded Wall Street: "A free market was never meant to be a free license to take whatever you can get, however you can get it." Big, fat executive bonuses, he said, "offend our fundamental values."[12]

Obama's main charge was that Wall Street had succumbed to "greed." But if you think about it, Wall Street is based on greed. People go there to make money. What inhibits greed on Wall Street is not public-minded altruism but rather fear. Greed drives the aggressive desire to make more money while caution is produced by the fear of losing money. If financial crises were merely the result of outbreaks of greed, Wall Street would be in perpetual crisis. Our economic system is based on directing or channeling greed in such a way that it serves the economic welfare of society. Somewhere along the way, this channeling system broke down, and that's what caused our financial system to go into a tailspin.

But how did it break down? While Obama conveniently blamed the investment bankers, in reality a good deal of the blame lay with the U.S. government.[13] For nearly two decades, both Congress and the Republican and Democratic administrations have been pushing to expand housing loans to more and more Americans. Activist groups such as ACORN—where Obama worked both in New York and Chicago—demanded that banks change their lending practices to benefit minorities and the poor. Now these lending practices had been in place for a long time. Traditionally you cannot buy a house unless you can afford a 20 percent down payment and show that you have a steady, dependable income. But since houses had been rising in value, many politicians and community activists figured that lending standards could be lowered. Even if people couldn't make the payments, the house could always be sold at a profit and no one would get hurt.

Consequently, Congress, which regulates banks and mortgage companies, began to push for easier lending standards. Fannie Mae and Freddie Mac, which were set up by the government and always had implicit government backing, virtually abandoned responsible lending criteria and encouraged private banks to do the same. In fact, when banks made irresponsible loans they could package and bundle them and then sell them to Fannie and Freddie, thus transferring the risk to these quasi-government entities. This lending binge was lubricated with interest rates that were kept low by another government entity, the Federal Reserve. The Federal Reserve also lowered bank reserve requirements—the minimum amount of capital that banks are required to maintain when they make loans of a certain size.

Once the government kicked off this reckless binge, it created an infectious mood across the country. Soon everyone got into the spirit. Bankers found they could make more federally guaranteed loans. Mortgage writers introduced all kinds of go-go financing schemes such as teaser rates and negative amortization. Wall Street found it could profitably trade bundles of these loans in a form called mortgage-backed securities. Ordinary Americans on shaky financial ground discovered that, hey, they could afford expensive houses with modest initial monthly payments and little or no money down.

The financial crisis occurred when interest rates began to rise and housing prices began to fall. That's when people began to default on those loans and, in some cases, to stop making payments and walk away from the houses they had bought. Suddenly the banks realized that this problem could be very widespread, and since no one knew what the default rate might turn out to be, no one knew what those mortgage-backed securities were really worth. Wall Street had been buying and selling the securities in the expectation of traditionally low default rates. When investment houses figured out that they were holding "toxic" assets that might be worth only a fraction of their list price, they began to sell those assets at fire-sale prices. Investors with money parked at these investment houses feared losing their capital and demanded it back. A "run" on the investment houses ensued, and many found themselves facing liquidation and, in some cases, bankruptcy. This, then, was the panic that produced the Great Recession of 2008.

But it was a recession, not a depression. Its speed caught everyone by surprise, but America had endured severe recessions before, most recently in 1981–1982. To this day, economists debate whether the financial sector faced a crisis of bankruptcy or merely a crisis of liquidity. Bankruptcy means that your liabilities outweigh your assets, you cannot meet your debts, and under ordinary circumstances you should go out of business. A liquidity crisis means that you have the assets but you cannot convert them into cash right away. Now behind the so-called mortgage-backed securities were real homes and real people, most of whom were making regular monthly mortgage payments. Sure, some of these people may end up defaulting on their loans, but they hadn't defaulted yet. The problem with the securities wasn't that they had little or no value, but that no one had a good idea of what their value was. Uncertainty, rather than bankruptcy, seemed to be the real problem.

The federal government needed to restore liquidity throughout the financial system, so that banks could make loans once again; but just as important, the government needed to revive business, consumer, and investor confidence in the economy. Obama's blasting of bankers and Wall Street executives could hardly be expected to restore business confidence. But even more revealing were Obama's policy remedies, which tell us a lot about his real economic objectives.

First, the administration not only provided bailout funds for banks, but it also wrote the terms of those bailouts in such a way that the federal government would retain control over the banks. This is not to say that the government had no control before; banks have always been federally regulated. But Obama has expanded federal power over the banking sector. One clue to Obama's intentions is that his administration insisted on bailing out not just banks that were failing but also banks that were not. Some 300 banks were force-fed a federal infusion of $200 billion. The largest banks all got infusions of capital, whether they wanted them or not.[14]

Some banks of course desperately needed the money, but others did not. Yet it seems that Obama wanted to exercise federal leverage over those banks as well. Most of the banks have now repaid their bailouts. But in some cases the Obama administration has refused to permit large banks to make repayments.[15] Now this is very strange: you might expect that the government would, on behalf of the taxpayer, welcome the idea of getting its money back. But if the government takes back the money, then it no longer has the same degree of control over that bank. So Obama has approved a "stress test" in which the government decides which banks are economically healthy enough to be allowed to pay their bailouts back.

Normally moneylenders don't need to do stress tests: if the guy is willing to pay his loan, it's safe to assume he is in a position to do so. But the stress test keeps the decision in the hands of the government, not the banks, no matter how eager the bank may be to escape the clutches of the government.

Now one might assume that a financially healthy bank that has passed Obama's stress test should be able to repay its bailout. Not so, according to Obama's Treasury Secretary Timothy Geithner. Geithner told the *Wall Street Journal* that the health of individual banks isn't enough to qualify them to repay the government. "We want to make sure that the financial system is not just stable but also not inducing a deeper contraction in economic activity. We want to have enough capital that it's going to be able to support a recovery."[16] In essence, the banks have to wait until the Obama administration decides that it's in the national interest for them to repay.

Second, the Obama administration diverted bailout money to rescue two of the Big Three Detroit auto companies, General Motors and Chrysler. Now as an economic solution, Obama's actions were both unwise and unnecessary. The auto companies have been mismanaged for decades—partly because of the ineptitude of the bosses, partly because of the millstone effect of the auto unions. In an attempt to extract as much as possible from management, the unions have raised the cost of making cars so high that Detroit is no longer competitive. Japanese companies can make better cars in American plants for a cheaper price. Detroit is going under because it deserves to go under. Sure, a bailout can postpone the day of reckoning in the faint hope that Detroit will get its act together. But only an investor who is using other people's money would be so careless as to take this kind of a chance.

No sooner did the Obama administration approve the General Motors bailout than Obama ordered the firing of General Motors chairman Rick Wagoner. Certainly Wagoner was an inept executive who deserved to go, but by this standard all the major Detroit auto executives deserve to go. To get an idea of what buffoons these people are, when Congress asked them to testify about their dire financial straits, they all traveled to Washington, D.C., in private jets. Congressmen had a great time castigating them for that in front of the TV cameras. So Wagoner was just one poor performer in a circus of poor performers. His ousting may have been overdue, but it is not usually the role of United States presidents to fire inept CEOs of big corporations. Obama was using the occasion to show who's in charge.

In the case of GM and Chrysler, the Obama administration renegotiated the terms of creditor contracts so that the union pension plans would get preferential treatment and Chrysler's investors would move to the back of the line. For Obama the recovery of GM and Chrysler seemed less important than figuring out how the spoils would be carved up. No one should have been surprised by Obama's behavior. As he wrote in *The Audacity of Hope*, "I owe those unions. When their leaders call, I do my best to call them back right away.... I got into politics to fight for these folks."[17] To put Obama's comments in their appropriate context, think of Chrysler's investors as part of the profit-seeking neocolonial overclass. And think of the unions as the struggling, lowly resisters who are fighting against that overclass. Now you can see why empowering the unions and weakening the claims of the investors took priority for Obama over everything else. Whether Chrysler can actually avoid future bankruptcy, or whether taxpayer money is being wisely spent—none of this seemed to matter. A very different battle was being fought, and Obama got the outcome he wanted.

A third measure taken by Obama to respond to the financial crisis was to sign into law a bill containing the most sweeping regulations of Wall Street since the 1930s. Working with Senator Chris Dodd and Representative Barney Frank, the Obama administration secured congressional support for a series of measures that would transfer power from the financial sector to the federal government. For instance, the government would now have new authority to oversee financial firms, hedge funds, insurance companies, and even car dealers. The Obama administration can now monitor these companies, alter their capital requirements, and even shut them down and restructure them if they are deemed to be in danger of insolvency.[18]

Now with Wall Street, as with the car companies, the issue is not whether some form of government intervention was necessary. In this case I think it was necessary. But the objectives of reducing Wall Street's go-go financing schemes could more easily be met by reestablishing something like the old banking and lending requirements. If banks make loans that are federally guaranteed, then they must have a stated level of reserves to back up those loans. Mortgages should have a specified down payment or at least a specified level of risk. And that's it. But once again Obama's objectives appeared to have more to do with castigating the financial industry ("The American people will never again be asked to foot the bill for Wall Street's mistakes") and bringing the financial sector under federal control than any kind of genuine "reform." Reform for Obama means: from now on I tell you what to do.[19]

Obama's final strategy to combat the financial crisis was to open up the federal money faucet in an attempt to produce "stimulus" and "create jobs." But how does the federal government "stimulate" an economy? And how does it "create" a job? Let's take the job question first. Sure, the government can create jobs by, say, doubling the number of people who work at the post office, or by hiring more bureaucrats in this or that agency. But how does a government create jobs in the private sector? There is only one way: by providing incentives for entrepreneurs to hire more people. The best way to do this is to reduce corporate tax rates or capital gains taxes. Neither of these options was even considered by the Obama administration; in fact, Obama has proposed raising the capital gains tax from 15 to 28 percent.

Obama's stimulus package started at around $800 billion and will end up costing the taxpayer something close to a trillion dollars.[20] Obama insisted that the government spending this kind of money would get the economy going again. According to the Department of Labor, unemployment was at 7.7 percent in January 2009, when Obama took office, and now it is 9.5 percent.[21] Some stimulus! If you want to know why such programs usually don't work, ask yourself this question: from where does the government get the funds to stimulate? The answer, of course, is from the private sector. In some form or other, the government has to take money from taxpayers in order to spend that money itself.

Now imagine that you take $100 from me and spend it. How have you stimulated anything? Sure, you have more cash to spend than you did before, but now I have less cash to spend than I did before. So when the federal government uses taxpayer funds to repair roads or fund artists or build unnecessary airports in the districts of influential Congressmen, the government is taking away money that could have been used for other things, such as starting new businesses, making new products, and hiring new employees. In sum, the stimulus was less a boost to the overall economy than a transfer of spending power from the private sector to the federal government.[22] Once again it was an issue of control, and once again Obama came out a winner.

In this case, however, the full measure of Obama's victory is yet to be appreciated. Not only did Obama increase the power of the federal government through stimulus, he also got his chance to stick it to the fat cats. Sticking it to the fat cats is an important part of the anti-colonial program. And Obama made it clear from the outset that this group—the group he calls "the rich"—would pay for the whole thing. No tax increases on the ordinary American or the middle class. The entire bill, Obama promised, would be delivered to those Americans who make $250,000 a year or more, the overclass that, in Obama's words, is not "paying their fair share."[23]

It's worth asking, for a moment, what is meant by this term "fair share." What is fair for rich people to pay? Obama never addresses this question. But now consider the fact that, under today's tax structure, a person who is earning $1 million a year pays around $375,000 in federal taxes. That's not counting a whole raft of other taxes that typically raises the tab to around $450,000. That means if you make $1 million, you only keep $550,000. The government basically takes $450,000 off the top. Aren't you already paying your "fair share"? According to Obama, you are not. Now consider how much revenue the federal government currently gets from the rich. According to government data, the top 1 percent of income-earners in the country pays about 40 percent of all the income tax revenues. The next 9 percent of income earners pays another 30 percent. So the top 10 percent of income-earners pays more than 70 percent of all the taxes. As for the bottom 40 percent of income earners, they pay nothing.[24]

Now I don't know about you, but to my way of thinking this is an unfair system—it is unfair to the rich. First of all, I think that everyone except the truly poor should pay some taxes. If we believe in "no taxation without representation," then we should also believe in "no representation without taxation." In a democratic society, it is good for citizens to have at least some stake in the system. Moreover, we can all agree that the rich should pay more, but I think they should pay proportionately more. If we have an across-the-board income tax of say 20 percent, that would mean that the guy who makes $50,000 a year would pay $10,000; the guy who makes $500,000 a year would pay $100,000; and the guy who makes $5 million a year would pay $1,000,000. So people are paying different amounts, but they are paying at the same rate. That's fair—and I think that's fairness as most people understand the term.

But to the anti-colonial mindset, none of this is even relevant. The anti-colonialist believes that the rich have become rich at the expense of the poor; the wealth of the rich doesn't really belong to them; therefore whatever can be extracted from them is automatically just. If you could take everything they have, that would mean they were paying their "fair share," because their fair share is actually 100 percent. Recall what Obama's father said in his 1965 paper: there is no tax rate that is too high, and even a 100 percent tax rate can be justified under certain circumstances.

Now certainly President Obama can't say any of this, but if he believes it, that would explain why he seems indifferent to the magnitude of bills that he is racking up on behalf of the taxpayer. Obama's intention is to extract all that money from the overclass, and this to him is the hidden benefit of all this stimulus. It's not simply where the money goes; it's also a matter of making the fat cats pay. How delicious it must be for President Obama to run a trillion-dollar tab and hand it over to the overclass. How much he must wish he could tell his father about it so that they could both laugh their heads off at how the tables have been turned. Yes, dad sure would be proud if he could see him now.

Obama's most significant economic achievement to date is not financial regulation but health care reform. While the financial regulations were a response to an acknowledged crisis, the health care reform was not. Admittedly Obama acted as though this was all part of some grand economic strategy to put the country back on track. But if anything, the high cost of Obama's health care program will further burden the economy and stall future growth. We have to admire Obama's persistence here. The Clintons tried with health care and failed. Obama suffered some stinging setbacks, especially with Scott Brown's election in Massachusetts. Even so, Obama got the job done and signed America's biggest new federal program since the Great Society in the 1960s.

Now Obama was certainly right that health care in America is expensive and costs in recent years have soared. He also identified some other problems with the system, such as the fact that people who went from one company to another couldn't take their health insurance with them. Obama neglected to point out that the government was largely responsible for health insurance not being portable. That's because during the federal government-imposed wage and price controls of World War II, companies found that providing health insurance was a way to give employees compensation that went beyond the limits imposed by the law; that's how we got employer-provided, rather than individual-purchased, health insurance. But the biggest problem with America's health care system was, of course, cost. Obama made it sound as though high costs were preventing millions of Americans from getting health care. This was totally bogus. Even Americans who didn't have health insurance, either because they couldn't afford it or because they chose not to buy it, could still get treatment. No one, for instance, with a serious condition gets turned away from a hospital emergency room. Hospitals are absorbing those costs and, of course, passing them on to paying customers. So, granted, this is one factor driving up insurance premiums.

But the most important reason America's health care system is so costly is that it's the best health care system in the world. America leads the world in new drug development, and Americans have higher survival rates for most major illnesses, from cancer to heart disease. Better quality costs more. Also, people are living longer these days, and when we get older our health needs, and the cost of meeting those needs, rise. Technology now makes it possible to treat more illnesses and to prolong longevity, and all of this is very expensive.

Now of course we want to keep that quality, while reducing costs. Is there a way to do that? Yes. Perhaps the single biggest factor driving up costs is that the health care customer is not the one who is typically paying. If I go to my doctor and say my head hurts, the doctor is going to want to run a bunch of tests. He's probably going to do every possible test, because he doesn't want to leave even the slightest chance that he'll miss something and get sued. Now the reasonable question for me to ask is, "What tests do you think are the most effective? And how much is each one going to cost?" But in fact I never ask that question, because I'm not the one who is paying for the tests. My insurance company is paying; I'm only going to fork over the $20 copayment. So my attitude is, "Test away!"

Clearly the best way to reduce health care costs and reduce health insurance premiums is to restore customer control to the process. Why not leave America's health care system in place but alter the incentives that people face? If there was a way to put the money in the customer's pocket, then the customer would make sure that the money—*his* money—was wisely spent.[25] This was not Obama's approach; in fact, it did not receive serious consideration.

When Republicans proposed market-based approaches that empowered consumers, Obama was respectful but uninterested. Consequently, not a single Republican voted for Obama's health bill. Obama could have modified his plan by incorporating some Republican suggestions. This would not only have brought some GOP moderates to his side, it would also have increased public support for his program. Obama made no such effort. He completely ignored the Republicans. Politically, Obama's conduct is strange. Every Great Society program enjoyed substantial bipartisan support. Even the controversial Bush tax cuts, enacted shortly after George W. Bush was elected, were supported by twenty-eight Democrats in the House and twelve Democrats in the Senate. Obama could have won at least modest Republican support if he really wanted to. So why didn't he want to? The reason, I suspect, is that for Obama the Republicans are the neocolonial party. They are not just wrong; they are evil. Consequently Obama will "play nice," but only for show: in reality he has no desire to work with the enemy.

But what about the health insurance companies; aren't they Obama's real enemy? Yes and no. Obama has mercilessly lashed out at the insurance companies. The *Washington Post* reports that in a single speech he "castigated insurance companies 22 times." Among his comments: "We allow the insurance industry to run wild in this country."[26] For him, the insurance companies are part of the neocolonial problem. But here is the key point: they are only part of the problem as long as they are operating freely, raising prices, and exploiting the customer. But if the insurance companies can be brought under government supervision and government mandate, then they have been decolonized and become part of the solution. The ingenuity of Obama is to devise a comprehensive health care plan that the insurance industry would support. And indeed they did support it. They even agreed to spend $150 million in ads to promote it to the public.[27] Why would insurance companies do this? Is this a case of Lenin's prediction that the capitalists would sell the rope which would then be used to hang them?

Let's return to what genuine health care reform would look like. Such reform would be limited to providing catastrophic health insurance to Americans who could not afford it. Think about it: if I drop a lamp in my study and it breaks, I don't need insurance to replace it. Why not? Because I can afford to buy a new lamp. But if my house floods or burns to the ground, I need insurance. Why? Because that's a catastrophic loss that I cannot afford. Similarly with health care, if I have a cold, I and most Americans can afford $100 to go to the doctor, or even realize that a cold will go away on its own and I don't need to see a doctor at all. But if I need open heart surgery, then I need insurance. Now catastrophic health insurance is much cheaper than full-coverage insurance because catastrophic events are rare. Consequently Obama could have mandated catastrophic coverage for all Americans, with the government subsidizing the cost for low-income Americans. This, arguably, would have been reasonable and affordable health care reform that could have won bipartisan support.

Instead, Obama opted to force every American to buy comprehensive health insurance, and to force companies to provide insurance to people with pre-existing conditions. Predictably the health insurance companies didn't like the latter provision. In fact, from an insurance point of view, it made no sense to insure people who were already sick. The whole point of insurance is for healthy people to put money into a pot so that if someone gets sick in the future, there is a pool of money to pay for treatment. But Obama brought the insurance companies around by showing them that his overall scheme actually meant much more business for them. If all Americans are compelled by law to buy comprehensive health insurance, where are they going to buy it from except from the insurance companies? So rally around the president, boys, because there is money to be made. You see here why the charge that Obama is a socialist is once again off the mark? Obama is quite happy to rally the corporate capitalists to his side with the promise of big bucks—as long as the corporate capitalists are willing to succumb to a government leash and to being told what to do by Big Daddy Obama. The president is eager to create an alliance between the government and big corporations when it serves the anti-colonial agenda. The cost, of course, is borne by the American taxpayer. In the case of health insurance, the tab is estimated to be in the range of $1.6 trillion over the next decade.

I'm not a math major, but even I can add up the numbers. The bank bailout: $700 billion this year. Stimulus: between $800 billion and $1 trillion this year. Proposed environmental and energy regulations: approximately $1 trillion over the next several years. Health care: $1.6 trillion over the next decade. What is Obama doing to America? The U.S. government is now $14 trillion in debt, and the Congressional Budget Office projects that another $12 trillion will be added over the next decade. Obama didn't create these huge numbers, but he has been adding to them faster than any previous president. This fiscal year alone the Obama deficit is $1.4 trillion. These debts are liabilities owed by the American taxpayer, and they have to be paid now or in the future. About 45 percent of our public debt is held by individuals and governments of foreign countries, especially China and the oil-rich Muslim countries. China alone is sitting on reserves in excess of $2 trillion; if the Chinese demanded their money right now, it's hard to see how America could afford to pay.[28]

Debts, like ideas, have consequences. In their book, *The End of Influence*, economists Stephen Cohen and Bradford Long argue that as a consequence of American indebtedness to the rest of the world, American influence is likely to decline. "The United States will continue to be a world leader . . . but it will no longer be the boss." A similar point is made by Fareed Zakaria in *The Post-American World*. America's economic position "does not, despite the opinions of some pundits, signal the end of capitalism. But it might well mean the end of a certain kind of global dominance for the United States. . . . The crisis has had the effect of delegitimizing America's economic power. . . . The current economic upheaval will only hasten the move to a post-American world."[29] While most Americans are likely to view this change with foreboding, I see a lone man in the Oval Office watching these trends that he has helped to exacerbate, cheering them on and grinning in triumph.

CHAPTER 9

TAMING THE ROGUE NATION

For nearly a decade, America has been fighting a "war on terrorism" aimed at rooting out terrorist networks and undermining the "rogue states" that support terrorism. President Obama has called an end to this "war on terror"; indeed, he has instructed his leading Cabinet officials not to use the term, but to speak instead of police action against criminals.[1] Even as he attempts to wind down America's war on terrorist networks and rogue states, Obama is fighting his own war. Perhaps more precisely I should say that he is fighting his father's war. Barack Obama Sr. didn't write about foreign policy—he was, after all, an economist. Even so, he espoused a broad anti-colonial perspective that viewed the West and specifically America as the invader, occupier and terrorizer of the world. In line with the senior Obama's thinking, President Obama is conducting a war against what he considers to be the biggest rogue state of all: the United States of America.

I am not suggesting that Obama is anti-American. On the contrary, he seeks a radical change in America's policies because he considers those policies bad for America and bad for the world. America is, in Obama's view, the last of the neocolonial powers. Obama sees America as having invaded and occupied two sovereign nations, Iraq and Afghanistan. Now America is, in effect, ruling those nations in much the same way that the British and the French ruled their colonies either directly or through surrogates. For Obama, America is a kind of rogue elephant, and Obama views his anti-colonial mission as one of taming that elephant. Once you understand this about Obama, all his foreign policy actions become coherent and intelligible.

It may seem odd to hear America described as a colonial or imperial power. After all, the United States was itself once a colony of Great Britain. After World War II, the United States used its influence to compel Britain and France to grant independence to many of their colonies, giving America an anti-colonial reputation. Even now Americans don't think of themselves as colonialists; on the contrary, we see ourselves as champions of self-government and liberty. But anti-colonial writers point out that the white man settled America by displacing the native Indians and taking their land. The United States forcibly took large tracts of land from Mexico and annexed Hawaii. America also occupied the Philippines from 1899 to 1946, perhaps the closest thing to direct colonialism by the United States, and America still possesses other colonial spoils like Puerto Rico, Guam, and American Samoa.

After World War II, America became the heir to European supremacy. The baton of Western leadership passed from Europe to America. In *The Audacity of Hope*, Obama faults America for its role in supporting the repressive Suharto regime in Indonesia. "Suharto's army . . . targeted not just guerillas but civilians for swift retribution— murder, rape, villages set afire. And throughout the seventies and eighties, all this was done with the knowledge, if not outright approval, of U.S. administrations."[2] Still, that was the era of the Cold War, and the Soviet Union provided a rival and a balance to America's global engagements.

Once the Cold War ended, however, America became the world's sole superpower, a top dog without a rival, what one French minister termed a "hyperpower." This power became evident after 9/11. President George W. Bush issued a new national security strategy that explicitly stated that America would seek global and unchallenged military dominance. This wasn't mere rhetoric; during this period America responded to the 9/11 attacks by invading two countries, Afghanistan and Iraq. One of these countries, Iraq, seemed to have nothing to do with 9/11. America didn't get in and get out; it is still calling the shots in both countries, if not directly then through its local allies. This is precisely what the British and the French did in parts of Asia, Africa, and the Middle East.

Deepak Lal writes in a book on empire, "The United States since the Second World War has at first surreptitiously, and since 9/11 more openly, taken on the imperial role." Obama's teacher Edward Said concurred. "Much of the rhetoric of the New World Order promulgated by the American government since the end of the Cold War—with its redolent self-congratulation, its unconcealed triumphalism, its grave proclamations of responsibility—all too easily produces an illusion of benevolence when deployed in an imperial setting. It is a rhetoric whose most damning characteristic is that it has been used before, not just by Spain and Portugal but with deafeningly repetitive frequency by the British, the French, the Belgians, the Japanese, the Russians and now the Americans." And this is the way Obama sees it. In *The Audacity of Hope* Obama writes, "Roosevelt's version of the Monroe Doctrine—the notion that we could preemptively remove governments not to our liking—was now the Bush Doctrine, only extended beyond the Western

Hemisphere to span the globe. Manifest Destiny was back in fashion; all that was needed, according to Bush, was American firepower, American resolve, and a 'coalition of the willing.'"[3]

If America's current president sees America this way, he is joined in this respect by many of America's adversaries. Venezuela strongman Hugo Chavez, for example, employs a rhetoric that is militantly anti-colonial and hostile to American foreign policy. Similar strains are occasionally heard from Russia, Zimbabwe, and North Korea. Radical Islam takes a similar view of the United States. A generation ago, the Egyptian writer Sayyid Qutb, who has become the leading intellectual guru of Islamic radicalism, wrote of Islam as the only force resisting first European and then American colonialism. "The spirit of Islam is like a rock blocking the spread of imperialism." Today the influential Muslim cleric Yusuf al-Qaradawi, who broadcasts frequently on Al-Jazeera, routinely calls on Muslims to fight against "American occupation." In his video-tapes and messages over the years, Osama bin Laden accuses America of leading a "Judeo-Crusader alliance" to massacre Muslims and dispossess them of their land and oil wealth. Bin Laden has said that terrorism is merely the Muslim defense against "the blatant imperial arrogance of America," a nation seeking "to occupy our countries, steal our resources, and install collaborators to rule us."[4]

Obama clearly had no sympathy for Bin Laden and his radical cohorts, whom he views as gangsters and criminals. Even so, he appears to agree with their assessment that America is the neocolonial aggressor and that the best way to promote peace and security in the world is to curb America's power and influence. Jonathan Alter reports in *Newsweek* that one of Obama's first objectives upon taking office was to reduce the size and resources of the U.S. armed forces. Alter quotes Obama saying, "For the past eight years, whatever the military asked for they got. My job was to slow things down." Writing in the influential journal *Foreign Policy*,

Walter Russell Mead notes that Obama seeks to "create conditions that would allow him to dismantle some of the national security state inherited from the Cold War and given new life and vigor after 9/11."[5]

But Obama must be supremely careful in how he carries this out. He cannot announce to his fellow Americans that he intends to scale down the nation's defenses and reduce his country's influence in the world; even many of his supporters believe they elected him to boost our national security and enhance or at least preserve America's leadership. So Obama's challenge is to achieve as many of his anti-colonial objectives as are politically feasible. Moreover, he must always camouflage his overall aim and take specific actions that can be defended in more conventional terms.

One of Obama's first actions in the Oval Office was to repeal Bush's national security doctrine. His rationale seemed reasonable at the time: "The burden of this century cannot fall on our soldiers alone."[6] Many Americans were pleased that Obama should solicit foreign support for America's objectives, especially from our longtime allies in Europe. Why do things by ourselves when we can find others to join us? Yes, this sounds like a great idea.

But when we look more closely we see that Obama is up to something quite different. A few months into his presidency, Obama embarked on a kind of world tour. Visiting London in early April 2009, Obama told his English audience he had come "to listen, not to lecture." In Germany, he confessed, "I don't come bearing grand designs." Rather, "I'm here to . . . share ideas and to jointly . . . help shape our vision for the future."[7] The Europeans got the message: Obama was on an apology tour, repenting for the sins of the Bush administration. The real message of his "sharing" was that without European approval, there would be no more U.S. invasions, no more unilateral American military action. In a way, Obama was paying the former colonial powers the compliment of using them as a restraint on American power. Barely able to contain its excitement, the Norwegian Parliament promptly conferred on Obama the Nobel Peace Prize. Not that he had done anything to deserve it. The honor was basically for endorsing the Norwegian view of America's role in the world.

Next Obama carried his self-abasement routine from the colonizers to the colonized, from Europe to the more hostile regions of the world. At a meeting of South American nations on April 17, 2009, Obama told the leaders of Cuba, Venezuela, Bolivia, and Haiti, "I pledge to you that we seek an equal partnership. There is no senior partner and no junior partner. The United States will be willing to acknowledge past errors where those errors have been made." How nice for this motley Third World crew to discover that henceforth they would be operating on an equal plane with the United States. Warming to Obama's promise to acknowledge American misdeeds, Hugo Chavez presented Obama with a copy of Eduardo Galeano's *The Open Veins of Latin America*. The book's theme is conveyed by its subtitle, *Five Centuries of the Pillage of a Continent*. The continent, of course, is South America, and guess who is doing the pillaging? Too bad the book was in Spanish, a language Obama doesn't read, because its anti-colonial themes would have thoroughly resonated with him. Chavez may have addressed Obama in the wrong medium, but he was entirely on target in his message.[8]

Visiting China in November 2009, Obama did not hesitate to criticize the Chinese government for its violation of human rights. But this criticism was carefully balanced by his lamentations for America's own human rights record. Obama noted that while China was responsible for forced abortions and the coerced trafficking in women for prostitution, "We are not perfect.... If you talk to women in America, they will tell you that there are still men who have a lot of old-fashioned ideals about the role of women in society." Obama struck a similar note of moral equivalence in Turkey, where his criticism of the Turkish geno-cide of Armenians was qualified by his acknowledgment of America's own sins, such as its "treatment of native Americans."[9]

Some conservatives chastised Obama, pointing out the indignity of an American president giving such short shrift to his own country. These critics also noted the absurdity of Obama's comparisons between Amer-ica's past misdeeds and the ongoing, and vastly more serious, abuses by the nations the president was addressing. This criticism became even louder when Obama cancelled the deployment of antimissile defenses to Poland and the Czech Republic. Many on the right faulted Obama for his inability to distinguish between America's friends and America's enemies. Summing up these arguments, Victor Davis Hanson argued in a recent broadside that when you treat your enemies well and your friends badly, it seems that you have lost your compass.[10]

But these criticisms in a way miss the point, not because they are wrong but because they are not strong enough. Obama is too intelligent a man to intend his "you do sex slavery but we have husbands who won't do the dishes" analogies seriously. His larger point was to telegraph to the world that he intended to be a different kind of president, one whose main focus would be not on controlling the destiny of other nations, but rather on controlling the actions of his own country. Rather than Amer-ican foreign policy seeking to regulate the world, Obama was soliciting the world to help regulate American foreign policy. In other words, Obama hasn't lost his compass, as the critics allege; he seems to be oper-ating with a different compass.

Consider Obama's decision to deny Poland and the Czech Republic missile defense technology. The ostensible purpose of this was to appease Russia, and the goal of appeasing Russia was to win Russian cooperation on sanctions against Iran. If this was the goal, it manifestly failed. The Russians—just like the Chinese—have been dawdling on

sanctions since the idea was first proposed. Neither country believes it
is in its interest to impose severe sanctions on Iran because both have
valuable commercial contacts there. The Chinese continue to buy Iranian oil; the Russians sell military technology to Iran. Every time the Russians signal, however tentatively, that they will consider sanctions, the
White House is ecstatic. But somehow the Russians never come through
in supporting strong sanctions—the only kind of sanctions that have a
chance to make an impact.

Actually, it's doubtful that any kind of sanctions would work. They
haven't worked in restricting nuclear weapons anywhere else; for
instance, military analyst Graham Allison points out in *Foreign Affairs*
that America has had sanctions against North Korea for decades, and
the North Koreans have gone ahead and built ten nuclear bombs.[11] The
reason sanctions are a long shot with Iran is simple: the mullahs really
want to build a nuclear bomb. If you and I were mullahs, we'd want to
build a bomb. The Iranian regime has two good reasons to acquire
nuclear weapons. First, there are Jewish and Christian bombs in the
Middle East, but there is no Islamic bomb. An Iranian bomb would strike
real fear in both Israel and America; no longer could the West have its
way—not with Iran capable of setting off a regional nuclear holocaust.
Second, several Muslim countries are vying for supremacy in the Middle
East. The leading contenders are Iran, Egypt, and Saudi Arabia. Certainly
the Muslim country that goes nuclear immediately emerges as the top
dog. Yes, the Saudis have the two holy sites, but we have the nukes, baby.
Nukes bring you real respect. Twentieth century proverb: what do you
call a dictator who has nuclear weapons? Answer: Sir!

So the mullahs desperately want a bomb, and they have the capability to build it. Is there a way to stop them? Actually, yes. It is to support
Iranians who are eager to overthrow their repressive government. This
does not require an American invasion of Iran or any kind of a direct

military operation. Rather, it requires supporting indigenous groups ready to fight for freedom in their own country. This would be akin to what America did with the Afghan mujahedeen who were trying to push out their Soviet oppressors. America did not send troops, but it did send military and economic assistance. The Afghans did the fighting; Afghanistan became what Gorbachev termed a "bleeding wound," and the Soviets got out.

Is there a similar window of opportunity with Iran? In June 2009, there was. And think of the significance: Iran is the one important country whose government is in the hands of the radical Muslims. Countries like Syria and Egypt, for instance, are under secular rulers; Saudi Arabia and other sheikdoms of the Gulf are actually fighting their own wars against Al Qaeda. If America could help eject the Iranian regime, it would be a devastating blow to radical Islam. Not that there have been easy openings to do this. But just six months into his term in office, Obama had a rare chance when tens of thousands of Iranians took to the street to protest Mahmoud Ahmadinejad's blatant rigging of the Iranian presidential election.

Of course the Iranian mullahs have been rigging elections since 1979 when Khomeini first came to power. But this time many people had had enough. Controversy over the election rapidly led to demands for an end to the regime. True, the protests lacked a unifying leader, someone with the capacity of a Lech Walesa or Boris Yeltsin who could have rallied the people into effective action. Yet with the right kind of encouragement, such a leader might have emerged. So here was a magnificent opportunity for the Obama administration to embrace the rebel cause and actively support efforts to topple the regime.

In fact, Obama did nothing. He let the opportunity pass. And while the mullahs were cracking down on the protesters, Obama remarked that "they are in the middle of an extraordinary debate taking place in

Iran." Debate? I suppose you could call the sight of Iranian police beating up civilians on the street a debate. Obama also specified what he intended to do: "We are going to monitor the situation and see how this plays itself out before we make any judgments about how we proceed."[12] In other words, he intended to do nothing. He would wait for the protests to end and then he would figure out how, if at all, to respond. Eventually the protests were shut down, and Obama decided that no response was, after all, necessary. So that was the end of that.

Having ignored the best chance to stop the Iranian bomb, and to help overthrow the regime itself, Obama continues with his laborious exercise of collecting signatures for sanctions. And as we saw in an earlier chapter, there is a second tier to Obama's strategy: example-setting. Obama has managed to convince the Russians that both America and Russia should substantially reduce their nuclear arsenals, presumably so that other countries like Iran will appreciate the gesture and decide not to build their own nuclear weapons.

There is a certain preposterousness to all this that Obama's conservative critics have highlighted and even thoughtful Obama supporters have quietly recognized. Anyone who thinks Iran will not build its bomb because America and Russia are paring down their stockpiles needs his head examined. Moreover, the Iranian government is clearly not scared of sanctions. Iran is an oil-rich country and it can always find a market for this most useful product. Besides, sanctions would only hurt the Iranian people; no one in the Iranian parliament would miss a meal. Not that Iran is even close to having to endure international sanctions. The Obama regime's slow-motion attempts to build diplomatic support for sanctions have only moved the ball a few yards down the field. We are a long way from the goal line, and even if we get there, it may not matter.

What, then, is the point? If you plug in the anti-colonial model, you will see it right away. The point is to allow the Iranians to get nuclear weapons while the Obama administration pretends to try to stop them. I'm not suggesting that Obama actually favors placing nukes in the hands of mullahs. Rather, I'm saying that he has no interest in using American power to prevent that from happening. For Obama, it is the huge American arsenal, and possibly the Israeli arsenal, that pose a far greater danger to world peace and stability than a single bomb or a handful of bombs that the Iranians may build. For political reasons, however, Obama can't adopt a ho-hum attitude toward an Iranian bomb. He has to make it look like he's doing something. So he selects the strategy that is least likely to work.

Actually, from Obama's point of view, it's even better than that. Obama's strategy works beautifully in achieving his own anti-colonial objectives. In denying the Poles and the Czechs missile defenses, Obama weakens America's association with two key allies. Then Obama sits down with the Russians and negotiates steep mutual cuts in the two nations' arsenals. The Russians don't have to do much: their arsenal is mostly old and decayed. The Russians can just junk some of the old missiles that aren't much good anyway. Meanwhile, America cuts its arsenal by a third. Thus, in the name of building support for sanctions and setting a good example for Iran, Obama has managed to substantially reduce America's military power as well as its links to two small but reliable European allies. Far from being clumsy and stupid, the Obama approach seems to have been both ingenious and largely successful in doing what it set out to do: reduce the power of the neocolonial United States.

If we follow Obama's policies in Iraq and Afghanistan, we see Obama acting with the same singularity of purpose and ingenuity in executing that purpose. This is not to say that Obama always gets his way. He has to operate within the parameters of what is politically possible. But within these goalposts Obama does exactly what the anti-colonial model predicts. His rhetoric is also illuminating in revealing what he wants to do. We have to read him carefully, because his statements are meticulously packaged for domestic political consumption. But even so, Obama cannot completely hide what he intends because he needs other people in his administration to actually carry out his wishes. So his packaging needs to have real content, and if we look we can usually get a peek at what's underneath the fine rhetorical wrapping.

Obama's first important foreign policy statement was on October 2, 2002, when he spoke at a rally in Chicago and condemned the looming Iraq war. In the Democratic primaries, Obama was able to use this fact against his main rival, Hillary Clinton: Obama claimed that his criticism of a then-popular but now-unpopular war had been prophetic. Obama's anti-war rationale, however, was hardly stable or consistent. During the primary debates, Obama implied that his original opposition to the Iraq war had been based on the absence of weapons of mass destruction. Yet Obama himself admitted in *The Audacity of Hope* that "I assumed that Saddam had chemical and biological weapons and coveted nuclear arms. I believed that he had repeatedly flouted UN resolutions and weapons inspectors and that such behavior had to have consequences."[13] So Obama's view on this matter was actually very close to that of President Bush.

Why then did Obama oppose the Iraq war? He told us quite clearly in his 2002 speech. "What I am opposed to is a dumb war. What I am opposed to is a rash war...to distract us from a rise in the uninsured, a rise in the poverty rate, a drop in the median income—to distract us from corporate scandals and a stock market that has just gone through its worst month since the Great Depression. That's what I'm opposed to....A war based...not on principle but on politics."[14] Now this is an argument that is lifted right out of Lenin's *Imperialism: The Highest Stage of Capitalism*. As discussed in an earlier chapter, Lenin's view was that capitalism is in an advanced stage of crisis, but the capitalists have figured out how to postpone that internal crisis by invading and occupying foreign countries, and stealing their resources. Thus, in Lenin's view, imperialism is a way to save capitalism and postpone its ultimate collapse. This is also Obama's argument. According to him, the Bush administration is facing disastrous economic problems at home, and therefore decided to invade Iraq not because of any threat posed by Saddam, but to divert attention from domestic woes and possibly also to ameliorate those woes by seizing Iraqi oil.

I don't want to dwell here on the outrageousness of accusing Bush of putting thousands of American lives at risk for the purpose of saving his own political hide. Rather, I want to draw attention to Obama's anti-colonial rhetoric, to show how in his own words he portrays the Iraq war as a war of imperial occupation. And this, we will see, is Obama's view of America's presence in Afghanistan as well. So from the outset Obama has been looking to get America out of those two places. To repeat: this is not because Obama hates America or because Obama wants the Iraqi insurgents or the Taliban to take power. Rather, Obama's primary focus is to curb the rogue elephant that is America, to bring American power under control. This is how Obama defines success; what else happens in those countries is secondary.

Obama's anti-colonial mentality is shown in *The Audacity of Hope*, where he writes that "when we seek to impose democracy with the barrel of a gun" we are "setting ourselves up for failure."[15] This is the anti-colonial critique: Western powers should not try to impose their form of government or their cultural norms on other nations—and certainly not by military force or occupation. That's how Obama views the wars in Afghanistan and Iraq, as colonial adventures inevitably, and rightly, doomed to failure. But most Americans, not thinking in these terms, would recognize that in the aftermath of World War II the United States imposed democracy with the barrel of a gun on Germany and Japan, and the results have been excellent. Even using the colonial model, one could say that former colonies that have democratic governments have them because of the example impressed on them by the former colonial powers; there is no other reason why Kenya should have a parliamentary system of government and judges who wear white wigs. We can debate whether democracy is likely to work in Iraq, but clearly Obama's historical lesson about the impossibility of forcing democracy on a country is invalid.

But who cares about these historical facts? Obama certainly doesn't seem to. From the outset he has been doing everything he can to get American troops out of Iraq. That's why as a United States senator he opposed General David Petraeus's "surge" strategy in Iraq and called it a "mistake that I and others will actively oppose." He termed the Petraeus plan a "reckless escalation" and introduced legislation to begin withdrawing American troops from Iraq in May 2007 "with the goal of removing all United States combat forces from Iraq by March 31, 2008."[16]

To Obama's chagrin, his political stance proved to be spectacularly and embarrassingly wrong. The surge worked. And now Iraq has stabilized. Weeks, even months, go by without a single American death in Iraq. Even Saddam's fellow Sunnis voted in the recent election. The *New York Times* reports that people are now going to the movies once again in Baghdad. Democracy in Iraq remains fragile, but it is working better than many thought it would under such difficult circumstances.[17]

So Obama's problem, once he became president, was what to do about Iraq. He recognized that if he precipitously withdrew American troops and Iraq fell back into chaos, then he would get the blame. Consequently he seems to have figured that there might be a better way to get the troops out: wait for Iraq to stabilize, and then say the troops aren't needed any more. Paradoxically Obama found that the best way for him to achieve his goal of withdrawal was to follow the Bush policy in Iraq and stay for a while. That's why Obama has continually postponed his date for withdrawal. His current plan is to get around 100,000 troops out in 2010 and the remaining 50,000 or so by the end of 2011.[18] This time he may do it. If he does, he is likely to give no credit to Bush, but rather to claim that his own enlightened approach has finally paid off. Can he once again fool the Choir? Count on it!

Afghanistan is a tougher problem for Obama. His challenge can be summarized in this way: how to get out without taking the political heat for perceived failure? Let's be clear: a victory in Afghanistan would pose serious problems for Obama. For an anti-colonialist like him, winning in Iraq is bad enough, but to win in Afghanistan also would be a nightmare! Think of what two victories in a row would do to America's arrogance, and to its appetite for further wars of imperial aggression. In Afghanistan, Obama has to figure out how to withdraw American troops in a way that avoids both American victory and Taliban victory.

While Obama may view the Taliban as a resister against American imperialism, it's obvious he would have no sympathy for the kind of regime they are intent on reestablishing in Afghanistan. So Obama seems to be after a kind of compromise: the administration has already suggested that it may be open to a negotiated settlement, so that the Taliban can share power with the current regime. Still, Obama knows he can't appear to be openly pursuing an agreement that permits a substantial Taliban role in Afghanistan's future.

As we saw in an earlier chapter, Obama limited his options in Afghanistan by portraying Afghanistan as a good war while depicting Iraq as a bad war. Obama insisted that we should get out of Iraq so we can focus on the real threat in Afghanistan. As Obama put it, Iraq was peripheral, but Afghanistan was the nation responsible for the 9/11 attacks. A little scrutiny, however, will expose the fatuity of this argument.

How many of those involved in 9/11 actually came from Afghanistan? Not one. 9/11 was primarily a Saudi operation, organized by a Saudi (bin Laden) and an Egyptian (Ayman al-Zawahiri) and carried out by a Pakistani (Khalid Sheikh Mohammed) and a group of hijackers mostly made up of Saudis. The membership of Al Qaeda is mostly Saudi and Egyptian. So Islamic terrorism is primarily a Middle Eastern operation. Afghanistan only came into the picture because the Taliban contacted bin Laden and offered him free use of the monkey bars. While Afghanistan was indeed the launching pad of 9/11, the toxic fumes of Islamic terrorism are far more concentrated in the Middle East.

Again, none of this seems to matter to Obama. His arguments function as a squid-like cloud of rhetoric, aimed at blinding people from seeing what's actually going on. If you want to know what Obama really thinks about Afghanistan, listen to this off-the-cuff statement he made during the presidential campaign. He said America should divert its resources from Iraq to Afghanistan "so that we're not just air raiding villages and killing civilians which is causing enormous problems there."[19] What? Is that what America has been doing in Afghanistan? Not in the least. The raids have been aimed at terrorist targets, and the military goes to great effort to minimize collateral damage to civilians. No American leader, not even during Vietnam, has described the foreign policy of his own country in such a harsh manner. And note that Obama is not talking about Iraq, a war he opposes, but about Afghanistan, a war he supposedly supports.

Let's focus on what Obama has actually done in Afghanistan. Having contrasted the "war of necessity" in Afghanistan with the "war of choice" in Iraq, Obama was from the outset stuck with Afghanistan. How, now, to switch paths and get out? Obama's difficulty was heightened when the enterprising General Stanley McChrystal proposed his own troop surge to turn things around and win the war. Oh no, Obama was not looking for a way to win. Yet it would look really bad for him to throw out his top general's victory strategy. Obama didn't give McChrystal everything he wanted, but he did agree to send 30,000 additional troops. At the same time he announced this surge, Obama pledged a U.S. troop withdrawal from Afghanistan starting in twelve months. As David Gergen summarized the logic of Obama's policy: "The cavalry is coming—but not for long."[20]

The reason Obama's withdrawal announcement was so damaging is that the McChrystal strategy relied on building the confidence of the Afghan people that they could count on the U.S. military to protect them and to restore normality to their lives. Obviously this whole approach is undercut if it has a one-year expiration date. So Obama had figured out a very clever stance. He would seem to be giving victory a chance while maximizing the chances that there would be no victory. McChrystal and the Afghan people saw the futility of Obama's strategy right away, and this was reflected in comments by Afghan president Hamid Karzai and in McChrystal's stated frustration with his commander in chief. Obama, however, had no interest in what McChrystal or the Afghans thought; his approach was carefully packaged for the consumption of the American media and the American people.

Around the same time, the Obama administration intensified its campaign to undermine the leadership of Karzai. Obama had been giving Karzai the cold shoulder from the beginning. While President Bush twice a month held a videoconference with Karzai, going over in detail the situation in Afghanistan, Obama decided to stop holding those meetings. In March 2010, as Karzai prepared for a scheduled visit to the White House, he received a note from the Obama administration that his invitation was canceled. White House officials told the press they were monitoring the Karzai regime for corruption, and criticized Karzai for vanity and hypersensitivity. So annoyed was Karzai by U.S. conduct that he invited Iranian president Mahmoud Ahmadinejad to deliver an anti-American speech inside Kabul's presidential palace. Karzai also told members of his parliament that if this harassment and interference continued he would "join the Taliban."[21]

Now that would be a big embarrassment for Obama, to have America's key ally in Afghanistan join the Islamic radicals. So the Obama administration backtracked and brought Karzai to Washington for a fancy state dinner. Obama was less forgiving, however, when McChrystal told *Rolling Stone* what he really thought of the Great One. McChrystal's publicly expressed frustrations with Obama—revealing for what they show about Obama's psyche—played into Obama's hands by giving Obama a good reason to fire McChrystal. Of course Obama had to preserve his political capital by naming a tough replacement. So he settled for Petraeus, while trusting that Petraeus won't possibly be able to figure out a way to win in Afghanistan in the time Obama has allotted him. And this provides an additional benefit for Obama: if America is defeated, he can hang defeat on America's most respected general, discredit the idea of "surges," and thus further discourage American neo-colonial wars.

In the White House, Obama is probably even now formulating what he can say next year: "We tried, we really tried. But unfortunately there's a limit to what American power can do in these faraway countries. I wish my misguided predecessor had realized this. He is the one responsible for this failure, and for the Americans who have died in Afghanistan. It is now time for me to finally bring the troops home. Let's learn from this and avoid these military misadventures in the future." That's how you tame a rogue elephant.

Finally I want to say a few words about the Obama administration's solicitous treatment of terrorists and Islamic militants who are captured abroad. From the anti-colonial point of view, these terrorists are simply

resisting American imperialism. This does not make them virtuous individuals, but it does put them on the "right side of history," at least from
the anti-colonial point of view. Obama has been careful to define Al
Qaeda operatives not as terrorists or enemy combatants, as President
Bush did, but rather as common criminals. For conservatives, this is a
classic case of political correctness, but I don't think "P.C." has anything
to do with it. Rather, Obama has a deeper, more fundamental reason for
making this distinction. By defining the enemy as common criminals,
Obama can separate them from the anti-colonial cause and move in
good conscience to take action against them. If they were truly soldiers
fighting against American imperialism, Obama's conscience would be
tempted to take their side.

But the evidence shows that once these bad guys have been identified, Obama has no hesitation in attacking them. As Jonathan Alter
reports in *The Promise*, Obama in his first year ordered some fifty strikes
by unmanned CIA drones against Al Qaeda targets in Pakistan.[22] When
terrorist suspects are tried and convicted in American courts, Obama is
completely in favor of locking them up or even carrying out the death
penalty. Obama understands his duty to protect Americans from terrorist attacks, and clearly he has no qualms about putting away people
seeking to harm American citizens. Interestingly Obama has approved
special scrutiny for people coming to America from fourteen Muslim
countries, including Algeria, Lebanon, Libya, Pakistan, Saudi Arabia,
Syria, and Yemen; he has tried to keep this ethnic and racial profiling
policy under wraps; but it shows once again that Obama's primary concerns have nothing to do with political correctness or even race.

Treating Al Qaeda operatives as criminals who deserve swift and
severe punishment is one thing; holding them in military detention
camps and interrogating them is quite another. Waterboarding and
other forms of coercion quite likely are, to Obama, reminiscent of the

tortures employed by the French in Algeria, not to mention the British in Kenya during the Mau Mau revolt. Just a few months after assuming office, Obama ordered the release of several classified memos from the Bush administration detailing terrorist interrogation methods. Predictably the memos produced outrage in the press, because they described in some detail such procedures as sleep deprivation, keeping detainees in cold and dark cells, and in a few cases dunking the suspect under water to give him the idea that he may be drowning. During the controversy, former vice president Dick Cheney pointed out that "the released memos were carefully redacted to leave out references to what our government learned through the methods in question. Other memos, laying out specific terrorist plots that were averted, apparently were not even considered for release."[23] Obama—now in control of what information gets out and what information stays under wraps—selected the facts that would make his case.

Obama has announced his intention to close the prison at Guantanamo Bay and to try terrorists like Khalid Sheikh Mohammed in civilian courts. He has been forced to keep postponing the Guantanamo shutdown because, evidently, congressmen and senators are appalled at the idea of Islamic terrorists and militants being housed on U.S. territory. Obama swears that he really will close the base, but he hasn't yet determined when or how. Obama's plans for Khalid Sheikh Mohammed are also on hold. When Obama's attorney general Eric Holder announced plans to have this man, the leading architect of 9/11, tried in New York City, there were a host of objections. Republicans complained about the risk of giving Mohammed a global platform to air his grievances, and even Democrats worried about the cost and security issues of such a high-profile civilian trial. As of this writing, Obama is still trying to figure out how to get Mohammed out of the hands of the military.

While one might expect a president to be mostly concerned with protecting the American people from terrorist attack, Obama's primary concern seems to be with protecting captured terrorists from the American military. Obama has hired several radical lawyers who have made a reputation providing free assistance to Islamic radicals and terrorists. Now these lawyers can provide those same services at the taxpayer's expense. All of this is done in the name of constitutional rights. What Obama has never explained, however, is why the rights of the U.S. Constitution extend to people who are not U.S. citizens. The Constitution after all is a social compact. Through mutual consent, citizens give to their government the power to protect certain rights. These rights do not extend to those who stand outside the social contract. Americans have no obligation to extend them to aliens, and they are most certainly inapplicable to those who are apprehended in foreign jihads against America. But Obama does not seem to view things in this way. One of the things that Obama learned in law school is that law can be used as an instrument of politics, and here he has chosen to make it an instrument of anti-colonial resistance, of giving jihadis the full legal protection of United States citizens.

As Americans, we can only hope that Obama's narrow focus on terrorist protections doesn't increase America's vulnerability to future attacks. Already there have been close calls, such as the cases of Nigerian Umar Farouk Abdulmutallab who attempted to bring down an airliner over Detroit, and Faisal Shahzad, who sought to set off car explosives in Times Square. So far the incompetence of the terrorists has contributed to the safety of Americans. But we may not always be able to count on "stupid terrorism" in the future. Wishful thinking may not seem like a very effective remedy to ensure the safety of America in these dangerous times, but with Obama in the White House this remedy may be all that we have.

The United States at the dawn of the twenty-first century is in approximately the same position that Britain was at the dawn of the twentieth.
We are on top of the world, but the view is precarious from up there.
The twentieth century has been the American century and, with effective leadership, there is no reason America should not also dominate the
twenty-first century. Yet there are many threats on the horizon. Britain's
shining moment did not last, and the sun eventually set on the British
empire. Remarkably, America now has a president who seems to want
his country to go the way of Britain, one collapsed empire following
another, so that we can all recite the somber words of Kipling's *Reces-
sional*, "Lo, all our pomp of yesterday, is one with Nineveh and Tyre."
And this is indeed one option, for those who are tired of American leadership in the world. But there is a second, for those who are not. We can
give up on America or we can give up on this president: we are, it seems,
at a time for choosing.

CHAPTER 10

THE LAST
ANTI-COLONIAL

W hile soliciting Senator Ted Kennedy to endorse the presidential aspirations of Hillary Clinton rather than Barack Obama, Bill Clinton could not hide his disdain for the man who seemed to be stealing the Democratic nomination. "A few years ago," he told Kennedy, "this guy would have been getting us coffee." Kennedy was offended by the remark, and when it was reported in the press, some thought Clinton was being racist. In one respect, I have to agree, but in another, I can see that Clinton's point was the exact opposite. As Clinton told Kennedy, "Let's just be clear—the only reason you're endorsing him is because he's black." From Clinton's point of view, only a perverted sort of affirmative action could explain why people would go for a virtually unknown and for the most part unaccomplished fellow like Obama. Is this the person whose script America was ready to follow? Clinton found the situation frustrating and absolutely incredible.[1]

But the real situation is actually more incredible than Clinton ever imagined. We are today living out the script for America and the world that was dreamt up not by Obama but by Obama's father. How do I know this? Because Obama says so himself. Reflect for a moment on the title of his book: it's not *Dreams of My Father* but rather *Dreams from My Father*. In other words, Obama is not writing a book about his father's dreams; he is writing a book about the dreams that he got from his father.

Think about what this means. The most powerful country in the world is being governed according to the dreams of a Luo tribesman of the 1950s—a polygamist who abandoned his wives, drank himself into stupors, and bounced around on two iron legs (after his real legs had to be amputated because of a car crash), raging against the world for denying him the realization of his anti-colonial ambitions. This philandering, inebriated African socialist is now setting the nation's agenda through the reincarnation of his dreams in his son. The son is the one who is making it happen, but the son is, as he candidly admits, only living out his father's dream. The invisible father provides the inspiration, and the son dutifully gets the job done. America today is being governed by a ghost.

Now we can understand why President Obama seems so distant, detached, and even bored. This is not merely a matter of "acting white." It is also the result of Obama living in his time machine. Obama inhabits a world of memories that harken back to continents far away and wars long ago. It was a world of marauding colonial armies and guerillas hiding in the Aberdare mountains. It was a world of pageantry and broken dreams. In Obama's view, great men lived in those days, men who stood athwart the colonial juggernaut crying "Stop." Sometimes they were crushed, but their bravery lives on in the hearts of those who knew and remember them. Compared to all this, today's world of global summits and credit card bailouts and ribbon-cutting seems dull and thin. In terms of sheer human drama, nothing today seems to rise to the level of the way things used to be.

This is not to say Obama is ideologically passive, that he lacks an agenda. On the contrary, Obama is a man on a mission, and he is obsessed with executing that mission. He is like the lead character in a movie who has come home to find his whole family wiped out. The incident brings forth an emotional outpouring of grief and of rage, but in time the emotions settle, leaving behind a more controlled anger combined with a steely resolve. From that point, the man's course is set: the rest of his life is dedicated to a campaign of revenge. In Obama's case the villains are dead, and so the rage takes a different form and settles on a different target. Rather than focus on the specific people who wronged his family, Obama is on a systematic campaign against the colonial system that destroyed his father's dreams. With a kind of suppressed fury, he is committed to keep going until he has brought that system down. And according to his father's anti-colonial ideology, which Obama has internalized for himself, that system is the military and economic power of the United States of America.

For many, it still may seem too fantastic to be true. Yet it is true. The great strength of our anti-colonial theory is not only its psychological plausibility—it is rooted in Obama's vivid and persuasive self-description—but also its explanatory power. The anti-colonial hypothesis explains both Obama's economic and his foreign policy. Obama's domestic and foreign agenda operate in a kind of reverse action: Obama wants to expand government power at home even as he works to contract America's power abroad. The *Weekly Standard* glibly summarizes this as: omnipotence at home, impotence abroad.[2] No other theory accounts for this dual action, but ours does. It also explains lots of little things—like Obama moving the Churchill bust out of the White

House—that no rival theory can even begin to do. Can our theory do even better than this? Perhaps it can. If our theory can forecast the future, if it can account for developments that occur after it has been formulated, then it satisfies the scientific criteria of both explanation and prediction. In that case we can not only account for Obama's actions, but also tell what he is likely to do in the future.

As I was completing this book, I saw news reports quoting NASA chief Charles Bolden announcing that from now on the primary mission of America's space agency would be to improve relations with the Muslim world. Come again? Bolden said he got the word directly from the president. "He wanted me to find a way to reach out to the Muslim world and engage much more with dominantly Muslim nations to help them feel good about their historic contribution to science and math and engineering." Bolden added that the International Space Station was a kind of model for NASA's future, since it was not just a U.S. operation but included the Russians and the Chinese. Bolden, who made these remarks in an interview with Al-Jazeera, timed them to coincide with the one-year anniversary of Obama's own Cairo address to the Muslim world.[3]

Bolden's remarks provoked consternation not only among conservatives but also among famous former astronauts Neil Armstrong and John Glenn and others involved in America's space programs. No surprise: most people think of NASA's job as one of landing on the moon and Mars and exploring other faraway destinations. Even some of Obama's supporters expressed puzzlement. Sure, we are all for Islamic self-esteem, and seven or eight hundred years ago the Muslims did make a couple of important discoveries, but what on earth was Obama up to here?

One of England's great colonial figures was the mining magnate Cecil Rhodes, one of the few people in history to get a country (Rhodesia) named after him. Rhodes is today remembered for the diamond mining company he founded, De Beers, and also for the Rhodes Scholarship. But in his time he commanded something of a private army, he got mixed up in the Matabele Wars and the Boer War, and his political and economic tentacles reached across most of southern Africa. At the peak of his power, Rhodes was asked by a journalist how far he intended his influence to spread. He replied, "I would annex the planets if I could. I often think of that."[4] This is the colonial mindset carried to the final frontier: even possession of the whole earth is not enough! You can imagine how the anti-colonialists reacted to Rhodes. Rhodes's comment can help us understand how the anti-colonial mind perceives America's space program—it is a projection of American power and arrogance into the solar system.

Recall the Moon Landing of Apollo 11 in 1969. "One small step for man," Neil Armstrong said. "One giant leap for mankind." But that's not how the rest of the world saw it. I was eight years old at the time and still living in my native India. I remember my grandfather telling me about how there was a great race between America and Russia to put a man on the moon, and America had won. And everybody knew it because Neil Armstrong placed the American flag on the moon. So it wasn't one giant leap for mankind, but one giant leap for the United States. It was as if that flag signified, "We Americans did this. We Americans now own the moon." I can understand how many in the Third World might see the Moon landing that way, because I'm from the Third World and that's the way I saw it.

If Obama shares this view, no wonder he wants to blunt NASA's space program, to divert it from being a symbol of American greatness to a more modest public relations operation that builds ties with Muslims and other peoples. Even when the Muslims aren't involved, Obama wants to make sure the Russians and the Chinese share the credit. Space, you see, is for human and not merely American exploration. Plug in our anti-colonial model and what at first seems inexplicable—converting NASA into a community outreach program for Muslims—suddenly makes complete sense. Remove the theory and it is almost impossibly difficult to account for what Obama is doing.

Here's a second example to test our theory's predictive power. On August 13, 2010, just as I was reviewing the final galleys for this book, President Obama held a White House dinner celebrating the Islamic holy month of Ramadan. At the event, he praised the plan to construct a mosque and Islamic community center two blocks from Ground Zero—the site of the 9/11 attacks in lower Manhattan. "This is America," Obama solemnly declared, "and our commitment to religious freedom must be unshakable.... The writ of our founders must endure." This is Obama in full translation mode, blurring the issue with his usual agility. The issue raised by the Ground Zero mosque is not one of religious freedom: of course Muslims have a right to build mosques and worship in them. Rather, the issue is whether it is right to have a mosque and Islamic center in virtually the exact spot where so many Americans were killed in the name of Islamic holy war. I don't think it is right, any more than I would support the idea of a neo-Nazi recruiting center at Auschwitz. My sympathies in this case are not with religiously deprived Muslims, but rather with Debra Burlingame, a spokesperson for a 9/11 victims group. "Barack Obama has abandoned America at the place where America's heart was broken nine years ago," she said.[5]

Some supporters of the mosque, such as New York mayor Michael Bloomberg, clearly missed the distinction being made here between the right to worship and how and where that right is exercised. Fareed Zakaria, writer and CNN host, recognizes the distinction; even so, he argues in favor of the mosque on the grounds that the folks building it are traditional Muslims who have condemned terrorism.[6] Still, it's not clear why these moderate Muslims disregarded the sentiments of the 9/11 victims' families and decided on a site so close to Ground Zero. Undoubtedly radical Muslims around the world will view the mosque as a kind of triumphal monument. There is historical precedent for this. Muslims have a long tradition of building monuments to commemorate triumphs over adversaries, as when they built the Dome of the Rock on the site of Solomon's Temple, or when Mehmet the Conqueror rode his horse into the Byzantine church Hagia Sophia and declared that it would be turned into a mosque. Many Americans may not know this history, but the radical Muslims do, and Obama does as well. The radical Muslims would like the Ground Zero mosque built so it can stand as an enduring symbol of resistance to American power, and President Obama evidently agrees with them.

My confidence in the anti-colonial model emboldens me to make three specific predictions about Obama's future conduct. The first prediction concerns deficit reduction. Obama's position has been that we need to spend trillions right now, but once the economy recovers it will be time to get serious about deficit reduction. Now there is one kind of deficit reduction that Obama clearly likes: tax increases on the rich. Already he has announced that he is going to let the Bush tax cuts lapse, at least for the higher brackets. But of course deficits can also be reduced through spending cuts. Since I don't think Obama cares about deficits per se, only about reducing concentrations of power and wealth in America, I do not expect to see any significant spending reductions during an Obama administration. Cutting spending is simply not a priority for the anti-colonial agenda.

Second, I predict that even as Iran develops the full capacity to build nuclear weapons, Obama will do little or nothing to stop it. My theory holds that Obama has no serious interest in preventing Iran from having a bomb; his main concern is with reducing the American arsenal. Therefore I believe that the Obama administration will huff and puff and take all kinds of meaningless steps but no effective action to actually prevent Iran from reaching its nuclear objective. Of course it is possible that Israel will launch airstrikes to disable the Iranian nuclear facilities, but in this case I predict the Obama administration will do its best to prevent Israel from taking any such action. From the anti-colonial point of view, an Israeli strike would be an unconscionable act of aggression against a country that is only seeking something that Israel and the West already possess.

My third prediction is more risky, because it relies on the political atmosphere being favorable to Obama and unfavorable to the military. If that becomes the case, then I predict that Obama will go beyond his attempt to try terrorists and foreign captives in civilian courts. He will initiate procedures to try U.S. military officers and soldiers for war crimes committed in Iraq and Afghanistan. Right now this is politically impossible, but the atmosphere can change quickly if there are more Abu Ghraib type scandals that provoke public outrage. I suspect that Obama is looking for something like this to launch an all-out campaign against the military. So if the circumstances permit him to do it, I believe that Obama will do it. This would be his way to call the colonial occupation forces to account.

Throughout this book, I have been outlining the formulation of Obama's anti-colonial ideology and showing the harmful impact of that ideology on America's economy and America's position in the world. But this is to judge Obama on terms that he would not accept. In this final chapter I intend to assess Obama's anti-colonialism on its own terms. How effectively does it meet its goals of bringing down the rich and powerful and raising up the wretched of the earth? I intend to argue that in the one place that it has been tried—namely, Africa—Obama's anti-colonialism has been a complete failure. Moreover, there is now a new ideology on the scene that is antithetical to Obama's and yet delivers precisely the goods that Obama claims to have been seeking all along.

That ideology is globalization or, to spell it out more clearly, global free trade. Apart from a tariff here and a tariff there, Obama hasn't done much to stop global free trade, but he isn't really a supporter of it, either. While previous presidents—Reagan, George H. W. Bush, Clinton, George W. Bush—all promoted agreements that expanded free trade, Obama does not even seem to be seeking one. In fact, the Obama administration has raised so many labor and environmental objections to free trade treaties that not one is likely to pass its muster. When Obama was in the Senate he voted against the Central America Free Trade Agreement (CAFTA).

How strange this is, because free trade has done more for the wretched of the earth than all the UN programs and foreign aid schemes ever implemented. Consider this: in the past few decades, two of the poorest countries in the world, India and China, have raised hundreds of millions of people out of poverty and tens of millions of people into the comforts of middle-class life. Fareed Zakaria notes that largely as a consequence of China and India's growth rates, "the share of people living on a dollar a day or less plummeted from 40 percent in 1981 to 18 percent in 2004 and it is estimated to fall to 12 percent by 2015."[7] No foreign assistance program comes close to achieving results like this.

How did the Chinese and the Indians do it? They exploited what economist Thorstein Veblen once termed "the advantages of backwardness." Poorer countries have lower labor costs, so if they figure out how to export their goods and services to richer countries, they have a competitive advantage. Think of all the Chinese-made goods you can now buy at Walmart, or of Mumbai call centers staffed by Indians. As these examples illustrate, the Chinese initially focused on producing manufacturing goods more cheaply than Western manufacturers could. India focused on information technology, telecommunications services, and data processing. Still, it was presumed by most observers that the West was driving globalization, as Western corporations looked to cut their costs and increase their profits. But now it seems that countries like India and China are not merely benefiting from Western "outsourcing"; rather, as *The Economist* reports, they are driving the process by becoming juggernauts of innovation.[8]

India and China have together refuted the anti-colonial economics of the 1950s, the economics that shaped the mind of a whole generation of Asian, South American, and African thinkers, including Obama's father. In Chinweizu's *The West and the Rest of Us*, we find the erroneous premise of that economics: "The poor have no way of influencing or changing the world market prices to their benefit."[9] Chinweizu's assumption was that the poor countries have the raw materials and the rich countries have the manufacturing capacity. Since the rich countries are powerful, they can set the world price, and the poor countries have no choice but to go along. Chinweizu could think of nothing better than to rage against this unjust system. Never did it occur to him, or for that matter to Barack Obama Sr., that poor countries could use their low labor costs to their advantage, making themselves wealthier in the process. Indeed, they would probably have dismissed such a prospect as neocolonial thinking at its worst.

India and China aren't the only poor countries that are on the upswing. Today we see impressive growth rates in a wide swath of emerging market economies, from Chile to Indonesia to Romania. Recently World Bank president Bob Zoellick remarked that given these trends the term "third world" is already obsolete.[10] The new term is "emerging markets." Remarkably it is these emerging markets that are now the main source of growth in the world economy. In a startling reversal, the economies of the old colonial powers are stagnant or growing at a very slow pace, while their former territories are racing to catch up.

One might expect a supposed advocate for the developing world like Obama to celebrate these trends, but he doesn't. Why not? Recall his father's rejection of the consumer capitalism that Jomo Kenyatta wanted for Kenya. The Kenyatta model is the forerunner of the global capitalism of today, in which the whole world becomes a single interconnected market. Barack Obama Sr. rejected the Kenyatta model in favor of African socialism. He wanted Kenya, and more broadly Africa, to control its own economic destiny through state supervision and regulation. For him, submitting to economic interdependence was another form of neocolonialism—a prospect to be feared and avoided. President Obama has adopted his father's model, and consequently, as his own writings and speeches confirm, he views global, entrepreneurial capitalism and free trade as a threat and an embarrassment.

Obama would be even more chagrined if he knew that the legacy of colonialism itself is now being reconsidered in several developing nations. India is a perfect example. The Indians are super-excited about their turbo-charged economy; one Indian entrepreneur was quoted saying that the technological revolution in India would realize Gandhi's dream of wiping a tear from every Indian face. But how have the Indians managed to do so well in the global economy? Well, one reason is that so many of them speak English. Another is that the Indians have a very good education system that places a high emphasis on mathematics and science. A third is that India has a system of laws, contracts, and property rights. When you ask the simple question, "How did the Indians get all these things?" the unavoidable answer is, "Colonialism."

No one is suggesting that the British came to India to provide the Indians with a universal language or scientific education or anything like that. The British, like previous conquerors before them, came to rule for their own benefit. In order to administer the empire, however, the British had to educate a native class of Indians. This required teaching them English. Education exposed the Indians to new ideas that were largely alien in traditional Indian culture: democracy, rule of law, human rights, self-determination, individualism, and so on. Ultimately the Indians learned the very language of political liberation from their captors. Several of the leaders of Indian independence were educated in Britain, including Gandhi and India's first prime minister, Nehru.

Remarkably this development was predicted by Lord Thomas Babington Macaulay in the nineteenth century. In his famous Minute on Education, Macaulay said the English sought to create an English-speaking native middle class "who may be interpreters between us and the millions whom we govern; a class of persons, Indian in blood and color, but English in taste, in opinions, in morals and in intellect." Macaulay foresaw that over time this group would challenge and replace their rulers. In 1833, Macaulay told the British parliament, "It may be that the public mind of India may expand under our system until it has outgrown that system, that by good government we may educate our subjects into a capacity for better government; that, having become instructed in European knowledge, they may in some future age demand European institutions. Whether such a day will ever come I know not. But never will I attempt to avert or retard it. Whenever it comes, it will be the proudest day in English history."[11]

Macaulay has been proven right. Even so, for several decades after independence, it was politically impossible for the colonized to say anything good about their former colonizers. All that has now changed.

Recently India's Prime Minister Manmohan Singh, gave a talk at Oxford University in which he did something that no Indian politician dared do when I was growing up. He openly praised the British legacy in India. "Today with the balance and perspective offered by the passage of time and the benefit of hindsight, it is possible for an Indian prime minister to assert that India's experience with Britain had its beneficial consequences. Our notions of the rule of law, of a Constitutional government, of a free press, of a professional civil service, of modern universities and research laboratories have all been fashioned in the crucible where an age-old civilization met the dominant Empire of the day."[12]

When Singh attributed Indian success to the groundwork laid by British institutions, he wasn't just talking about the Indian nation being able to stand on its own—which was the original meaning of independence—but also of India becoming fully integrated and competing effectively in the global economy. Now political independence operates in conjunction with economic interdependence. Obama may not join me, but as an Indian myself who has greatly benefited from this colonial legacy, I am quite willing to give two cheers for colonialism. I say "two" and not "three" in deference to my ancestors, who had a hard time under colonialism. But while colonialism was bad for them, it has been good for me. Hey, it's thanks to the Brits that English is my first language and that's how I was able to write this book. So while Obama fumes, I am happy to raise my glass and toast that curmudgeonly old defender of the British empire, Winston Churchill.

Alas, there is one continent that largely missed out on the growth curve, and that's Africa. With the exception of South Africa with its diamonds and mineral wealth, and a few other African countries that have oil revenues, the rest of Africa is, as former UN Secretary General Kofi Annan put it, a "cocktail of disasters."[13] A lethal combination of poverty, repression, civil war, and AIDS is now the distinguishing characteristic

of this continent. Systemic poverty was once considered an Asian phenomenon; now it is mostly an African phenomenon. Economist Xavier
Sala-i-Martin writes that in the 1970s only 11 percent of the world's
poor were in Africa while 76 percent were in Asia; today Africa hosts 66
percent of the world's poor and Asia's share has fallen to 15 percent.[14]
The sad truth is that most of Africa is simply irrelevant: if sub-Saharan
Africa were to sink into the ocean tomorrow, the world economy would
be largely unaffected.

It is tempting to blame Africa's problems on colonialism, but let's
remember that most of Africa was only colonized in the late nineteenth
and early twentieth century. In 1875 more than 90 percent of Africa was
still ruled by Africans. For centuries, the white man stayed on the coast
of Africa, scared to penetrate the interior because of malaria, yellow
fever, and a host of deadly diseases. In fact, the central regions of Africa
had the reputation of being the "white man's grave." Only with the discovery in the mid-nineteenth century of quinine as a prophylactic
against malaria could the white man go into the heart of Africa. The
European "scramble for Africa" did not begin in earnest until the 1880s.
European rule over the vast majority of Africa was not consolidated until
1914. And the whole colonial enterprise was done by the mid-1960s:
Kenya, for example, became a British Protectorate in 1895, officially a
British colony in 1920, and was free in 1963. So Africa was colonized for
little more than half a century, or a single lifetime.

A strong case can be made that Africa's problem isn't colonialism but
too little colonialism. Economist P. T. Bauer noted that if you make a list
of the poorest regions in the world today—a list that would include Tibet,
Nepal, Liberia, and Ethiopia—they are by and large the regions that have
had the least contact with the West. Some of the far outposts of the world
have aboriginal communities and desert people who remain outside the
orbit of Western influence; they are still living at the subsistence levels of

three thousand years ago. When we consider the world as a whole, Bauer writes that "the level of material achievement usually diminishes as one moves away from the foci of Western impact."[15]

Ethiopia is a good example of Bauer's point. Except for a three-year period of Italian occupation during the 1930s, Ethiopia was never colonized; it has remained a free country for two millennia. Ethiopia is on the African coast, has an ancient cultural heritage, and has a plentiful supply of natural resources. Still, Ethiopia today is one of the world's most wretched countries, always on the edge of famine and starvation. If a country is more likely to be poor the farther it is from Western influence, the reverse is also true: the longer a country has been exposed to the West, the more likely it is to have a promising, developing economy. India had the benefit of being colonized for the longest time: the British came in the 1600s, established themselves in the 1700s, ruled virtually the whole country by the mid-1800s, and got out in the middle of the 1900s. So there was plenty of time for Western institutions and indeed the Western worldview to take hold.

In Africa, however, the white man got in and very promptly got out. True, the Europeans in that half-century did little to develop the continent. The Portuguese and the Belgians left almost nothing. The British did stop slavery in Africa, reduce if not prevent tribal conflict, and construct a railway network through Uganda and Kenya—built, by the way, by importing 30,000 "coolies" from India. (Obama knows about this because he writes about it, and I know because my great grandfather was one of those coolies.) But only a tiny fraction of Africans under British rule were provided with decent jobs or a decent education. During this period of ruling Africa, the Western powers were hampered in their attention to the needs of the continent by two world wars and the Great Depression. On the whole, colonization in Africa was a tragedy—but it might not have been had colonization lasted longer, as it did in India.

In any event, what is more important than colonialism is what route countries took after colonialism. For the most part, Africa rejected the route of free market capitalism and adopted a route of centralized planning and African socialism. Overall, Africa rejected Jomo Kenyatta's approach in favor of the approach of Barack Obama Sr. Over the past half-century, Africa has witnessed a succession of dictators and strongmen such as Mobutu Sese Seko in Zaire, Idi Amin in Uganda, and Hastings Kamuzu Banda in Malawi. These thugs quickly learned the language of anti-colonialism and used it as a pretext to confiscate property and appropriate it for themselves and their cronies. Moreover, these men continued for decades to blame the failures of their societies on the legacy of colonialism, freeing them from the responsibility of raising the people's standard of living. Even today Robert Mugabe of Zimbabwe, one of the last of the Big Daddy despots, has declared his mission as one of rooting out the last vestiges of colonial rule from his country. His strategy for doing that is to drive the European and Asian entrepreneurs out of the country and to seize the most productive lands of the white farmers. As a result, Mugabe's once productive country has been reduced to economic ruins, and most of the population is either starving or running away.

Even as they contemplate their own miseries, however, the Africans can see the progress that is being made around the world. Younger Africans, in particular, are weary of the anti-colonial claptrap and socialist power-grabbing. They want more Western investment in their countries, more free trade, and greater integration into the global economy. The wretched of the earth now realize that they don't have to remain wretched. They too can exploit "the advantages of backwardness" and become productive citizens who flourish in the world economy. Globalization has opened up new possibilities.

How is Obama responding to those possibilities? We can see the answer by comparing Obama's attitude to the two countries that shaped his outlook when he was growing up: Indonesia and Kenya. Indonesia is a former colonial country that is moving quickly to become part of the global capitalist economy. Led by President Susilo Bambang Yudhoyono, Indonesia is following in the way of China and India. Currently it is growing at 6 percent, one of the fastest growth rates in the world.[16] So how has Obama treated Indonesia? With "benign neglect," according to Bara Hasibuan, a leading Indonesian politician. "More talk than substance," editorialized the *Bangkok Post* recently. When Obama was elected, the Indonesians erected a statue of him in a public park in Jakarta. Now in response to more than 50,000 local signatures, the government has taken the statue down. As Protus Tanuhandaru, who organized the signature campaign, told *Time* magazine, "I'm not against Obama, but it's wrong to have a statue in a public park of someone who has contributed nothing to Indonesia." *Time*'s article was about how Obama is perceived not just in Indonesia but throughout a continent: "Why Obama is Disappointing Asia."[17]

No one can deny, however, that Obama cares deeply about Kenya, and more generally about Africa. So let us follow his sojourns there. In July 2009 President Obama traveled to Africa and spoke to the parliament of Ghana. There was great anticipation, and of course his message was transmitted across Africa. Obama was in a remarkable position. He was the first U.S. president of African descent whose very identity was shaped by his African father. Now he had the power to actually do something about the terrible problems plaguing the continent. What, then, did Obama have to offer today's Africa?

Obama began his speech in a familiar manner: he blamed Africa's past problems on colonialism. "I can give you chapter and verse on why the colonial maps that were drawn helped to spur on conflict, and the terms of trade that were uneven emerging out of colonialism." Then Obama moved to a detailed account of his family history, noting that in his grandfather's life "colonialism wasn't simply the creation of unnatural borders or unfair terms of trade—it was something he experienced personally, day after day, year after year."

Obama recognized, however, that colonialism could not entirely account for Africa's current situation. Getting to the heart of the matter, he said, "Countries like Kenya had a per capita economy larger than South Korea's when I was born." One might expect Obama at this point to advocate that Africa learn from South Korea and liberalize its economy, open up its markets, exploit the advantages of backwardness, and integrate into the world economy. America could provide some of the technological and entrepreneurial knowhow.

But Obama said none of this. Instead, he offered some useless exhortation. "I have come here, to Ghana, for a simple reason: the twenty-first century will be shaped by what happens not just in Rome or Moscow or Washington, but what happens in Accra as well." And some more useless exhortation. "With strong institutions and a strong will, I know that Africans can live their dreams in Nairobi and Lagos, Kigali, Kinshasa, Harare, and right here in Accra." Earlier that day Obama had taken his family to the Cape Coast Castle which for centuries served as a Portuguese depot for slaves bound for America and the Caribbean. There Obama had offered still more useless exhortation: "I think that [this site] helps to teach all of us that we have to do what we can to fight against the kinds of evils that sadly still exist in our world not just on this continent but in every corner of the globe."

Speaking before Ghana's parliament, he did finally get down to practical issues. He called on Africa to set up "public-private partnerships that invest in better roads and electricity." He called for a U.S.–Africa partnership to combat climate change since "Africa gives off less greenhouse gas than any other part of the world, but it is the most threatened by climate change." He did pledge "substantial increases in our foreign assistance," including technical assistance for crop production. Obama expressed his hope that Ghana would not only feed its population but one day become a food exporter. And that was it. Falling back into campaign mode, Obama concluded, "Yes, we can! Thank you very much."[18]

So this is what this son of Africa came to offer Africa: virtually nothing. He now has the power, but he doesn't know how to use it effectively. That's because Obama still cannot bring himself to abandon his father's anti-colonial ideology. That ideology calls for transfers of wealth from the colonizers to the colonized. If Obama can't convince Congress to approve more foreign aid for Africa, then he has no idea what else to do. The tragedy is that even if Congress were to approve the aid, it would not provide any lasting benefit. President Obama is still trying to apply his father's discredited formulas from the 1950s even though they have no relevance to the world we live in today.

The blunt truth is that anti-colonialism is dead; no one in today's world cares about it—except the man in the White House. He is the last anti-colonial. The rest of the world has no interest in how many schools the Belgians built, or didn't build, in the Congo, or how British officials in Kenya used to beat their house servants with canes. We are now living in a new world. And while most of the world is facing the challenges and seizing the opportunities of the twenty-first century, Obama refuses to embrace the promise of that growth—for his African homeland or for the country he was elected to lead. Instead, President Obama is committed to bring down the "neocolonial" forces in the economy and to lasso the rogue elephant that is America.

Sometimes he wins and sometimes he loses, but his intent is immutable. He is like the toy soldier; even when he walks into the wall, he keeps going. Don't expect him to change direction or turn around. He cannot change; he is in too deep. Moreover, he doesn't want to change; he thinks of himself as on a righteous course, one that demands his own singular leadership at this crucial moment in history. While Obama regards himself as a model of confident cosmopolitanism, in fact he has the narrow clarity of the one-eyed man.

But what harm can one man do? Obama may have nothing to offer Africa, but are his policies harming people today? Even with the power of the presidency, Obama is not going to stop globalization or the information revolution. But there is another way that he could gravely damage the engine of global prosperity: that is by removing its cordon of protection, a cordon that is provided by the United States. Trade, after all, is vulnerable; it has always been vulnerable to thugs who want to disrupt trade routes and save themselves the trouble of buying and selling by taking and plundering. That's why, contrary to the views of some economists, global free trade cannot by itself solve the world's problems of scarcity and want. The world needs a policeman, and in case you haven't yet figured it out, the United States has that job.

Call it empire if you will, but America's role is very different from that of previous empires. Contrary to the charges of the anti-colonialists, the United States today has no intention of ruling or seeking tribute from other countries; America's foreign policy goals are basically to encourage people to trade with us and to make sure they don't bomb us. That's pretty much it. Of course America could stop being the global policeman, but then there wouldn't be anyone to deter North Korea from nuking South Korea or to prevent China from kicking around the small countries in its neighborhood, or to put a stop to genocidal wars in Bosnia or Rwanda or the Middle East. Someone has got to be the cop, and it's a role I wouldn't want to hand over to China, Russia, or the United Nations. There is currently no alternative to American leadership in the world, and deep down even American liberals know this.

So one great threat posed by Obama is that in weakening America he will jeopardize the security and stability that America provides not only for its own citizens but for the world. Then there is a second threat that Obama poses to his own country. America is currently the world leader, but it is faced with serious competitive challenges from leaner, hungrier nations like China and India. The economic balance has tipped in favor of these countries; they are growing five times faster than the United States. Chinese cities are bigger, newer, and glitzier than anything in America today. Also, China and India have larger populations and this too has economic significance. Since China has more than three times the number of people that America has, even if the Chinese per capita income only rises to one-third that of the United States, China will have a bigger GNP than America. At current rates, the Chinese economy will overtake that of the United States in a few decades. The American era will be over and, if history is any guide, it will never return.

What are we going to do about this? Here we are at a fork in the road. We can either draw from the wellsprings of American strength and get about the business of competing in the world, or we can give up on the American dream and lapse into a second-class position as indeed Britain eventually did. If Obama has his way, America would look a lot like Obama's father wanted Kenya to look: government-run peasant cooperatives rationing land and natural resources in order to enjoy a modest self-sufficiency.

Recall Obama's granny outlining for him the simple life in the village before the white man came. Each family had its own hut. The men tilled the land and the women drew the water. The boys learned to throw their spears and the girls learned to grind millet. The elders watched over everything and made all the rules. I understand the appeal of growing up in a simple, settled society, because I grew up in one. We didn't have all the problems of modern life. But then we also didn't have basic amenities that most people today take for granted. Equally important, there is very little mobility and opportunity in settled societies. That's why so many people from the old country would be thrilled to have a chance to move to the United States. Consequently I understand Obama, but I don't sympathize with him. In fact, his warped ideology really scares me. His vision for America may be therapeutic for his psyche, but it is a ridiculous one for America in the twenty-first century. The dream of the two Obamas is not the dream that I want for America. Obama's dream is actually an American nightmare.

It's time to act. Yes, we need change, and this time the change we need is to change the man in the White House. America isn't the rogue elephant: Obama is. It's not a matter of putting him out of his misery; it's a matter of putting him out of our misery. We also have to get rid of his team of sycophants and enablers. I am thinking of Harry Reid, Chris Dodd, Nancy Pelosi, Barney Frank: the entire liberal Democratic menagerie. Do all these enablers, or even his own private staff, know who Obama really is and what his goals really are? I suspect they do not, because Obama's philosophy derives from his own unique experience. So they are, in a way, dupes of Obama and of his translation strategy; this would make Obama a true loner. But it makes no difference. The sycophants and enablers are the ones who are clearing the path for this Pied Piper, and we had better get rid of the whole crew before they take us off the cliff.

More than this, we need to ask ourselves how we got into this situation. We need to reexamine what it is to be an American. This means we must no longer respond so lethargically to the competitive challenges we face. Ronald Reagan once noted that the American national anthem is the only one in the world that ends with a question: "Oh say does that Star Spangled banner yet wave, o'er the land of the free and the home of the brave?" Only we, through our resolution and through our action, can answer that question.

ACKNOWLEDGMENTS

This book could not have been written without the love and care of Dixie and Danielle, my two pillars of support. Dixie reads all my stuff and is also the original source of the rumor that I am actually the "front man" for her ideas. I have to remember this when I am invited to a friendly "let's sort this out" dinner at the White House; she can be my food taster. Harry Crocker, my editor, championed this project from the start and went with me when I kept changing my mind and direction. Mary Beth Baker did the editing that makes my work flow so well; if at any time it doesn't flow so well, direct all complaints to Mary Beth. I am also grateful to my research assistant, Gregory Hirshman, who finds time to work with me when he is not playing tennis for Stanford or doing genius-level math or applying for the Rhodes Scholarship. I wish to thank Stan Guthrie for his critiques of the manuscript and help with editing it; Stan provides the level-headed, outsider perspective that every writer needs. Peter Marsh is an inspiration and a friend and his support, through the Peter Marsh Foundation, was indispensable to this project. With Pete comes B. J. Marsh, who doesn't have a foundation to her name, but is certainly a lot more attractive than Pete. I also appreciate the useful suggestions of Andrew Accardy and Byron Van Kley. I am grateful to Ed and Caroline Hoffman, Spencer Masloff, Andy Mills, Larry Taunton, and John and Carol Saeman for their assistance in my work. My regular breakfasts with Ed McVaney are a constant source of ideas and suggestions, and several of those are reflected in this book. In fact, a single line by Ed launched me on the right path with regard to my subject. I'd also like to thank "Engels." He has been with this project from the beginning, even helping to shape the original idea. I call him "Engels" because he sometimes jokes that as a team we are like Marx and Engels. Some individuals who have helped me with this book have asked that their names not be used; they are worried they might attract the unhelpful scrutiny of the Obama administration. "Trust me," says one of them, "You don't want those guys coming after you." As you see from these pages, I am not waiting for them to come after me; I am going after them, and with the greatest weapon of all, the truth.

NOTES

Chapter 1

1. Richard Cohen, "Who is Barack Obama?" *Washington Post*, July 20, 2010; available at: http://www.washingtonpost.com/wp-dyn/content/article/2010/07/19/AR2010071904224.html [accessed August 2, 2010].

2. Nick Pisa, "Barack Obama's Lost Brother Found in Kenya," *Telegraph*, August 20, 2008; available at: http://www.telegraph.co.uk/news/worldnews/northamerica/usa/barackobama/2590614/Barack-Obamas-lost-brother-found-in-Kenya.html [accessed August 2, 2010]. See also, David McKenzie, "Behind the Scenes: Meet George Obama," CNN, August 22, 2008; available at: http://www.cnn.com/2008/POLITICS/08/22/ bts.obama.brother/ [accessed August 2, 2010]; and Dinesh D'Souza, "George Obama, Start Packing," September 22, 2008; available at: http://townhall.com/columnists/DineshDSouza/2008/09/22/george_obama,_start_packing [accessed August 2, 2010].

3. Dinesh D'Souza, "Obama and Post-Racist America," January 28, 2009; available at: http://townhall.com/columnists/DineshDSouza/2009/01/28/obama_and_post-racist_america [accessed August 2, 2010].

4. See, e.g., Jeffrey Jones, "Blacks More Pessimistic Than Whites About Economic Opportunities," Gallup News Service, July 9, 2004; available at: http://www.gallup.com/poll/12307/blacks-more-pessimistic-than-whites-about-economic-opportunities.aspx [accessed August 2, 2010].

5. Hamil Harris, "From Tavis Smiley, love and criticism for Obama," *Washington Post*, March 24, 2010; available at: http://voices.washingtonpost.com/44/2010/03/from-tavis-smiley-love-and-cri.html [accessed August 2, 2010]. See also, Michael Eric Dyson, comments on MSNBC, January 11, 2010; video available at: http://www.youtube.com/watch?v=WA3oqycCBvQ [accessed August 2, 2010].

6. Kathleen Wells, "A Conversation with Cornel West," February 23, 2010; available at: http://www.huffingtonpost.com/kathleen-wells/a-conversation-with-corne_b_472853.html [accessed August 2, 2010].

7. Barack Obama, *Dreams from My Father* (New York: Three Rivers Press, 2004), 29–30.

8. David Remnick, *The Bridge* (New York: Alfred Knopf, 2010), 239.

9. See, e.g., "Barack Obama's Speech on Race," *New York Times*, March 18, 2008; available at: http://www.nytimes.com/2008/03/18/us/politics/18text-obama.html [accessed August 2, 2010].

10. James Fallows, "Obama on Exceptionalism," *The Atlantic*, April 4, 2009; available at: http://www.theatlantic.com/science/archive/2009/04/obama-on-exceptionalism/9874/ [accessed August 2, 2010].

11. Frantz Fanon, *Black Skin, White Masks* (New York: Grove Press, 2008), 91.

12. Barack Obama, *The Audacity of Hope* (New York: Three Rivers Press, 2006), 11.

Chapter 2

1. "Newsweek Editor Evan Thomas: Obama is 'Sort of God,'" June 5, 2009; video available at: http://www.realclearpolitics.com/video/2009/06/05/ newsweek_editor_evan_thomas_obama_is_sort_of_god.html [accessed August 2, 2010].

2. Barack Obama, Inauguration Address, January 20, 2009, www.msnbc.com.

3. Barack Obama, *The Audacity of Hope* (New York: Three Rivers Press, 2006), 9, 25. See also, Barack Obama, speech at the Democratic National Convention, July 27, 2004; transcript available at: http://www.washingtonpost.com/wp-dyn/articles/A19751-2004Jul27.html [accessed August 2, 2010].

4. Obama, *The Audacity of Hope*, 204; Barack Obama, *Dreams from My Father* (New York: Three Rivers Press, 2004), 154.

5. Jonathan Alter, *The Promise* (New York: Simon & Schuster, 2010), 63.

6. Bernard Goldberg, *A Slobbering Love Affair* (Washington, D.C.: Regnery, 2009), 24, 26. See also, Mark Morford, "Is Obama an Enlightened Being?" *San Francisco Chronicle*, June 6, 2008; available at: http://articles.sfgate.com/2008-06-06/entertainment/17120245_1_obama-s-presence-new-age-black-president [accessed August 2, 2010].

7. Maureen Dowd, "Spock at the Bridge," *New York Times*, March 1, 2009; available at: http://www.nytimes.com/2009/03/01/opinion/01dowd.html [accessed August 2, 2010]. See also, Jacob

Weisberg, "Only Connect!" *Slate*, January 23, 2010; available at: http://www.slate.com/id/2242223 [accessed August 2, 2010].

8. Cited by Bernard Goldberg, *A Slobbering Love Affair* (Washington, D.C: Regnery, 2009), 135–36.

9. David Remnick, *The Bridge* (New York: Alfred Knopf, 2010).

10. Obama, *Dreams from My Father*, xvi, 220. See also, Jon Meacham, "On His Own," *Newsweek*, August 22, 2008; available at: http://www.newsweek.com/2008/08/22/on-his-own.html [accessed August 9, 2010].

11. Richard Wolffe, Jessica Ramirez, and Jeffrey Bartholet, "When Barry Became Barack," *Newsweek*, March 31, 2008; available at: http://www.newsweek.com/2008/03/22/when-barry-became-barack.html [accessed August 2, 2010].

12. Thomas Pakenham, *The Scramble for Africa* (New York: Avon Books, 1991).

13. Chinweizu, *The West and the Rest of Us* (New York: Vintage, 1975), 3; Aimé Césaire cited by Frantz Fanon, *Toward the African Revolution* (New York: Grove Press, 1967), 72, 166.

14. Edward Said, *Culture and Imperialism* (New York: Alfred A. Knopf, 1993), 22; Albert Memmi, *The Colonizer and the Colonized* (Boston: Beacon Press, 1991), 52; Aimé Césaire, *Discourse on Colonialism* (New York: Monthly Review Press, 2000), 33, 41.

15. Frantz Fanon, *The Wretched of the Earth* (New York: Grove Press, 1963), 76; Walter Rodney, *How Europe Underdeveloped Africa* (Washington, D.C.: Howard University Press, 1982).

16. Said, *Culture and Imperialism*, 55; Michael Omi and Howard Winant, *Racial Formation in the United States* (New York: Routledge & Kegan Paul, 1986), 72.

17. Chinweizu, *The West and the Rest of Us*, 3; Gayatri Chakravorty Spivak, "Three Women's Texts and a Critique of Imperialism," in

Henry Louis Gates, Jr., ed., *Race, Writing and Difference* (Chicago: University of Chicago Press, 196), 262.

18. Kwame Nkrumah, *Neocolonialism: The Last Stage of Imperialism* (New York: International Publishers, 1965), ix–x, 239.

19. Karl Marx, "The Future Results of British Rule in India," in Shlomo Aveni, ed., *Marx on Colonialism and Modernization* (New York: Doubleday, 1969), 94–95, 132–34; V. I. Lenin, *Imperialism: the Highest Stage of Capitalism* (London: Pluto Press, 1996), 17.

Chapter 3

1. Barack Obama, *The Audacity of Hope* (New York: Three Rivers Press, 2006), 192. See also, The Scrapbook, "The Thinness of His Skin," *The Weekly Standard*, May 24, 2010; available at: http://www.weeklystandard.com/articles/thinness-his-skin, p. 2 [accessed August 3, 2010].

2. Barack Obama, *Dreams from My Father* (New York: Three Rivers Press, 2004), 136. See also, Dan Armstrong, "Barack Obama Embellishes His Resume," July 9, 2005; available at: http://www.analyzethis.net/2005/07/09/barack-obama-embellishes-his-resume/ [accessed August 3, 2010].

3. Bob Young, "Obama's Big Time Fumble," *The Arizona Republic*, May 17, 2009; available at: http://www.azcentral.com/sports/heatindex/articles/2009/05/17/20090517spt-p2mainyoung.html [accessed August 3, 2010].

4. Obama, *Dreams from My Father*, 301.

5. Charles Bremner, "Barack and Michelle Obama Decline Dinner with the Sarkozys," *Times*, June 5, 2009; available at: http://www.timesonline.co.uk/tol/news/world/europe/article6434141.ece [accessed August 3, 2010]. See also, Tom Diemer, "Obama, Struggling on Homefront, Still a Global Pop Star, Poll Finds,"

Politics Daily, June 17, 2010; available at: http://www.politicsdaily. com/2010/06/17/obama-struggling-on-homefront-still-a-global-pop-star-poll-fi/ [accessed August 3, 2010].

6. Remarks by President Obama at Strasbourg Town Hall, April 3, 2009; available at: http://www.whitehouse.gov/the_press_office/ Remarks-by-President-Obama-at-Strasbourg-Town-Hall/ [accessed August 3, 2010].

7. Jimmy Orr, "Obama Gives the Queen of England an iPod," *Christian Science Monitor*, April 1, 2009; available at: http://www.csmonitor. com/USA/Politics/The-Vote/2009/0401/obama-gives-the-queen-of-england-an-ipod [accessed August 3, 2010]. See also, Jim Shipman, "Barack Obama Sends Bust of Winston Churchill on Its Way Back to Britain," *Telegraph*, February 14, 2009; available at: http://www.telegraph.co.uk/news/worldnews/northamerica/usa/ barackobama/4623148/Barack-Obama-sends-bust-of-Winston-Churchill-on-its-way-back-to-Britain.html [accessed August 3, 2010].

8. Winston Churchill, "The End of the Beginning," November 10, 1942, Churchill Society, London; available at: http://www. churchill-society-london.org.uk/EndoBegn.html [accessed August 3, 2010]. See also, Tom Schachtman, *Airlift to America* (New York: St. Martin's Press, 2009), 30–31.

9. Associated Press, "Obama Stops Wearing American Flag Pin," April 10, 2007; available at: http://www.msnbc.msn.com/id/21138728/ [accessed August 3, 2010].

10. Severin Carrell, "Barack Obama faces rising pressure to publish Lockerbie bomber release letter," London *Guardian*, July 25, 2010; available at: http://www.guardian.co.uk/uk/2010/jul/25/barack-obama-megrahi-release-lockerbie [accessed August 9, 2010]. See also, CNN, "Obama, Cameron blast release of Lockerbie bomber," CNN, July 20, 2010; available at: http://politicalticker.blogs.

cnn.com/2010/07/20/obama-cameron-blast-release-of-lockerbie-bomber/ [accessed August 9, 2010]. "White House Reportedly Preferred Scotland to Libya for Released Lockerbie Bomber," FOX News, July 25, 2010; available at: http://www.foxnews.com/ politics/2010/07/25/obama-administration-reportedly-backed-lockerbie-release-transfer-libyan-prison/ [accessed August 9, 2010].

11. Alexis de Tocqueville, *Democracy in America* (New York: Vintage, 1990), Volume I, 394, 427, Volume II, 22, 38.

12. Seymour Martin Lipset, *American Exceptionalism* (New York: W.W. Norton, 1997), 51, 63, 66, 77.

13. Edward Wyatt and David Herszenhorn, "In Deal, New Authority Over Wall Street," *New York Times*, June 28, 2010; available at: http://www.nytimes.com/2010/06/26/us/politics/ 26regulate.html [accessed August 9, 2010].

14. Stephanie Condon, "James Carville Slams Obama on Oil Spill Response," CBS News May 26, 2010; available at: http://www. cbsnews.com/8301-503544_162-20006016-503544.html [accessed August 3, 2010]. See also, James Taranto, "Keith Olbermann's Wisdom," *Wall Street Journal*, June 21, 2010; available at: http://online. wsj.com/article/NA_WSJ_PUB:SB10001424052748704895204575320670422192984.html [accessed August 3, 2010].

15. Barack Obama, "Remarks by the President to the Nation on the BP Oil Spill," June 15, 2010; available at: http://www.whitehouse.gov/ the-press-office/remarks-president-nation-bp-oil-spill [accessed August 3, 2010].

16. "Obama Decries Political Posturing on Immigration," My Fox Phoenix, July 1, 2010; available at: http://www.myfoxphoenix.com/dpp/news/ immigration/apx-obama-speech-immigration-overhaul-07012010.

17. Edward Said, *Culture and Imperialism* (New York: Alfred A. Knopf, 1991), xx, 17.

18. Michael Hastings, "The Runaway General," *Rolling Stone*, June 22, 2010; available at: http://www.rollingstone.com/politics/news/17390/119236 [accessed August 3, 2010].

19. Thomas Friedman, "What's Second Prize?" *New York Times*, June 22, 2010; available at: http://www.nytimes.com/2010/06/23/opinion/23friedman.html [accessed August 3, 2010].

20. Helene Cooper, "Obama Says a Way Out of Afghanistan Is Needed," *New York Times*, March 23, 2009; available at: http://www.nytimes.com/2009/03/23/us/politics/23obama.html [accessed August 3, 2010].

21. "More Than a One-Man Problem," *The Economist*, June 24, 2010, p. 30; available at: http://www.economist.com/node/16425992.

22. "Obama, Netanyahu Agree to Focus on Peace Talks," *Washington Post*, July 6, 2010; video available at: http://www.washingtonpost.com/wp-dyn/content/video/2010/07/06/VI2010070602814.html [accessed August 3, 2010]. See also, Dan Ephron, "Israel Holds the Line on East Jerusalem," *Newsweek*, July 26, 2010, p. 6.

23. AP, "Obama Under Fire for Comment on Palestinians," March 15, 2007; video and transcript available at: http://www.msnbc.msn.com/id/17631015/ [accessed August 3, 2010]. See also, Ali Abunimah, "How Barack Obama Learned to Love Israel," *The Guardian*, March 5, 2007; available at: http://www.guardian.co.uk/commentisfree/2007/mar/05/howbarackobamalearnedtolo [accessed August 3, 2010].

24. "Old worry, new ideas," *The Economist*, April 15, 2010, p. 67; available at: http://www.economist.com/node/15915393. See also, "An Awkward Guest List," *The Economist*, April 29, 2010, p. 60; available at: http://www.economist.com/node/16010410.

25. Mark Steyn, "Obama's Nuke Summit Dangerously Delusional," April 18, 2010; available at: http://www.jewishworldreview.com/ 0410/steyn041810.php3 [accessed August 3, 2010]; and Charles Krauthammer, "Obama's Nuclear Strutting and Fretting," *Washington Post*, April 16, 2010; available at: http://www.washingtonpost. com/wp-dyn/content/article/2010/04/15/ AR2010041504663.html [accessed August 3, 2010]. See also, Charles Krauthammer, "Plumage—But at A Price," *Washington Post*, July 9, 2009; available at: http://www.washingtonpost.com/ wp-dyn/content/article/2009/07/09/AR2009070902363.html [accessed August 3, 2010].

Chapter 4

1. Michael Dobbs, "Aide says Obama erred on Kennedy tie," *Boston Globe*, March 30, 2008; available at: http://www.boston.com/ news/nation/articles/2008/03/30/aide_says_obama_erred_on_ kennedy_tie/ [accessed August 3, 2010].

2. Tom Schachtman, *Airlift to America* (New York: St. Martin's Press, 2009), 6, 9; Elsa Dixler, "How Obama Sr. Came to Hawaii," *New York Times*, May 7, 2010; available at: http://papercuts.blogs.nytimes. com/2010/05/07/how-obama-sr-came-to-hawaii/ [accessed August 3, 2010].

3. Sally Jacobs, "A Father's Charm, Absence," *Boston Globe*, September 21, 2008; available at: http://www.boston.com/news/politics/ 2008/articles/2008/09/21/a_fathers_charm_absence/ [accessed August 3, 2010]. See also, Tom Schachtman, *Airlift to America*, 10.

4. Gavan Daws, *Shoal of Time* (Honolulu: University Press of Hawaii, 1968), 291.

5. Barack Obama, *Dreams from My Father*, 23.

6. Ibid., 52, 80; Constance Ramos, *Our Friend Barry: Classmates' Recollections of Barack Obama and Punahou School* (Lulu, 2008), www.lulu.com; Kristen Scharnberg and Kim Barker, "The not-so-simple story of Barack Obama's youth," *Chicago Tribune*, March 25, 2007; available at: http://www.chicagotribune.com/news/politics/obama/chi-070325obama-youth-story-archive,0,3864722.story [accessed August 3, 2010].

7. Obama, *Dreams from My Father*, xv; W. E. B. Du Bois, *The Souls of Black Folk* (New York: Barnes and Noble Classics, 2003), 9.

8. Obama, *Dreams from My Father*, 9.

9. Ibid., 220; Barack Obama, *The Audacity of Hope*, 205.

10. Ibid., 363–64.

11. Keith Richburg, "Obama's Half Brother Steps Into Spotlight to Tell His Own Story," *Washington Post*, November 5, 2009; available at: http://www.washingtonpost.com/wp-dyn/content/article/2009/11/04/AR2009110401214.html [accessed August 3, 2010]. See also, William Foreman, "Obama's Half-Brother Recalls Their Abusive Father in Novel," *USA Today*, November 4, 2009; available at: http://www.usatoday.com/life/books/news/2009-11-03-obama-half-brother-novel_N.htm [accessed August 3, 2010].

12. Sally Jacobs, "A Father's Charm, Absence," *op. cit.* See also, David Remnick, *The Bridge*, 54; Obama, *Dreams from My Father*, 76; Schachtman, *Airlift to America*, 187.

13. Obama, *Dreams from My Father*, 63, 69.

14. Ibid., 70.

15. Liza Mundy, "When Michelle Met Barack," *Washington Post*, October 5, 2008; available at: http://www.washingtonpost.com/wp-dyn/content/story/2008/10/03/ST2008100302144.html [accessed August 3, 2010].

16. Jomo Kenyatta, *Suffering Without Bitterness* (Nairobi: East African Publishing, 1968), 161.
17. For an analysis of Mboya's paper, see William Ochieng, "Structural and Political Changes," in B. A. Ogot and W. R. Ochieng, *Decolonization and Independence in Kenya* (London: James Currey, 1995), 83–85.
18. Barak H. Obama, "Problems Facing Our Socialism," *East Africa Journal*, July 1965; available at: http://www.politico.com/static/ PPM41_eastafrica.html, p. 3.
19. Jon Meacham, "On His Own," *Newsweek*, August 23, 2008; available at: http://www.newsweek.com/2008/08/22/on-his-own.html [accessed August 3, 2010]. See also, Obama, *Dreams from My Father*, 50.
20. Remnick, *The Bridge*, 60; Obama, *Dreams from My Father*, 51.
21. K. M. Panikkar, *Asia and Western Dominance* (New York: Collier Books, 1969), 92.
22. Obama, *Dreams from My Father*, 37
23. Scharnberg and Barker, "The Not-So-Simple Story of Barack Obama's Youth," *Chicago Tribune*.
24. Obama, *Dreams from My Father*, 41–43.
25. Ibid., 46–47, 50.
26. Ibid., 129.

Chapter 5

1. Associated Press, "Obama's Census Choice: Just African-American," CBS News, April 2, 2010; available at: http://www.cbsnews.com/stories/2010/04/02/politics/main6357568.shtml [accessed August 4, 2010].
2. Marie Arana, "He's Not Black," *Washington Post*, November 30, 2008; available at: http://www.washingtonpost.com/wp-dyn/

content/article/2008/11/28/AR2008112802219.html [accessed August 4, 2010].

3. Jesse Washington, "Many Insisting that Obama Is Not Black," AP Report, *Huffington Post*, December 14, 2008; available at: http://www.huffingtonpost.com/2008/12/14/ap-many-insisting-that-ob_n_150846.html [accessed August 4, 2010]. See also, Ta-Nehisi Paul Coates, "Is Obama Black Enough?" *Time*, February 1, 2007; available at: http://www.time.com/time/nation/article/0,8599,1584736,00.html [accessed August 4, 2010].

4. Barack Obama, *Dreams from My Father*, xi.

5. David Mendell, *Obama: From Promise to Power* (New York: Harper, 2007), 73.

6. David Garrow, *Bearing the Cross* (New York: Vintage Books, 1988), 90–91. See also, "Interview: Martin Luther King Comes to Ghana," Martin Luther King Estate; available at: http://www.ghanaweb.com/GhanaHomePage/NewsArchive/artikel.php?ID=53300 [accessed August 4, 2010]; and "Birth of a New Nation: Martin Luther King on Ghana," April 7, 1957; full text of speech available at: http://news.peacefmonline.com/features/200909/27185.php [accessed August 4, 2010].

7. "Malcolm X: Youth More Filled with Urge to Eliminate Oppression," interview with Jack Barnes and Barry Sheppard, January 18, 1965; available at: http://www.africaresource.com/index.php?option=com_content&view=article&id=266:malcolm-x-youth-more-filled-with-urge-to-eliminate-oppression&catid=85:oral-history&Itemid=341 [accessed August 4, 2010]. And "Jackson to Ask U.N. for Cash to Help Finance Rights Group," *Chicago Tribune*, December 25, 1971.

8. Obama, *Dreams from My Father*, 79, 85–86.

9. Ibid., 87–89.

10. "Poet advised young Obama," *Washington Times*, August 12, 2009; available at: http://www.washingtontimes.com/news/2008/aug/ 12/poet-advised-young-obama/ [accessed August 4, 2010]. See also, John Edgar Tidwell, Introduction to *Writings of Frank Marshall Davis* (Jackson, MS: University Press of Mississippi, 2007), xxv.

11. Obama, *Dreams from My Father*, 90–91.

12. Ibid., 98; Tidwell, Introduction to *Writings of Frank Marshall Davis*, xxvi.

13. Tidwell, ed., *Writings of Frank Marshall Davis*, 91–98.

14. Obama, *Dreams from My Father*, 97.

15. Ibid., 100, 103.

16. Chinua Achebe, "An Image of Africa: Racism in Conrad's 'Heart of Darkness,'" *Massachusetts Review* 18, 1977; available at: http://kirbyk. net/hod/image.of.africa.html [accessed August 4, 2010].

17. Joseph Conrad, *Heart of Darkness* (London, Arcturus Publishing, 2010), 15.

18. David Remnick, *The Bridge*, 109–10.

19. Ibid., 101, 112.

20. Janny Scott, "Obama's Account of New York Years Often Differs From What Others Say," *New York Times*, October 30, 2007; available at: http://www.nytimes.com/2007/10/30/us/politics/30 obama.html [accessed August 4, 2010].

21. Barack Obama, "Breaking the War Mentality," *Sundial*, March 10, 1983; full text available at: http://www.freerepublic.com/focus/ news/2286251/posts [accessed August 4, 2010].

22. Shira Schoenberg, "Law Expert: Obama Will Preserve Constitution," *Concord Monitor*, November 14, 2007; available at: http://www.concordmonitor.com/article/law-expert-obama-will-preserve-constitution [accessed August 4, 2010]; and Remnick, *The Bridge*, 191.

23. Derrick Bell, *Faces at the Bottom of the Well* (New York: Basic Books, 1992), ix, 158–94.
24. Albert Memmi, *The Colonizer and the Colonized*, 9.
25. Roberto Mangabeira Unger, *Knowledge and Politics* (New York: Free Press, 1975), 4; Roberto Mangabeira Unger, *The Critical Legal Studies Movement* (Cambridge: Harvard University Press, 1986).
26. Remnick, *The Bridge*, 184–85.

Chapter 6

1. Shiva Naipaul, *Black and White* (London: Abacus, 1980), 15.
2. Richard Wolffe, Jessica Ramirez, and Jeffrey Bartholet, "When Barry Became Barack," *Newsweek*, March 22, 2008; available at: http://www.newsweek.com/2008/03/22/when-barry-became-barack.html.
3. Barack Obama, *Dreams from My Father*, 201.
4. See, e.g., Kenneth Timmerman, *Shakedown* (Washington, D.C.: Regnery, 2002).
5. Saul Alinsky, *Rules for Radicals* (New York: Vintage Press, 1989), 3, 184–96; Saul Alinsky interview, *Playboy*, March 1972.
6. Barack Obama, *The Audacity of Hope*, 207.
7. Obama, *Dreams from My Father*, 292–93.
8. "Obama Releases 2000-2006 Tax Returns," March 15, 2008; available at: http://taxprof.typepad.com/taxprof_blog/2008/03/obama-releases.html [accessed August 2, 2010].
9. Tom Leonard, "Jeremiah Wright, Obama's Pastor, 'Stole my Wife,'" *Telegraph*, May 4, 2008; available at: http://www.telegraph.co.uk/news/1927227/Jeremiah-Wright-Barack-Obamas-pastor-stole-my-wife.html [accessed August 2, 2010].
10. Colin Dayan, "Out of Defeat," *Boston Review*, September 10, 2008; available at: http://bostonreview.net/BR33.5/dayan.php [accessed August 2, 2010].

11. *Hannity & Colmes*, Fox News Channel, March 1, 2007; partial transcript available at: http://www.foxnews.com/story/0,2933,256078,00. html [accessed August 2, 2010]. See also, "Reverend Wright at the National Press Club," *New York Times*, April 28, 2008; available at: http://www.nytimes.com/2008/04/28/us/politics/28text-wright.html [accessed August 2, 2010].

12. The Reverend Jeremiah Wright, "The day of Jerusalem's fall," *The Guardian*, March 27, 2008; transcript available at: http://www. guardian.co.uk/commentisfree/2008/mar/27/ thedayofjerusalemsfall [accessed August 2, 2010].

13. Obama, *Dreams from My Father*, 116, 220.

14. Ibid., 299–300.

15. Ibid., 307, 369.

16. Ibid., 312–14.

17. Ibid., 311–12.

18. Edward Said, *Orientalism* (New York: Vintage Books, 1978), 41, 322.

19. Wunyabari O. Maloba, *Mau Mau and Kenya* (Bloomington: Indiana University Press, 1998), 86.

20. David Anderson, *Histories of the Hanged* (New York: W.W. Norton, 2005), 5; Caroline Elkins, *Imperial Reckoning* (New York: Henry Holt, 2005), xiv. Her numbers have been disputed as exaggerated.

21. Anderson, *Histories of the Hanged*, 5–7.

22. Elkins, *Imperial Reckonings*, 304–5, 361. Revelations of abuses in the detention camps later led to their closure.

23. Anderson, *Histories of the Hanged*, 78.

24. B. A. Ogot and W. R. Ochieng, *Decolonization and Independence in Kenya* (London: James Currey, 1995), 40.

25. Ben Macintyre and Paul Orengoh, "Beatings and Abuse Made Barack Obama's Grandfather Loathe the British," *Times*, December 3,

2008; available at: http://www.timesonline.co.uk/tol/news/
world/africa/article5276010.ece [accessed August 2, 2010]. See
also, Obama, *Dreams from My Father*, 418.

26. Obama, *Dreams from My Father*, 406–7, 414, 417.

27. Ibid., 406.

28. Ibid., 341–44.

29. Ibid., 356.

30. Ibid., 394.

31. Ibid., 396.

32. Ibid., 376–77.

33. Ibid., 367–68.

34. Ibid., 425–27.

35. Ibid., 429–30.

36. Ibid., xv.

Chapter 7

1. "Jackson Apologizes for 'Crude' Obama Remarks," CNN, July 9,
   2008; available at: http://www.cnn.com/2008/POLITICS/07/
   09/jesse.jackson.comment/ [accessed August 2, 2010].

2. Krissah Thompson, "Activist Al Sharpton Takes on New Role as
   Administration Ally," *Washington Post*, April 17, 2010; available
   at: http://www.washingtonpost.com/wp-dyn/content/article/
   2010/04/16/AR2010041602381.html [accessed August 2,
   2010].

3. Barack Obama, *The Audacity of Hope*, 287.

4. Michelle Obama, Interview with Steve Croft, *60 Minutes*, CBS, February 11, 2007; video available at: http://www.cbsnews.com/
   video/watch/?id=2454398n&tag=related;photovideo [accessed
   August 2, 2010].

5. Andrew Kull, *The Color-Blind Constitution* (Cambridge: Harvard
   University Press, 1992), viii, 183.

6. Frantz Fanon, *Toward the African Revolution* (New York: Grove Press, 1967), 33, 35, 43, 66, 81, 105; and *The Wretched of the Earth*, 37, 39, 53.

7. Dinitia Smith, "No Regrets for a Love of Explosives," *New York Times*, September 11, 2001; available at: http://www.nytimes.com/2001/09/11/books/no-regrets-for-love-explosives-memoir-sorts-war-protester-talks-life-with.html [accessed August 3, 2010].

8. Bill Ayers, letter to the *New York Times*, September 15, 2001; available at: http://billayers.wordpress.com/2008/04/21/clarifying-the-facts-a-letter-to-the-new-york-times-9-15-2001/ [accessed August 3, 2010]; Bill Ayers, *Fugitive Days* (Boston: Beacon Press, 2009), 61, 241.

9. Frantz Fanon, *Black Skin, White Masks*, 2–3, 29, 91.

10. Saul Alinsky, *Rules for Radicals*, 70, 184–87, 195.

11. Shelby Steele, *A Bound Man* (New York: Free Press, 2008).

12. "Obama regrets his attack on 'stupid' police for 'racist' arrest of Harvard scholar," London *Daily Mail*, July 25, 2009; available at: http://www.dailymail.co.uk/news/article-1201199/Obama-regrets-attack-stupid-police-racist-arrest-Harvard-scholar.html [accessed August 3, 2010].

13. Obama, *The Audacity of Hope*, 11, 247; Lexington, "Angry White Men," *The Economist*, March 4, 2010, p. 46; available at: http://www.economist.com/blogs/lexington/2010/03/angry_white_men_and_obama.

14. Jennifer Senior, "Dreaming of Obama," *New York* magazine, September 24, 2006; available at: http://nymag.com/news/politics/21681/ [accessed August 3, 2010].

15. Obama, *The Audacity of Hope*, 37.

16. David Callahan, "Traitors to Their Class," *The New Republic*, June 25, 2010, p. 13; available at: http://www.tnr.com/article/politics/75615/traitors-their-class [accessed August 9, 2010].

17. Obama, *The Audacity of Hope*, 18.

18. Don Terry, "The Skin Game," *Chicago Tribune Magazine*, October 24, 2004; available at: http://www.chicagotribune.com/chi-0410240530oct24,0,6470102.story [accessed August 3, 2010]. See also, Xuan Thai and Ted Barrett, "Biden's Description of Obama Draws Scrutiny," CNN, posted February 9, 2007; available at: http://www.cnn.com/2007/POLITICS/01/31/biden.obama/ [accessed August 3, 2010].

19. Joann Price, *Barack Obama* (Westport, Connecticut: Greenwood Press, 2008), 61; David Mendell, *Obama: From Promise to Power*, 10.

20. Jodi Kantor, "A Candidate, His Minister and the Search for Faith," *New York Times*, April 30, 2007; available at: http://www.nytimes.com/2007/04/30/us/politics/30obama.html [accessed August 3, 2010].

21. "Barack Obama's Speech on Race," *New York Times*, March 18, 2008; available at: http://www.nytimes.com/2008/03/18/us/politics/18text-obama.html [accessed August 3, 2010].

22. Janny Scott, "Obama Chooses Reconciliation Over Rancor," *New York Times*, March 19, 2008; available at: http://www.nytimes.com/2008/03/19/us/politics/19assess.html [accessed August 3, 2010]. See also, Editorial, "Mr. Obama's Profile in Courage," *New York Times*, March 19, 2008, http://www.nytimes.com/2008/03/19/opinion/19wed1.html [accessed August 3, 2010]; and Chris Matthews, "Hardball," MSNBC, March 18, 2008; video available at: http://www.youtube.com/watch?v=t_J46peAVzw.

23. Barack Obama's Election Night Remarks, *Politico*, November 5, 2008; available at: http://www.politico.com/news/stories/1108/15294.html [accessed August 3, 2010].

Chapter 8

1. Amilcar Cabral, *Unity and Struggle* (New York: Monthly Review Press, 1979), 143; Frantz Fanon, *The Wretched of the Earth* (New York: Grove Press, 1963), 101–3.

2. "Obama Underwrites Offshore Drilling," *Wall Street Journal*, Review and Outlook, August 18, 2009; available at: http://online.wsj.com/article/NA_WSJ_PUB:SB10001424052970203863204574346610120524166.html [accessed August 6, 2010]. See also, Mario Loyola, "Rule by Decree," *National Review*, July 26, 2010; available at: http://www.nationalreview.com/articles/243537/rule-by-decree-mario-loyola.

3. See e.g., Jillian K. Melchior, "Ignoring Climategate," *Commentary*, February 2010; available at: http://www.commentarymagazine.com/viewarticle.cfm/ignoring—climategate—15339 [accessed August 6, 2010].

4. Roy Spencer, *The Great Global Warming Blunder* (New York: Encounter Books, 2010), xii, 2, 4, 6.

5. Elisabeth Rosenthal, "China Increases Lead as Biggest Carbon Dioxide Emitter," *New York Times*, June 14, 2008; available at: http://www.nytimes.com/2008/06/14/world/asia/14china.html [accessed August 6, 2010].

6. Martin Feldstein, "Cap and Trade: All Cost, No Benefit," *Washington Post*, June 1, 2009; available at: http://www.washingtonpost.com/wp-dyn/content/article/2009/05/31/AR2009053102077.html [accessed August 6, 2010].

7. "Remarks by the President at United Nations Secretary General Ban Ki-Moon's Climate Change Summit," Office of the Press Secretary, the White House, September 22, 2009; text available at: http://www.whitehouse.gov/the_press_office/Remarks-by-the-

President-at-UN-Secretary-General-Ban-Ki-moons-Climate-
Change-Summit/ [accessed August 6, 2010].

8. Walter Russell Mead, "The Politics of Climategate," *The American Interest*, January–February 2010, pp. 125–26; available at: http://www.the-american-interest.com/article.cfm?piece=821 [accessed August 6, 2010].

9. Cliff Kincaid, "Obama's Global Tax Proposal Up for Senate Vote," *AIM Report*, February 12, 2008; available at: http://www.aim.org/aim-column/obamas-global-tax-proposal-up-for-senate-vote/ [accessed August 9, 2010].

10. Obama interview with Steve Kroft, *60 Minutes*, CBS, November 16, 2008; available at: http://www.cbsnews.com/stories/2008/11/16/60minutes/main4607893_page3.shtml [accessed August 6, 2010].

11. David Leonhardt, "The Big Fix," *New York Times*, January 27, 2009; available at: http://www.nytimes.com/2009/02/01/magazine/01Economy-t.html [accessed August 6, 2010].

12. Massimo Calabresi, "Obama vs. the Banks," *Time*, December 13, 2009; available at: http://www.time.com/time/business/article/0,8599,1947411,00.html [accessed August 6, 2010]. See also, Michael Muskal, "Obama channels his inner populist and attacks bankers," *Los Angeles Times*, January 14, 2010; available at: http://latimesblogs.latimes.com/washington/2010/01/president-obama-channels-his-inner-populist-banks-bailout.html [accessed August 6, 2010]; and "Obama Makes Case About Capitalism's Drift," AOL News, April 22, 2010; available at: http://www.aol-news.com/nation/article/obama-makes-case-about-capitalisms-drift/19450218 [accessed August 6, 2010].

13. For a detailed presentation of this case, see Thomas Sowell, *The Housing Boom and Bust* (New York: Basic Books, 2009).

14. Robert Pozen, *Too Big to Save?* (New York: John Wiley, 2010), 211, 215.

15. Stuart Varney, "Obama Wants to Control the Banks," *Wall Street Journal*, April 4, 2009; available at: http://online.wsj.com/article/NA_WSJ_PUB:SB123879833094588163.html [accessed August 6, 2010].

16. Deborah Solomon, "Geithner Weighs Bank Repayments," *Wall Street Journal*, April 21, 2009; available at: http://online.wsj.com/article/NA_WSJ_PUB:SB124027087650836931.html [accessed August 6, 2010].

17. Barack Obama, *The Audacity of Hope*, 119.

18. David Herszenhorn, "Democrats Corral Votes on Bank Bill," *New York Times*, July 12, 2010, p. B-1; available at: http://www.nytimes.com/2010/07/12/business/12regulate.html [accessed August 6, 2010]. See also, David Sessions, "Financial Reform Will Become Law, So What's in the Bill?" *Politics Daily*, July 15, 2010; available at: http://www.politicsdaily.com/2010/07/15/financial-reform-will-become-law-so-whats-in-the-bill/ [accessed August 6, 2010].

19. "Obama's Remarks at the Signing Ceremony," *New York Times*, July 21, 2010; available at: http://www.nytimes.com/2010/07/22/business/22regulate-text.html [accessed August 6, 2010].

20. "A sticky gas pedal," *The Economist*, May 29, 2010, p. 27; available at: http://www.economist.com/node/16216567.

21. Motoko Rich, "U.S. Lost 131,000 Jobs As Governments Cut Back," *New York Times*, August 6, 2010, p. A-1; available at: http://www.nytimes.com/2010/08/07/business/economy/07econ.html [accessed August 9, 2010].

22. This point is effectively made in Arthur Laffer and Stephen Moore, *Return to Prosperity* (New York: Threshold Editions, 2010), 43–45.

23. See, e.g., William McGurn, "For Obama, Taxes Are About Fairness," *Wall Street Journal*, August 19, 2008. See also, "President Obama's Address to Congress," *New York Times*, February 24,

2009; available at: http://video.nytimes.com/video/2009/02/25/us/politics/1194838132344/president-obama-s-address-to-congress.html [accessed August 9, 2010].

24. "Who Pays Income Taxes and How Much?" Tax Year 2007, National Taxpayers Union, Washington, D.C, www.ntu.org

25. Peter J. Hansen, "Put the Patient in Charge," *The Weekly Standard*, May 24, 2010, p. 21–26; available at: http://www.weeklystandard.com/articles/put-patient-charge [accessed August 6, 2010].

26. Amy Goldstein and Scott Wilson, "Obama Launches Attack on Health Insurance Companies," *Washington Post*, March 9, 2010; available at: http://www.washingtonpost.com/wp-dyn/content/article/2010/03/08/AR2010030801703.html [accessed August 6, 2010].

27. Tim Carney, "Big Business, Big Government and Libertarian Populism," *Cato Policy Report*, March–April 2010, p. 9; available at: http://www.cato.org/pubs/policy_report/v32n2/cpr32n2-3.html [accessed August 6, 2010].

28. Robert Samuelson, "China's $2.4 Trillion Stash," *Newsweek*, February 1, 2010, p. 17; available at: http://www.newsweek.com/2010/01/22/china-s-2-4-trillion-stash.html [accessed August 9, 2010].

29. Stephen Cohen and J. Bradford Delong, *The End of Influence* (New York: Basic Books, 2010), 14; Fareed Zakaria, *The Post-American World* (New York: W.W. Norton, 2009), xxi.

Chapter 9

1. Jonathan Alter, *The Promise* (New York: Simon & Schuster, 2010), 348.

2. Barack Obama, *The Audacity of Hope*, 276.

3. Deepak Lal, *In Praise of Empires* (New York: Palgrave, 2004), xxiv; Edward Said, *Culture and Imperialism*, xvii; Obama, *The Audacity of Hope*, 293.

4. Sayyid Qutb, *Social Justice in Islam* (Oneonta, New York: Islamic Publications, 2000), 273; "The Battle for a Religion's Heart," *The Economist*, August 6, 2009, p. 52; available at: http://www.economist.com/node/14179219; Osama bin Laden, *Messages to the World* (London: Verso, 2005), 5, 25.

5. Jonathan Alter, "Secrets from Inside the Obama War Room," *Newsweek*, May 15, 2010; available at: http://www.newsweek.com/2010/05/15/secrets-from-inside-the-obama-war-room.html [accessed August 9, 2010]. See also, Walter Russell Mead, "The Carter Syndrome," *Foreign Policy*, January-February 2010, p. 61; available at: http://www.foreignpolicy.com/articles/2010/01/04/the_carter_syndrome [accessed August 9, 2010].

6. "Obama Breaks With Bush Doctrine in New Security Policy," AOL News, May 26, 2009; available at: aolnews.com/2010/05/26/obama-breaks-with-bush-in-new-security-policy.

7. Michael Scherer, "Barack Obama's New World Order," *Time*, April 3, 2009; available at: http://www.time.com/time/world/article/0,8599,1889512,00.html [accessed August 9, 2010].

8. Barack Obama, "Remarks by the President at the Summit of the Americas," April 17, 2009; available at: http://www.whitehouse.gov/the_press_office/Remarks-by-the-President-at-the-Summit-of-the-Americas-Opening-Ceremony/ [accessed August 9, 2010]. See also, Katie Pickert, "Chavez's Gift: Open Veins of Latin America," *Time*, April 21, 2009; available at: http://www.time.com/time/arts/article/0,8599,1892801,00.html [accessed August 9, 2010].

9. Barack Obama, "Remarks by President Obama to the Turkish Parliament," April 6, 2009; available at: http://www.whitehouse.gov/the-press-office/remarks-president-obama-turkish-parliament [accessed August 9, 2010].

10. Victor Davis Hanson, *How the Obama Administration Threatens Our National Security* (New York: Encounter, 2009), Broadside No. 5; Robert

Kagan, "Obama Year One: Contra," *World Affairs*, January-February 2010, pp. 12–18; available at: http://www.worldaffairsjournal.org/articles/2010-JanFeb/full-Kagan-JF-2010.html.

11. Graham Allison, "Nuclear Disorder," *Foreign Affairs*, January-February 2010, p. 76; available at: http://www.foreignaffairs.com/articles/65732/graham-allison/nuclear-disorder.

12. Lara Setrakian, "Iranian President Tells Obama to Back Off," *ABC News*, June 25, 2009; available at: http://abcnews.go.com/International/story?id=7932217 [accessed August 9, 2010].

13. Obama, *The Audacity of Hope*, 294.

14. Barack Obama, speech on the Iraq war, October 2, 2002; available at: http://www.barackobama.com/2002/10/02/remarks_of_illinois_state_sen.php [accessed August 9, 2010].

15. Obama, *The Audacity of Hope*, 316–17.

16. Jon Ward, "Democrats Ready to Fight New War Plan," *Washington Times*, January 11, 2007, p. A-1; available at: http://www.washingtontimes.com/news/2007/jan/11/20070111-121645-6413r/?page=1 [accessed August 9, 2010]. See also, Shailagh Murray, "Obama Bill Sets Date for Troop Withdrawal," *Washington Post*, January 31, 2007, p. A-4; available at: http://www.washingtonpost.com/wp-dyn/content/article/2007/01/30/AR2007013001586.html [accessed August 9, 2010].

17. "No promised land at the end of all this," *The Economist*, March 6, 2010, p. 31; available at: http://www.economist.com/node/15603901. See also, Anthony Shadid, "In a Baghdad Cinema, Celebrating a Return of Iraqi Culture," *New York Times*, May 6, 2010, p. A-4; available at: http://www.nytimes.com/2010/05/07/world/middleeast/07baghdad.html [accessed August 9, 2010].

18. Peter Baker and Rod Nortland, "Obama Sticks to a Deadline in Iraq," *New York Times*, April 27, 2010; available at: http://www.

nytimes.com/2010/04/28/world/middleeast/28iraq.html [accessed August 9, 2010].

19. Associated Press, "Obama: U.S. Troops in Afghanistan Must Do More than Kill Civilians," FOX News, August 14, 2007; available at: http://www.foxnews.com/story/0,2933,293187,00.html [accessed August 9, 2010].

20. Alter, *The Promise*, 391

21. Ibid., 368; Dexter Filkins and Mark Landler, "Afghan Leader Is Seen to Flout Influence of U.S.," *New York Times*, March 29, 2010, p. A-1; available at: http://www.nytimes.com/2010/03/30/world/asia/30karzai.html [accessed August 9, 2010]. See also, Fareed Zakaria, "Our Man in Afghanistan," *Newsweek*, April 19, 2010, p. 20; available at: http://www.newsweek.com/2010/04/08/our-man-in-afghanistan.html [accessed August 9, 2010]; and Ken Dilanian, "Karzai's Remarks About Taliban Give White House Pause," *USA Today*, April 7, 2010, p. 6-A; available at: http://www.usatoday.com/news/washington/2010-04-06-Karzai_N.htm [accessed August 9, 2010].

22. Alter, *The Promise*, 347–48.

23. "Cheney Defends Use of Harsh Interrogation Methods in Speech to AEI," *Washington Post*, May 21, 2009; available at: http://voices.washingtonpost.com/44/2009/05/21/cheney_speaks.html [accessed August 9, 2010].

Chapter 10

1. John Heilemann and Mark Halperin, *Game Change* (New York: Harper, 2010), 218–19.

2. Irwin Stelzer, "The Obama Formula," *Weekly Standard*, July 5–July 12, 2010, p. 16; available at: http://www.weeklystandard.com/articles/obama-formula [accessed August 9, 2010].

3. "NASA Chief: Next Frontier Better Relations With Muslim World," FOX News, July 5, 2010; available at: http://www.foxnews.com/politics/2010/07/05/nasa-chief-frontier-better-relations-muslims/ [accessed August 9, 2010].

4. Matthew Sweet, "Cecil Rhodes: A Bad Man in Africa," *Independent*, March 16, 2002; available at: http://www.independent.co.uk/news/world/africa/cecil-rhodes-a-bad-man-in-africa-654195.html [accessed August 9, 2010].

5. Hugh Collins, "President Obama Supports Ground Zero Mosque," AOL News, August 14, 2010; available at: http://www.aolnews.com/surge-desk/article/president-obama-supports-ground-zero-mosque/19593492 [accessed August 16, 2010]; and Hugh Collins, "Obama Slammed, Praised for Backing Ground Zero Mosque," AOL News, August 14, 2010; available at: http://www.aolnews.com/nation/article/obama-slammed-praised-for-backing-ground-zero-mosque/19593700 [accessed August 16, 2010].

6. Fareed Zakaria, "Build the Ground Zero Mosque," *Newsweek*, August 6, 2010; available at: http://www.newsweek.com/2010/08/06/the-real-ground-zero.html [accessed August 16, 2010].

7. Fareed Zakaria, *The Post-American World* (New York: W.W. Norton, 2009), 3.

8. "The world turned upside down," *The Economist*, April 15, 2010, pp. 3–4; available at: http://www.economist.com/node/15879369.

9. Chinweizu, *The West and the Rest of Us*, 256.

10. "Seeing the world differently," *The Economist*, June 10, 2010, p. 65; available at: http://www.economist.com/node/16329442.

11. Cited by Deepak Lal, *In Praise of Empires* , 73–74.

12. Manmohan Singh, address by the prime minister at Oxford University, July 8, 2005; available at: http://www.hinduonnet.com/thehindu/nic/0046/pmspeech.htm [accessed August 9, 2010].

13. Kofi Annan, Address to the Security Council, January 10, 2000; available at: http://www.un.org/News/ossg/sg/stories/statments_search_full.asp?statID=9 [accessed August 9, 2010].

14. Cited by Jagdish Bhagwati, *In Defense of Globalization* (New York: Oxford University Press, 2007), 65.

15. P. T. Bauer, *Equality, the Third World and Economic Delusion* (Cambridge: Harvard University Press, 1981), 5, 70, 172.

16. Aubrey Belford, "After Years of Inefficiency, Indonesia Emerges as an Economic Model," *New York Times*, August 5, 2010, p. B-3; available at: http://www.nytimes.com/2010/08/06/business/global/06iht-rupiah.html [accessed August 9, 2010].

17. Hannah Beech, "Why Obama is Disappointing Asia—Even in Indonesia," *Time*, March 29, 2010; available at: http://www.time.com/time/magazine/article/0,9171,1973182,00.html [accessed August 9, 2010].

18. The White House, "Remarks by the President to the Ghanaian Parliament," July 11, 2009; available at: http://www.whitehouse.gov/the-press-office/remarks-president-ghanaian-parliament [accessed August 9, 2010]. See also, The White House, "Remarks by the President at Cape Coast Castle," July 11, 2009; available at: http://www.whitehouse.gov/the-press-office/Remarks-By-The-President-At-Cape-Coast-Castle/ [accessed August 9, 2010].

INDEX